EARLY AND MEDIEVAL RIT
THEOLOGIES OF BAF

Presenting a comprehensive survey of the historical underpinnings of baptismal liturgies and theologies, Bryan Spinks presents an ecumenically and geographically wide-ranging survey and discussion of contemporary baptismal rites, practice and reflection, and sacramental theology. Writing within a clear chronological framework, Bryan Spinks presents two simultaneous volumes on Baptismal Liturgy and Theology.

In the first volume, *Early and Medieval Rituals and Theologies of Baptism*, Bryan Spinks summarizes the understandings of baptism in the New Testament and the development of baptismal reflection and liturgical rites throughout Syrian, Egyptian, Roman and African regions. He focuses particularly on the Homilies of Chrysostom, Cyril of Jerusalem, Theodore and Ambrose, the post-nicene rites and commentaries and the impact of medieval theologies of baptism and Augustinian theology with reference to Western understanding.

In the second volume, *Reformation and Modern Rituals and Theologies of Baptism*, Spinks traces developments through the Reformation, liturgies in the eighteenth and nineteenth centuries, and explores important new ecumenical perspectives on developments of twentieth-century sacramental discussion.

LITURGY, WORSHIP AND SOCIETY

SERIES EDITORS

Dave Leal, Brasenose College, Oxford, UK
Bryan Spinks, Yale Divinity School, USA
Paul Bradshaw, University of Notre Dame, UK and USA
Gregory Woolfenden, St Mary's Orthodox Church, USA
Phillip Tovey, Ripon College, Cuddesdon, UK

The Ashgate Liturgy, Worship and Society series forms an important new 'library' on liturgical theory at a time of great change in the liturgy and much debate concerning traditional and new forms of worship, suitability and use of places of worship, and wider issues concerning interaction of liturgy, worship and contemporary society. Offering a thorough grounding in the historical and theological foundations of liturgy, this series explores and challenges many key issues of worship and liturgical theology, currently in hot debate within academe and within Christian churches worldwide – issues central to the future of the liturgy, to public and private worship, and set to make a significant impact on changing patterns of worship and the place of the church in contemporary society.

Other titles in the series include

Daily Liturgical Prayer
Origins and Theology
Gregory W. Woolfenden

West Syrian Liturgical Theology
Baby Varghese

Inculturation of Christian Worship
Exploring the Eucharist
Phillip Tovey

Early and Medieval Rituals and Theologies of Baptism

From the New Testament to the Council of Trent

BRYAN D. SPINKS
Yale University, USA

ASHGATE

Published by
Ashgate Publishing Limited
Gower House
Croft Road
Aldershot
Hants GU11 3HR
England

Ashgate Publishing Company
Suite 420
101 Cherry Street
Burlington, VT 05401-4405
USA

Ashgate website: http://www.ashgate.com

British Library Cataloguing in Publication Data
Spinks, Bryan D.
  Early and medieval rituals and theologies of baptism: from
  the New Testament to the Council of Trent - (Liturgy,
  worship and society)
  1.Baptism–History–To 1500
  I.Title
  265.1'0902

Library of Congress Cataloging-in-Publication Data
Spinks, Bryan D.
Early and medieval rituals and theologies of baptism: from
  the New Testament to the Council of Trent / Bryan D. Spinks.
    p. cm. – (Liturgy, worship and society series)
  Includes bibliographical references and index.
    ISBN 0-7546-1427-1 (hardback: alk. paper) – ISBN 0-7546-1428-X (pbk: alk.
paper) 1. Baptism (Liturgy)–History. 2. Baptism–History. I. Title. II.
Series: Liturgy, worship, and society.

  BV803.S65 2005
  265'.1'09–dc22

                                                          2005011594

ISBN-10: 0-7546-1427-1 (Hbk)
ISBN-10: 0-7546-1428-X (Pbk)

Typeset by Manton Typesetters, Louth, Lincolnshire, UK.
Printed and bound in Great Britain by TJ International Ltd, Padstow, Cornwall.

Contents

List of Figures and Tables

Figure

Tables

Acknowledgements

I began work on a book on baptism in 1992. It was to be short, and would focus on particular theological issues being debated in the Church of England at that time. A rough draft was completed, and then abandoned. I am therefore grateful to Sarah Lloyd and the series editors for inviting me to revisit the subject, and to write a much wider and deeper study on baptism and baptismal liturgies. The material in this book, from the New Testament to the ritual issued by the Council of Trent, is the first of two studies on baptismal liturgies. The second will cover the period from the Reformation to the present. Each book is designed to stand alone, but they are clearly related in terms of chronology and development, and will share a common bibliography.

A task such as this requires help and support from many others. Dr Daniel Findykian gave invaluable help on the Armenian rite; and I am indebted to Simon Jones for insights on the Syrian rites. I would like to express my thanks to the librarians at the Yale Divinity School, Cambridge University Library, and the Bodleian Library, Oxford. I would also like to express my thanks to my research assistants, the Revd Kate Heichler, and Ms Melanie Ross, who enabled the checking of quotations and footnotes to be a relatively speedy process, and for checking my prose and grammar.

Bryan D. Spinks

Yale Institute of Sacred Music and Yale Divinity School,
New Haven, Connecticut
Epiphany 2005

Introduction

We were walking carefully through the bamboo forest, trying to avoid the nettles with their fiery sting. Eventually, we arrived at a glade where small rivulets trickled through deep mounds of grass towards a small pond. There we would hold the first baptism for the Dorobo people ... My wife Kym and I, missionaries with Africa Inland Mission International, started working with the Dorobo tribe in 1992. The Dorobo are hunter-gatherers in the highland forests of Kenya who, because their villages are difficult to access, had never heard the gospel ... We had first visited the Dorobo village of Oloolbung'aiko in March 1997. To my surprise, five people prayed to receive Christ on our first visit. They began meeting in a clearing in the bamboo forest. It gets cold at 9,000 feet above sea level, even on the equator. So they built a bamboo building, which we helped them roof. Now, a year later in April 1998, we were going to have our first baptism ... The shallow pond had thick weeds with lily-pad-like leaves. I tried to push the weeds aside to clear a section of water, but they resisted. I ended up just dunking the Dorobo believers under the weeds. They emerged adorned with leaves on their heads, but baptized and beaming ... At another baptism I was conducting in a stream near Sakutiek, we had dug a hole in the river because the water was barely a foot deep. The hole had filled with miry mud by the time I stepped in. Each candidate slid in beside me – up to their waist in mud. I bent them over just enough to get their heads under water. With each candidate, I sank a little deeper. Fortunately, I only baptized eight people that day. At the end, I had to claw my way out of the sucking grasp of the mud.[1]

Why make these Dorobo undergo this ritual called baptism? The rite, of course, goes back to the baptism of Jesus in the River Jordan. The River Jordan was the boundary that the ancient Israelites had had to cross in order to gain the promised land. Moses had seen the land, but died before his people crossed the Jordan. According to the story recorded in Joshua 3, the Jordan was in full flood. However, the priests carrying the Ark of the Covenant crossed over first, and when they dipped their feet into the Jordan, the waters coming from upstream stopped, 'and all Israel passed over on dry ground until the whole nation had crossed the river'. Joshua set up twelve stones in the middle of the Jordan to mark this event of crossing the river without getting wet (Joshua 4:9).

In contrast, the call of John the Baptist for the people to come to the Jordan was for the purpose of getting wet. According to the Synoptic Gospels, John summoned the people of Israel to undergo a ritual washing in the Jordan for the remission of sins in preparation for one who was to come with apocalyptic judgement; once more the Jordan was serving as a boundary to a promised land. The Gospels record John's activity because Jesus responded to his call, underwent this ritual washing in the Jordan, and emerged to a divine voice declaring him to be 'my beloved Son, with

---

[1] *Today's Christian*, Christian Reader, March/April 2000, <http://www.christianitytoday.com/tc/2000/002/7/63.html>.

whom I am well pleased', and by implication, the one who was to come. This Christological narrative, together with the command the risen Jesus gave to his disciples to baptize (Matthew 28:19), provide the foundational rationale for the Christian ritual practice of baptism. This present study is concerned with the development of these rituals from the New Testament churches to the Council of Trent, tracing how they evolved beyond the Jordan in the major ancient Christian Churches of East and West.

It was the anthropologist Arnold Van Gennep who coined the term 'rite de passage' for certain rituals which societies, organizations and religions use to mark a person's passing from one state or stage to another.[2] Baptism is certainly a rite of passage. In New Testament phraseology, it is a rite in which a person dies and rises with Christ, or is born again, and it is the rite of membership – the ordinary means by which one becomes a member of the Church, the Body of Christ, the people of God of the New Covenant. In predominantly paedobaptist Christian cultures, it has also functioned as a birth ritual. However, according to ritual-studies exponent Ronald Grimes, to enact any kind of rite is to *per*form, but to enact a rite of passage is also to *trans*form.[3] Baptism, again in New Testament terminology, actualizes transformation – some of its metaphors are a new creation, regeneration, being cleansed from sins, and being in Christ, or putting on the Lord Jesus Christ. The washing is a crossing of several boundaries, and the beginning of a journey into the promised land, the Kingdom of God.

In Christian theological parlance, baptism is a ritual which has been termed a sacrament. Of such rituals Stanley Hauerwas writes:

> The sacraments enact the story of Jesus and, thus, form a community in his image. We could not be the church without them. For the story of Jesus is not simply one that is told: it must be enacted. The sacraments are means crucial to shaping and preparing us to tell and hear that story. Thus baptism is that rite of initiation necessary for us to become part of Jesus' death and resurrection. Through baptism we do not simply learn the story, but we become part of that story.[4]

Baptism rituals articulate in language, symbol and gesture the narrative of the salvific work of Christ.

Though the identities of the original compilers of the ancient baptismal rites are shrouded in the mists of antiquity, the evolved rites were mainly the work of clerics articulating the faith of the Church. Larry Hoffman has reminded us that liturgy has many layers of meaning. Certainly where there is a text, or commonly repeated form and structure, these themselves carry the meaning of the author(s), the official church body, and the tradition. Beyond the text, however, is the meaning given by the

---

[2] Arnold van Gennep, *The Rites of Passage*, University of Chicago Press, Chicago, IL, 1960.

[3] Ronald L. Grimes, *Deeply into the Bone: Re-inventing Rites of Passage*, University of California Press, Berkeley, CA, 2000, p. 7.

[4] Stanley Hauerwas, *The Peaceable Kingdom*, University of Notre Dame Press, Notre Dame, IN, 1983, pp. 107–108.

particular celebrants of the rite, in their interpretation of the text or forms. And beyond these 'public' meanings are the private interpretations – the existential impact (or lack of impact) and reflection on the mind, heart and body of the recipients and those witnessing the rituals.[5] The full meaning of the rite would therefore consist of multiple layers of meaning, and include the personal stories. Cyprian, later bishop of Carthage, writing *c.* 246, told something of his personal story:

> Once I lay in darkness and in the depths of night and was tossed to and fro in the waves of the turbulent world, uncertain of the correct way to go, ignorant of my true life and a stranger to the light of truth. At that time and on account of the life I then led, it seemed difficult to believe what divine mercy promised for my salvation, namely, that someone could be born again and to a new life by being immersed in the healing water of baptism. It was difficult to believe that though I would remain the same man in bodily form, my heart and mind would be transformed.
>
> How was it possible, I thought, that a change could be great enough to strip away in a single moment the innate hardness of our nature? How could the habits acquired over the course of many years disappear, since these are so deeply rooted within us? If someone is used to fine feasts and lavish banquets, how can they learn restraint? If someone is used to dressing conspicuously in gold and purple, how can they cast them aside for ordinary simple clothes? Someone who loves the trappings of public office cannot become an anonymous private person. Anyone who is attended by great crowds of supporters and is honored by a dense entourage of obsequious attendants would consider solitude a punishment. While temptation still holds us fast, we are seduced by wine, inflated with pride, inflamed by anger, troubled by greed, goaded by cruelty, enticed by ambition and cast headlong by lust.
>
> These were my frequent thoughts. For I was held fast by the many sins of my life from which it seemed impossible for me to extricate myself. Thus I yielded to my sins which clung fast to me. Since I despaired of improvement I took an indulgent view of my faults and regarded them as if they were slaves born in my house.
>
> But after the life-giving water of baptism came to my rescue and took away the stain of my former years and poured into my cleansed and purified heart the light which comes from above, and after I had drunk in the Heavenly Spirit and was made a new man by a second birth, then amazingly what I had previously doubted became clear to me. What had been hidden was revealed. What had been dark became light. What previously had seemed impossible now seemed possible. What was in me of the guilty flesh now confessed it was earthly. What was made alive in me by the Holy Spirit was now quickened by God.[6]

However, such testimonies from antiquity are something of an exception. On the whole we have only the evolved liturgical rites, and earlier catechetical commentaries and homilies on the rites, giving us the 'public' meanings of the liturgies. Working within

---

[5] L.A. Hoffman, *Beyond the Text: A Holistic Approach to Liturgy*, Indiana University Press, Indianapolis, 1987.

[6] Cyprian, *To Donatus*, English translation in Oliver Davies (ed.), *Born to New Life. Cyprian of Carthage*, New City Press, Brooklyn, NY, 1992, pp. 21–2.

such limitations, nevertheless, it is hoped that this study will disclose something of the nature and development of the rites in the ancient major Christian Churches. It is hoped that in places this study will break new ground in that some new suggestions are made regarding some currently accepted scholarly views. Where possible I have tried to go a little beyond the text, exploring how the ritual was taught in commentaries and homilies.

PART I
RISING SPRINGS

CHAPTER 1

The New Testament Foundations

Origins

When writing to the churches of Rome *c.* 56 CE, Paul asked what seems to have been a rhetorical question, 'Are you not aware that all of us who have been baptized into Christ Jesus have been baptized into his death?' (Romans 6:3). It may well be that some of the recipients were not fully aware of the connection between baptism and Christ's death, but Paul certainly seemed to assume that all knew of the particular rite of initiation which had brought them into the *koinonia* of the Christian church.[1] In his earlier letter to the Galatians, Paul had written, 'For as many of you as were baptized into Christ have put on Christ' (Galatians 3:27), and in 1 Corinthians he had referred to divisions stemming from baptism. In none of the letters did Paul pause to give any lengthy explanation of baptism; he assumes that the recipients will know precisely what is being referred to. Whatever may have been the case at an earlier date, by the time of Paul's ministry it seems that baptism was the established ritual of Christian initiation. According to Matthew's Gospel (28:19), it was commanded by Jesus, and though many commentators take this to be a post-resurrection redaction, it nevertheless reflects the conviction of the Matthean community that the practice could be traced to Jesus himself. This at least is correct in that the Synoptic Gospels all attest that Jesus himself was baptized by John the Baptist in the Jordan. While the Fourth Gospel seems quite deliberately to avoid any hint that Jesus was baptized, nevertheless it too is clear in asserting the one-time link between the Baptist and Jesus. As James Dunn points out, the Christian story begins uniformly across all four Gospels with John the Baptist.[2]

According to Mark's Gospel, the beginning of the Gospel of Jesus Christ the Son of God begins with the ministry of John the Baptist who appeared in the wilderness, 'preaching a baptism of repentance for the forgiveness of sins'. Mark associates John scripturally with Malachi and Isaiah, and has him dressed as Elijah of old. This

---

[1] Hans Dieter Betz, 'Transferring a Ritual: Paul's Interpretation of Baptism in Romans 6', in (ed.) Troels Engberg-Pederson, *Paul in His Hellenistic Context*, T & T Clark, Edinburgh, 1994, sees this as a development in Paul's own theology, subsequent to Galatians and 1 Corinthians, and therefore a new idea. But cf. Charles Cranfield: 'The inference that the belief that baptism into Christ involved baptism into His death must therefore have belonged to the common primitive Christian teaching (as opposed to being a Pauline contribution), while not absolutely certain, is highly probable'. *The Epistle to the Romans*, Vol. 1, ICC T & T Clark, Edinburgh, 1975, p. 300.

[2] James D.G. Dunn, '"Baptized" as Metaphor', in (eds) Stanley E. Porter and Anthony R. Cross, *Baptism in the New Testament and the Church. Historical and Contemporary Studies in Honour of R.E.O. White*, Sheffield Academic Press, Sheffield, 1999, pp. 294–310, 300.

evangelist also asserts that John not only baptized, but also spoke of a figure to come who would administer a different baptism: 'I have baptized you with water; but he will baptize you with the Holy Spirit.' The content of John's preaching is elaborated in Matthew and Luke. It is a baptism of repentance to escape the coming judgement. The one greater than John, according to Matthew and Luke (Q), will baptize with the Holy Spirit and fire.

According to all three Synoptics, Jesus was baptized by John in the Jordan. Matthew adds that this was in order to 'fulfill all righteousness'.[3] All three agree (though Luke suggests it happened after the baptism when Jesus was praying) that when Jesus was baptized, immediately as he came up from the waters, the heavens opened, the Spirit like a dove descended on him, and a voice from heaven said, 'This is my beloved Son, with whom I am well pleased.'[4]

In the Fourth Gospel, the Baptist bears witness to the 'Light'. He says that he himself is not Elijah or one of the prophets, but is the one spoken of by Isaiah, crying in the wilderness (John 1:19–23). He announces that, while he baptizes with water, a greater one is coming, but there is no reference to a baptism with the Holy Spirit. The Baptist sees the Spirit descend on Jesus, and he bears witness that this is the Son of God and the Lamb of God. According to John 3:23, Jesus baptized, whereas in 4:22 it is asserted that only his disciples baptized. The first disciples, according to John, were originally followers of the Baptist. Thus, even if silent on the actual baptism of Jesus, the Fourth Gospel – like the Synoptics – links baptism with Jesus via John the Baptist.

Various suggestions have been made concerning the possible antecedents of John's baptism:[5]

- *Jewish cleansing and lustrations, and proselyte baptism:*[6] At first sight these seem to be promising parents for John's baptism. However, Jesus was reputed to be critical of some lustration rites (Mark 7), and proselyte baptism seems to have been influenced in part by the Christian practice – the main evidence for Jewish proselyte baptism post-dates Christian baptism. T.F. Torrance pointed out that, whereas in proselyte baptism the bathing was self-administered unless for children, in John's baptism and Christian baptism, all were treated as though they were children, in that someone baptized them.[7]

---

[3] Usually assumed to be an apologia for the sinless Christ undergoing a baptism for repentance.

[4] There are differences in emphasis as to whether Jesus alone was aware of this, or whether it was for all to see and hear. As regards the words from heaven, there are variants, some indicating that Sonship was being conferred at this point, rather than reiterating the incarnation, and may have been changed for Christological reasons.

[5] See G.R. Beasley-Murray, *Baptism in the New Testament*, Macmillan, London, 1963; Adela Yarbro Collins, 'The Origin of Christian Baptism', in (ed.) Maxwell E. Johnson, *Living Water, Sealing Spirit*, Pueblo, Collegeville, MN, 1995, pp. 35–57.

[6] See Beasley-Murray, pp. 18–25; Collins, pp. 41–6.

[7] T.F. Torrance, in Report of the Special Commission on Baptism 1955, in *Reports to the General Assembly*, Church of Scotland, Edinburgh 1955, 623. Torrance wrote most of the report.

- *The ritual bathings of Qumran*: In this community we have evidence of a ritual bath which pre-dates Christianity.[8] Indeed, the late J.A.T. Robinson suggested that John the Baptist was himself from the Essene community.[9] This suggested link between the Baptist and Qumran is, however, extremely tenuous. Furthermore, like Jewish cleansing rituals, those of Qumran were repeated.
- *Old Testament foundations*: Markus Barth, among others, has suggested such passages as Isaiah 1:16–17 and Ezekiel 36:25–28.[10] If the Synoptic portrayal of John has some basis in history, then John appeared as one of the prophets of old, and Elijah and Ezekiel are prophets who certainly used prophetic symbolism. While not mimetic magic, this symbolism acted as a visible word, and helped bring about what it symbolised.[11] Adela Collins observes:

> The tradition of the prophetic symbolic action and the growing importance of ritual ablutions were contributing factors in making John a baptizer rather than simply a preacher or oracular prophet. The significance of John's baptism is best understood in terms of a prophetic reinterpretation of the sense of defilement in ethical terms and an apocalyptic expectation of judgment.[12]

None of these can probably be claimed to be the exclusive antecedent to John, but together they provide a religious and cultural milieu which allowed this wilderness preacher to institute his particular ritual. Jesus, it would seem, was originally allied with the Baptist, but later broke from him, and the Jesus movement became distinct with its own rite of baptism.

A Christocentric and Trinitarian Basis for Christian Baptism?

One of the several differences between the baptism of John the Baptist and that of the early Christian movement was that, whereas the former was a baptism of or for something (namely repentance), the latter was a baptism into something, namely into Jesus Christ, or into his Name, or into the Name of the Father, Son and Holy Spirit. Although the Greek does have 'in the name' (*en*), in the sense of 'by someone's authority' (Acts 10:48), it is to be understood in the sense of 'into' (*eis* or *epi*), as in Acts 8:36, 1 Corinthians 1:13, Matthew 28:19 – something recognized and stressed by the sixteenth-century Reformed theologian, Huldrych Zwingli.[13] Being baptized

---

[8] See for example CD 10:12–13; IQS 3:6–9. E.F. Sutcliffe, 'Baptism and Baptismal Rites at Qumran', *Heythrop Journal* 1 (1960), 69–101.

[9] J.A.T. Robinson, 'The Baptism of John and the Qumran Community', in *Twelve New Testament Studies*, SCM, London, 1962, pp. 11–17.

[10] Markus Barth, 'Baptism,' in (ed.) Keith Crim, *The Interpreter's Dictionary of the Bible, Supplementary Volumes*, Abingdon, Nashville, TN, 1972.

[11] Gerhard Von Rad, *Old Testament Theology*, Vol. 2, Oliver and Boyd, Edinburgh, 1965, 95ff.

[12] Collins, 'Origins of Christian Baptism', p. 40.

[13] See Lars Hartman, *Into the Name of the Lord Jesus. Baptism in the Early Church*, T & T Clark,

into the name has to do with identity and ownership. In the Semitic world the 'name' had considerable significance – that is why it was important for Moses to know the name of the 'Lord' who encountered him in the burning bush, or for Jacob to know the name of the one who wrestled with him till dawn, and probably why Jesus was interested in the name of the demons oppressing the Gerasene demoniac. The name was regarded as the bearer, the person, his or her whole reality; through a name a person made him or herself known. To be baptized into the name of Jesus may be regarded at the very least as to be dipped, immersed or poured into the person and identity of Jesus, and to participate in the sphere of his power, authority and Lordship. Whatever else may be said of baptism – remission of sins, new birth, covenant, adoption – it is first and foremost into the name of the Lord Jesus. Thus Paul speaks of putting on the Lord Jesus (Galatians 3:27), or of being baptized into one body (1 Corinthians 12:13), or, in the Romans 6 passage, of being baptized into Jesus' death and being united with him.

The Synoptic Gospels' account of the baptism of Jesus reveals his identity. It is quite possible that the incident has been shaped by the Testament of Levi, where in chapter 18, the Lord will raise up a new eschatological priest: 'The heavens will be opened, and from the temple of glory sanctification will come upon him, with a fatherly voice, as from Abraham to Isaac. And the spirit of understanding and sanctification shall rest upon him [in the water].'[14]

His will be a priesthood in which sin ceases, and paradise will be regained. Mark had already announced that he is Jesus the Messiah, the Son of God (Mark 1:1); Matthew had announced that he shall save his people because Yah saves (Matthew 1:21); and Luke that he is the Son of the Most High God, conceived by the power of the Most High (Luke 1:32, 35). In all these accounts, when Jesus emerged from the Jordan, the word of the Father addressed him as the Son, and the Spirit descended on him. Thus, through his baptism in the Jordan, the identity of Jesus as Son of God has a Trinitarian dimension, involving a disclosure of God the Father, and the work of the Holy Spirit. Whatever might be the judgement of Form Criticism on the origin of Matthew 28:19, the formula is a legitimate inference of the meaning of baptism into the name of Jesus, linking it to the triune disclosure at his own baptism.

A similar argument can be made for the Fourth Gospel. Some New Testament scholars believe that St John's Gospel is anti-sacramental, and thus find little of significance on baptism in it. Others argue that allusions to the sacraments abound throughout the Gospel. R.E. Brown took what seems to be the middle view, suggesting that we have to distinguish between the meaning of passages in their primary redaction, and the various resonances for readers of the final redaction.[15]

Edinburgh, 1997; T.F. Torrance, Report of the Commission on Baptism; Zwingli's formula was 'N. Ich touff dich in den namen des vatters und des suns und des heiligen geistes.'

[14] *Testament of Levi*, in (ed.) J.H. Charlesworth, *The Old Testament Pseudepigrapha*, Vol. 1, Doubleday, Garden City, NY, 1983, p. 795; 'in the water' is regarded as a Christian addition.

[15] R. Bultmann, *The Gospel of John*, E.T. Westminster Press, Philadelphia, PA, 1971; C.H. Dodd,

In several of the Johannine passages which seem possibly to allude to baptism there is a marked concern to reveal the identity of Jesus, who is the Logos made flesh. The high Christology of the final redaction of this Gospel is concerned to stress the humanity and divinity of Jesus. Thus in John 1–3 (or even 4), the themes of water, perhaps suggesting baptism, seem to be interwoven with the disclosure of the person of Jesus. In John 1:29–34, though it does not record the baptism of Jesus itself, John the Baptist recognizes Jesus as the Lamb of God, carrying sacrificial overtones; as the pre-existing One, pointing to the incarnation, the Word made flesh, and as the vehicle of the Spirit, pointing to glorification. In the account of the first miracle at Cana in John 2, the evangelist stresses that the stone vats filled with water which Jesus turned to wine were the kind used for Jewish purification rites, perhaps suggesting baptismal themes. In John 3, the theme of water and salvation, which at least echoes baptism, is inextricably linked to the one who came down from heaven and who will also be lifted up. The incident at the well in Samaria, although not directly concerned with baptism, nevertheless mentions Jesus as the living water, and may well have signalled the content of baptism for readers of the final redaction. This is probably true also of 1 John 5:5–8, with its reference to water and blood, even though its primary concern is almost certainly Christological, showing that Jesus was Son of God at his birth, and the same Son of God when he died on the cross. A similar secondary reference to baptism quite possibly underlies John 19:34, where the primary reference might be the imparting of the Spirit through the shedding of blood. If there are allusions to baptism, they are linked firmly with the person of Jesus.

The New Testament use of the term *baptisma* is also relevant for this discussion. Jesus is recorded as using it regarding his own destiny and death, though with clear echoes of his *Baptismos*, and it is not found elsewhere.[16] Jesus said he had a baptism with which he must be baptized, and James and John were asked if they were ready to be baptized with it. *Baptisma* thus contains not only the declaration of who Jesus is – the incarnate Son of the Father who is glorified by the Spirit – but also expresses his ignoble end, which the New Testament regards as a sacrifice, an atonement and the means of the New Covenant. It could be argued that the implications of Jesus' reference to his *baptisma* are echoed in Paul's teaching in Romans 6, that one is baptized into Jesus Christ, which means into his death and resurrection.

The link between the rite of baptism and *baptisma* as death raises the question of the significance of the term 'covenant' for understanding baptism. According to Gordon Kuhrt, covenant is the overriding theme of the canon of scripture, and is also the central concept for interpreting baptism.[17] As important as the theme might be, however, the death of Jesus inaugurated a *new* Covenant in his blood, not a continuation or fulfilment of the Old. As Aidan Kavanagh put it, 'In John's baptism of Jesus the Old

---

Interpretation of the Fourth Gospel, Cambridge University Press, Cambridge, 1951; R.E. Brown, *The Gospel According to John*, 2 vols, Doubleday, Garden City, NY, 1966/70.

[16] Beasley-Murray, *Baptism in the New Testament*, p. 73.

[17] Gordon Kuhrt, *Believing in Baptism*, Mowbray, London, 1987.

Covenant did not so much come to an end as mutate into the New by the agency of a divine act manifesting Jesus as the Messiah of God.'[18] The Son's obedience to the Father in the Spirit becomes the whole context of the new covenant. E.P. Sanders has outlined what he describes as 'covenantal nomism', which he believed was common to much of the literature of Judaism that has come down to us.[19] Although it includes the free grace of God in the election of Israel, the Law indicates both God's promises of election and the need for obedience. Obedience is necessary to remain in the covenant. In contrast, so Sanders argues, for Paul the Jewish covenant cannot be effective for salvation. Sanders concedes that a case can be made for seeing in Paul a Christianity on its way to becoming a new form of covenantal nomism, entered by baptism in place of circumcision. However, he argues that this is an inadequate assessment, because what is most important for Paul are the 'participationist transfer terms', such as partaking in the death, freedom, new creation, reconciliation and justification:

> The heart of Paul's thought is not that one ratifies and agrees to a covenant offered by God, becoming a member of a group with a covenantal relation with God and remaining in it on the condition of behaviour; but that one dies with Christ, obtaining new life and the initial transformation, that one is a member of the body of Christ and one Spirit with him, and that one remains so unless one breaks the participatory union by forming another.[20]

The point is that one is in the new covenant because one is baptized into the Name of him who is the new covenant. Ultimately baptism, the 'cultic actualization of the salvific work of Jesus',[21] is grounded in the whole person and work of Jesus Christ, the Son of the Father and giver of the Spirit. The Christian rite of baptism has an unmistakably Christocentric and Trinitarian basis.

Baptismal Themes

In his study of baptism in the New Testament, G.R. Beasley-Murray gave a penultimate chapter entitled 'The Doctrine of Christian Baptism', in which he drew together the conclusions of his detailed and thorough study. A rather looser approach is taken by Lars Hartman, who notes that the texts represent a variety of ways of thinking about baptism, and are not always in harmony with one another, and that the different emphases among the New Testament writers should not be overlooked.[22]

It has been suggested above that the foundation of Christian baptism – and that which differentiates it from the baptism of John the Baptist – is *Christocentric* and

---

[18] Aidan Kavanagh, *The Shape of Baptism*, Pueblo, New York, 1978, p. 11.

[19] E.P. Sanders, *Paul and Palestinian Judaism: A Comparison of Patterns of Religion*, SCM Press, London, 1977; Sanders, *Paul*, Oxford University Press, Oxford, 1991.

[20] Sanders, *Paul and Palestinian Judaism*, p. 514.

[21] Hartman, *Into the Name of the Lord Jesus*, p. 163.

[22] Ibid.

Trinitarian. But there are other important dimensions, some of which are in continuity with the baptism of John, and some of which are peculiar to Christian baptism.

John preached a baptism of preparation and repentance for the forgiveness of sins; those who flocked to him confessed their sins in the Jordan. This *soteriological* dimension is reproduced in the primitive *kerygma* as recorded by Luke in Acts. Peter called on his audience to repent and be baptized so that their sins may be forgiven (Acts 2:38), and in the Lukan account of Paul's testimony of his conversion, Ananias called upon him to 'be baptized and wash away your sins' (Acts 22:16). In 1 Corinthians 6:11, Paul writes, 'You have been through the purifying waters; you have been dedicated to God and justified through the name of the Lord Jesus and the Spirit of God.' Here the term 'justification', so important in Galatians and Romans, is associated with baptism and with purification. In Romans 5, Paul had discussed justification, Christ's sacrificial death and the sin of Adam. In Romans 6, he turns to the ritual of baptism to assert that Christians have died to sin. Just as Christ died and was raised again, so 'in the same way you must regard yourselves as dead to sin and alive to God, in union with Christ Jesus. So sin must no longer reign in your mortal body'.

Ephesians 5:25–7 speaks of Christ's love for the Church, giving himself up for it, to consecrate it, cleansing it by water and word, which may be a reference to baptism. The writer of Hebrews speaks of 'our guilty hearts sprinkled clean, our bodies washed with pure water' (Hebrews 10:22). In 1 Peter, the writer mentions the ark of Noah, which prefigures baptism.[23] The writer stresses that the washing is not of bodily pollution, but that it 'brings salvation'. Here we have a variety of approaches to a soteriological understanding of baptism: it washes, regenerates (1 Timothy 6:13), it justifies, saves, frees from the slavery of sin and brings forgiveness of sins.

If soteriology is a common theme between John's baptism and Christian baptism, a sharp difference is the *pneumatological* theme. John announced one who was to come, who would baptize with the Holy Spirit. In the Fourth Gospel there is rich teaching on the Paraclete who is breathed out on the disciples at the resurrection. In John 3, Nicodemus is told that he must be born again, and that this rebirth is by water and Spirit, for it is the Spirit that gives birth to the Spirit. In Acts a rather different but equally sophisticated theology of the Spirit is unfolded, with Pentecost – where the Spirit is also 'as fire' – being the outpouring of the Spirit on the Church. But the *kerygma* that Luke collects in Acts, the Old Testament text on which Peter preaches, is the prophecy of Joel with the promise of the outpouring of the Spirit. If the people repent and are baptized, they will receive the gift of the Holy Spirit. In Acts 10, the Gentiles receive the Spirit as Peter preaches, and then receive baptism. Also, in Acts 8, Samaritans are baptized by Philip, but the Spirit is given later through Peter and John. In 1 Corinthians 12:13, Paul asserts that we were all brought into one body by baptism, and that 'the one Holy Spirit was poured out for all of us to drink'. As

---

[23] For the possible local background to this, see Larry J. Kreitzer, 'On Board the Eschatological Ark of God: Noah-Deucalion and the "Phrygian Connection" in 1 Peter 3.19–22', in Porter and Cross, *Baptism*, pp. 228–72.

Wheeler-Robinson observed, 'Baptism, in its New Testament context, is always a baptism of the Spirit.'[24]

The baptism of John was concerned to call Jews to repentance, and John seemingly rejected the notion that the Jew had a right to the Kingdom, simply as a Jew.[25] The Gospels portray Jesus as founding a new people with twelve new leaders who would judge the twelve tribes of Israel. Continuity with old Israel there most certainly was, but also discontinuity. Jesus is portrayed as founding an *ekklesia*, and Paul too is concerned with *ekklesiae*, not synagogues. Christian initiation has a distinct *ecclesiological* emphasis, in that Christians become members of the Church. Paul's emphasis is on one baptism into one body, the body of Christ. 1 Peter speaks of a chosen race, a royal priesthood, a dedicated nation and a people claimed by God for his own (1 Peter 2:9). Paul, writing to the Galatians, says, 'For through faith you are all sons of God in union with Christ Jesus. Baptized into union with him, you have all put on Christ as a garment. There is no such thing as Jew nor Greek, slave nor free, male nor female, for you are all one in Christ Jesus' (Galatians 3:26–8). Hartman notes of baptism, 'It was not only a "rite de passage" for those who entered a new phase of God's history with his people. It was also the door into a new human community.'[26]

John's baptism took place in the context of preaching the coming judgement and the coming of one greater than John. In other words, there was an *eschatological* dimension. Jesus fulfils the preaching of John, and inaugurates the Kingdom. But the Jesus movement itself was and is a community which lives between the times – between the time of the resurrection, and that of the *parousia* or *telos*. Thus, Paul in Romans 6 can speak of dying in baptism, but with the hope that 'we shall also be one with him in a resurrection like his'. Some of the problems of the Corinthian community seem to have stemmed from the belief of some members that, having been baptized into an eschatological community, they were already in the resurrected state and free from all laws and responsibilities. If anything, baptism into the Church creates what might be called a liminal stage of a rite of passage, since the aggregation or reintegration comes about only with the *parousia*.

Another eschatological theme is that of new birth and new creation; the Fourth Gospel speaks of the need to be born again from above, and Paul in 2 Corinthians states that 'If anyone is in Christ, he is a new creation; the old has passed away, behold, the new has come' (2 Corinthians 5:17).

One important aspect of baptism in the New Testament is the place of *faith* and/or response. John's baptism was administered after preaching, and seemed to be regarded as itself a response to that preaching and a sign of repentance. Whether idealized or not, the response to Peter's preaching in Acts 2 – 'Those who accepted his word' (verse 41) – was apparently immediate baptism. In Acts 8, Philip gives some

---

[24] H. Wheeler-Robinson, *Baptist Principles*, London, 1938, p. 77, cited in Beasley-Murray, *Baptism in the New Testament*, p. 277.

[25] Beasley-Murray, *Baptism in the New Testament*, p. 33.

[26] Hartman, *Into the Name of the Lord Jesus*, p. 46.

rudimentary exegesis of the passage in Isaiah to the Ethiopian eunuch, who then receives baptism (in the next body of water they happen upon). Whether any prolonged instruction was received by, for example, the Corinthians, is difficult to say. The Word was preached, and the response of desiring baptism seems to have counted as a sign of repentance and faith. Likewise in Acts 16:30–34, the jailer hears the word of the Lord, and then he and his whole family are baptized. As Hartman notes, baptism is 'a ritual point of intersection between that which is preached and its acceptance'.[27]

Perhaps a final observation is that the New Testament writers employ a host of images in association with baptism and belonging to the Church. There are clothing images: stripping off and putting on, liberation from sin and the power of darkness, reconciliation, illumination, cleansing and building. It is also possible that marriage is an image: Ephesians 5:25–6, Revelation 22:17.

Baptismal Ritual Patterns?

Although there may be many allusions to baptismal rituals in the New Testament, some of which may be entirely lost on contemporary readers, the fact remains that it does not outline any ideal pattern or ritual of Christian initiation. It may well be that the accounts of the baptism of Jesus in the Synoptic Gospels, like the accounts of the Last Supper, are influenced by liturgical usage, but since we do not know what that liturgical usage was, we have no way of evaluating what the extent of that influence might have been. It may well be that the Synoptic sequence of Jesus going into the water, a voice from heaven, and the descent of the Spirit might suggest the ritual of dipping/immersion, a spoken formula, and some rite indicating the gift of the Spirit. Paul's discussion in Romans 6 has caused speculation on whether the Isis cult might have influenced the ritual he presupposes, or whether the dying/rising language suggests submersion.[28]

The accounts of initiation in Acts have caused considerable discussion, since there we find references not only to baptism, but also to the laying-on of hands associated with the gift of the Spirit as a ritual gesture after baptism. Equally, in the case of Cornelius, the gift of the Spirit comes prior to baptism. We also hear of those who had received the baptism of John, but whom Paul instructed, baptized and laid hands upon for the gift of the Spirit. Beasley-Murray observes:

> A well-known ordering of the evidence is provided by Johannes Weiss and by Jackson and Lake. By ranging the narratives of Pentecost along with the Cornelius

---

[27] Ibid., p. 163.

[28] See A.J.M. Wedderburn, *Baptism and Resurrection. Studies in Pauline Theology Against its Graeco-Roman Background*, J.C.B. Mohr, Tübingen 1987; Hans Dieter Betz, 'Transferring a Ritual: Paul's Interpretation of Baptism in Romans 6', in (ed.) Troels Engberg-Pedersen, *Paul in His Hellenistic Context*, pp. 84–118; Brook W.R. Pearson, 'Baptism and Initiation in the Cult of Isis and Sarapis', in Porter and Cross, *Baptism*, pp. 42–62.

incident (chs 2 and 10), and that of the Samaritan community with those of Apollos and the Ephesian disciples (chs 8, 18, 19), they produce a well-defined evolution of baptismal theology: first, the Spirit is believed to be given solely on the basis of faith in Jesus as Messiah (Peter's demand for baptism in 2.38 and the statements that he baptized converts at Pentecost and the members of Cornelius' household are to be viewed as editorial additions); secondly, the Spirit is mediated by baptism, as is seen in the additions just mentioned and in Paul's question to the Ephesian disciples, 'Did you receive the Holy Spirit when you believed?' (19.2); thirdly, the Spirit is mediated not through baptism but by the laying on of hands of Apostolic men (ch. 8).[29]

But, as Beasley-Murray observes, this neat evolutionary account is produced at a price. It may be better to see Acts as witness to a variety of ritual practices rather than a progression of fixed forms.

What is said of these texts also applies to speculation about whether chrism was used ('seal' in Ephesians 1:13–14) or whether the references to clothing (Galatians 3:27) signify a ritual stripping-off and a ritual putting-on of white garments. They might do so, but it is impossible to know whether the language is simply linguistic imagery, or whether it reflects a ritual action.

The Fourth Gospel's account of foot washing at the Last Supper has been regarded as having baptismal overtones. However, it has been suggested that bathing to the ankles (foot washing) was a form of baptism practiced by the Johannine community. This cannot be ruled out, but if it was so, this ritual did not survive as an initiation rite, though foot washing was part of the initiatory rites in fourth-century Milan, and may be alluded to in writings in baptism of Aphrahat, the Persian theologian.[30] Similarly, in 1 Corinthians, Paul refers to the practice of baptizing on behalf of the dead. Paul assumes his readers know the practice, and he does not elaborate. Nowhere else in the New Testament is there any reference to this practice, which seems not to have survived the New Testament period, though it resurfaced in the Church of Jesus Christ of Latter Day Saints.

Concluding Remarks

The New Testament is both the fulcrum from which emerges all theological reflections on baptism and all Christian baptismal rites, and the touchstone, or 'norming norm' against which they may be tested.[31] However, the books of the New Testament present neither a single doctrine of baptism, nor some archetypal liturgical rite. The various

---

[29] Beasley-Murray, *Baptism in the New Testament*, p. 106.

[30] See John Christopher Thomas, *Footwashing in John 13 and the Johannine Community*, Sheffield Academic Press, Sheffield, 1991.

[31] For the term 'norming norm', see Stanley J. Grenz and John R. Francke, *Beyond Foundationalism. Shaping Theology in a Postmodern Context*, Westminster John Knox Press, Louisville, KY, 2001, Chapter 3.

writers allude to baptism, or discuss baptism in passing, or are concerned to draw out Christological and salvific claims from the baptism of Jesus. We are presented with the fact of Jesus' baptism, but beyond that we have not so much a systematic baptismal theology as some kaleidoscopic pictures. The New Testament communicates these pictures through a rich tapestry of imagery. Jesus Christ is the eyepiece of the kaleidoscope, and all other concepts and images are focused through him. Much of this imagery forms part of a doctrinal understanding of baptism, and much of it features in liturgical rites. However, the history of the development of both poses questions: which elements in the kaleidoscope pictures are placed in the foreground, and which remain in the background? Which are major and indispensable, and which are minor and merely decorative? And how, beyond the use of water, are these ritualized? The chapters which follow discuss how churches at different times and places have answered these questions.

CHAPTER 2

Pre-Nicene Baptismal Practice and Faith

Both the liturgical and doctrinal evidence for baptism from the pre-Nicene period is sparse. First, the Christian churches seem to have grown through a period of orality, when rites and ceremonies were part of tradition handed on, but not necessarily written down. Once the tradition needed to be written down, antiquity was not in the habit of preserving old documents as collector's items. Worn-out manuscripts were discarded and replaced by new ones. This means that what liturgical fragments and documents have survived are fortunate accidents which enable us to have some idea of the rites and practices of this period. However, since the survivals are few, we should not infer that each one is a typical rite representative of all Christian churches everywhere at that time. The liturgical documents in particular witness to a particular area or group at a particular time, and how typical a rite may have been often must remain an open question.

With theological writings, we are only slightly more fortunate. Writers such as Tertullian and Origen do indeed reflect on the theological meaning of baptism, either directly or indirectly. But it is impossible to know how representative their views were, or how widely their writings were disseminated. They certainly give us some insight as to what certain articulate Christian thinkers thought. Within the parameters of these limitations, we may proceed to investigate these sources, by geographical grouping.

Syria and Asia Minor

The Testimony of the Didache

This work was discovered by Archbishop Philotheos Byrennios in 1873, and is named Manuscript 54 in the library of the Greek Orthodox Patriarchate in Jerusalem. It is a Greek text, and another Greek version is found in Ms. Poxy 1782. However, there is also a Coptic fragment in the British Library with significant variations. The Coptic fragment is older than the Greek manuscripts, and although it may not represent the oldest text, it cannot be simply dismissed.

The document is a Church Order. Niederwimmer divides it into four sections:[1]

---

[1] See Paul F. Bradshaw, *The Search for the Origins of Christian Worship*, Oxford University Press, New York, 2002 edition, Chapter 4 for the characteristics of Church Orders; Kurt Niederwimmer, *Didache*, ET Augsburg Fortress, Minneapolis, MN, 1998.

1   A Baptismal Catechesis: A Tract on the Two Ways (that is, a moral instruction), chapters 1–6
2   Agenda, or liturgical section, relating to baptism and a meal, chapters 7–10
3   Church Order, on ministry, chapters 11–15
4   Eschatological section, chapter 16.

The late Joan Hazelden Walker regarded the *Didache* as a pre-Marcan and possibly pre-Pauline document, and others have dated it to the late second century.[2] The majority of scholars seem to place it as contemporary with St Matthew's Gospel, *c.* 80 CE. Whereas some have suggested an Egyptian provenance, most scholars place it in the region of Antioch. There seems to be considerable agreement that it is a composite document, and Chapters 1–6 are probably the oldest stratum.[3]

In some books on liturgy, the *Didache* is treated as though it witnesses to what all churches did at the end of the first century CE. It seems rather to be the product of a conservative Jewish-Christian group, and may not be at all representative of Gentile ecclesial groups. It has a distinct Matthean flavour (and there is much discussion on whether the authors knew Matthew or drew on an independent Matthean tradition) and a glaring absence of Pauline theology. Jonathan Reed notes:

> While *Didache* 1–6 presents a code of ethics which is in continuity with the Israelite past of the community, and *Didache* 7–10 introduces communal rituals which are appropriate to the resumption of the true Israel, the 'church order' in *Didache* 11–15 elucidates the metamorphosis from Israel to the church with a particular focus upon social roles. The church's apostles and prophets are equated with the prophets of old (11.11), itinerant Christians are equated with the pilgrims of old (12.1), prophets and teachers are equated with the high priests of old (13.4), and the eucharist is equated with the temple sacrifices of old (14.1).[4]

In other words, for this community the church stands in line with the Mosaic Law, the Davidic lineage, the priestly system, and the Temple cult. Jonathan Draper believes that Chapters 7–10 are best interpreted against a background of initiation of Gentile converts into a Jewish-Christian community which looked to the authority of Jerusalem rather than to Paul.[5]

The information which the document gives is sparse. Willi Rordorff suggests that, at least in the composite document, Chapters 1–6 represent pre-baptismal instruction.[6]

---

[2] Joan Hazelden Walker, 'A pre-Marcan Dating for the Didache: Further Thoughts of a Liturgist', *Studia Biblica* (1978), Sheffield Academic Press, Sheffield, 1980, 403–11; F.E. Vokes, *The Riddle of the Didache: Fact or Fiction, Heresy or Catholicism?*, SPCK, London, 1938.

[3] See Clayton N. Jefford (ed.), *The Didache in Context*, E.J. Brill, Leiden, 1995; Jonathan A. Draper (ed.), *The Didache in Modern Research*, E.J. Brill, Leiden, 1996; Huub van de Sandt and David Flusser, *The Didache*, Fortress Press, Minneapolis, MN, 2002.

[4] Jonathan Reed, 'The Hebrew Epic and the *Didache*' in Jefford, *The Didache*, pp. 213–25.

[5] Jonathan A. Draper, 'Ritual Process and Ritual Symbol in Didache 7–10', *Vigiliae Christianae* 54 (2000), 121–58, p. 122.

[6] Willi Rordorf, 'Baptism according to the Didache', in Draper, *The Didache in Modern Research*, E.J. Brill, Leiden, 1996, pp. 212–22.

Certainly Chapter 7.1 refers back to what has been said previously. Baptism is in the name of the Father and of the Son and of the Holy Spirit, as in Matthew 28:19, though *Didache* 9.5 mentions baptism in the name of the Lord. The *Didache* allows baptism in living water, cold or warm, but also triple pouring as a default mode of baptism. In Jewish thought, 'living water' refers to water that is running rather than still or stagnant, but could nevertheless include a cistern, public baths or fountain. The earliest known font is that preserved in the house church at Dura Europos, and this was a cistern in which someone could stand and have water poured on them. The *Didache* instructs the baptizand and officiant to fast beforehand.

The Coptic version does not have the section on baptism, but immediately before the meal prayers has the following:

> Concerning the matter of the stinoufi give thanks thus, as you say: We give thanks to you, Father, concerning the stinoufi which you made known to us through Jesus, your child. Yours is the glory which is for ever. Amen.

Stinoufi means fragrance, and may refer to incense; some, however, have suggested that it refers to baptismal perfume or chrism.

On the whole we have little information here of the meaning of baptism, and little on its ritual practice. Pertinent, however, is the comment of Nathan Mitchell on its meaning within the context of this Jewish-Christian community which lived in the ambit of the Torah:

> For the Didachist, baptism does *not* create an egalitarian community. Gentile Christians are 'second-class citizens,' and are ultimately expected to embrace Torah observance. (One must become a Jew in order to be a Christian.) The baptismal liturgy of the *Didache* provides, therefore, yet another reflection of a Jewish-Christian group which wishes to remain faithful to the Torah, and is unwilling to follow either the 'extreme liberals' (Paul's party, a thoroughgoing affirmation of the legitimacy of gentile Christianity) or the 'extreme hardliners' (ultra-right-wing Jewish Christians who have abandoned the ekklesia [congregation] and returned to the synagogue). It is a community which preaches what Jesus preached, but which does not necessarily preach *Jesus*.[7]

Melito of Sardis

Flourishing sometime between 160–170 CE, Melito of Sardis wrote a *Homily on the Passion of Christ*, and other works of which only fragments have survived. One of the fragments is possibly from a work on baptism. It tells us nothing of the practice in Sardis, nor does it reveal much theological articulation. Melito had been trained in Greek rhetoric, and in this fragment he speaks of the heavenly bodies being reflected on the ocean and therefore being baptized. Speaking of the sun at sunset, and likening this to molten bronze being plunged in water, Melito says that it

---

[7] Nathan Mitchell, 'Baptism in the Didache', in Jefford, *The Didache*, pp. 226–55, p. 255.

... wholly undying bathes in cold water, but keeps the fire unsleeping; and when he has bathed in symbolic baptism, he exults greatly, taking the water as food. Though one and the same, he rises for men as a new sun, tempered from the deep, purified from the bath.[8]

From this he turns to speak of Christ's baptism in the Jordan. The fragment says little, and it would be hazardous to make any conclusions since we have no idea what the rest of the work might have said. The fragment does underscore the idea of purification and new birth from the waters of baptism.

The Odes of Solomon

There are four sources for the forty-two *Odes of Solomon*, namely the Pistis Sophia, manuscripts H and N, and more recently, the Bodmer Papyrus, G. Most of the *Odes* survive in Syriac, which is probably their original language, but five are preserved in Coptic and one in Greek.[9] According to J.H. Charlesworth, most scholars date them between 70–125 CE, and in Charlesworth's view they are Jewish-Christian.[10] When the *Odes* were published by J.H. Bernard, he argued that they were baptismal hymns, and K.A. Aytoun has argued that a baptismal liturgy can be reconstructed from them; on the other hand, Charlesworth argued that they had nothing to do with baptism, and were just simply hymns.[11] Mark Pierce has taken a middle view, namely that some of the hymns reflect an interest in the baptism of Jesus in the Jordan, and use baptismal imagery and allusions.[12] For example, Ode 24:

1 The dove fluttered over the head of our Lord Messiah,
   Because he was her head.
2 And she cooed over him
   And her voice was heard.

It is difficult not to hear echoes here of Genesis 1:2 and Deuteronomy 32:11. The Ode speaks of Jesus descending into Sheol and giving life, and it seems that this Ode depicts Jesus being anointed with the Spirit in order to carry out the work of salvation. In Ode 11 there seems to be a parallel between baptism and circumcision, and use of the term 'Way', which we also encounter in the *Didache*:

---

[8] Thomas M. Finn, *Early Christian Baptism and the Catechumenate – Volume 1: West and East Syria*, Liturgical Press, Collegeville, MN, 1992, hereafter, *ECBC*, 1, p. 36.

[9] J. Emerton, 'Some Problems of Text and Language in the Odes of Solomon', *Journal of Theological Studies* 18 (1967) 372–406.

[10] J.H. Charlesworth, *The Pseudepigrapha and Modern Research*, Scholars Press, Chico, CA, 1981, p. 190.

[11] J.H. Bernard, *The Odes of Solomon*, Cambridge University Press, Cambridge, 1912; K.A. Aytoun, 'The Mysteries of Baptism by Moses bar Kepha Compared with the Odes of Solomon', in J. Vellian (ed.), *The Syrian Churches Series* 6, CMS Press, Kottayam, Kerala, India, 1973, pp. 1–15; J.H. Charlesworth, 'The Odes of Solomon – not Gnostic', in *The Catholic Biblical Quarterly* 31 (1969), 357–69.

[12] Mark Pierce, 'Themes in the "Odes of Solomon" and other early Christian Writings and their Baptismal Character', *Ephemerides Liturgicae* 98 (1984), 35–59.

> For the Most High circumcised me by his Holy Spirit,
> then he uncovered my inward being toward him,
> and filled me with his love.
> And his circumcising became my salvation,
> and I ran in the way in his peace,
> in the way of truth.

More important, at least for some modern discussions, is the use of feminine language for the Spirit. It is possible to overplay this fact. Since *ruah* is feminine in Syriac grammar, it is quite natural that feminine imagery should have been suggested, particularly in terms of baptism as new birth. Ode 19 has:

> A cup of milk was offered to me,
> and I drank it in the sweetness of the Lord's kindness.
> The Son is the cup,
> and the Father is he who has milked;
> and the Holy Spirit is she who milked him;
>
> The Holy Spirit opened her bosom (or womb),
> and mixed the milk of the two breasts of the Father.

Simon Jones has noted that the Syriac word translated as 'bosom' might better here be rendered as 'womb', since the image develops in terms of the milk/grace of the Father being mixed in the womb of the Spirit, who gives birth to the mixture which is communicated to Mary in order that she might conceive.[13] In Ode 36 we find mention of the anointing of Christ by the Father which accompanies the presence of the Spirit. The allusions are certainly suggestive of concern for the imagery of new birth in baptism and anointing with the Spirit, but it would be anachronistic to attempt to reconstruct some rite based on later usage. Mark Pierce's judgement seems wise – that though

> ... the highly developed typology and the use of rich imageries characteristic of the author of the *Odes of Solomon* does seem to have a certain relationship with the baptismal theology of second and third century Syria, these allusions are not immediately and automatically identifiable with later baptismal practices that would surface in the Syrian communities.[14]

The Didascalia

Like the *Didache*, the *Didascalia* is a Church Order. It exists in Syriac, though the original language seems to have been Greek. It is thought to have originated in the region north-east of Antioch in the early third century, and the author is thought to be a Hellenized Syrian bishop. According to the study by Charlotte Methuen, one of its main purposes was to change the structure of ministry in the churches of Syria,

---

[13] Simon Jones, 'Womb of the Spirit. The Liturgical Implications of the Doctrine of the Spirit for the Syrian Baptismal Tradition', Ph.D thesis, University of Cambridge, 1999, p. 43.

[14] Pierce, 'Themes in the "Odes of Solomon"', p. 59.

in particular by imposing an episcopal structure on the churches and limiting the role of women.[15] Indeed, it is in the context of the bishop's ministry, and that of deacons, that baptism is discussed.

Chapter 9 speaks of the bishop as the one who 'loosed you from your sins, who by baptism has given new birth, and filled you with the Holy Spirit'. The bishop also gives the word 'as milk', teaches doctrine, confirms with admonition, and allows participation in the eucharist. Chapter 16 mentions that women deacons should be appointed to assist in the baptismal ceremonies for women, the implication being that the whole of the body was anointed. The bishop is to lay on hands and anoint the head only, 'as of old priests and kings were anointed in Israel' – presumably on the crown of the head. After this, apparently, the candidates were anointed all over, and then were baptized with a formula or invocation. Instruction followed, at least for women by the women deacons. Chapter 26 stresses that the Holy Spirit received by women does not depart from them during their menstruation period.

Clearly, in the churches represented by this document, the ceremonial of anointing with oil had become an established part of the rite. Whether the anointing was accompanied by the formula, 'Thou art my Son, this day I have begotten you', (Chapter 9) is uncertain, but it does suggest that the author saw the anointing as messianic and as symbolizing both coronation and new birth. The author intended that the rite should be presided over by the bishop, but various parts of the rite were delegated to others.

Most commentators have concluded that we have here a ritual sequence of anointing on the crown of the head, followed by the whole body, followed by baptism. In fact, the text presents a slightly more ambiguous picture; it is possible to read it as suggesting that if no female deacons are present, the bishop anoints the head only. It might be that the bishop at one time did the anointing of the whole body, but when the rite was delegated, he started with anointing the head (with proof texts about anointing priests and kings) and gave the remainder over to male and female deacons; in the event that there were no female deacons, only the heads of women were anointed.

The Acts of Judas Thomas

These apocryphal *Acts* are thought to have originated in East Syria, probably Edessa, somewhere between 220–230 CE.[16] Although existing in translation in a number of languages, the primary texts are in Syriac and Greek. It is generally thought that Syriac was the original language, but that some parts of the Greek preserve an earlier version than the present Syriac redaction.[17] This is particularly pertinent to the accounts of

---

[15] Charlotte Methuen, 'Widows, Bishops and the Struggle for Authority in the *Didascalia Apostolorum*', *Journal of Ecclesiastical History* 46 (1995), 197–213.

[16] See the discussion in Jan N. Bremmer, 'The *Acts of Thomas*: Place, Date and Women,' in Bremmer (ed.), *The Apocryphal Acts of Thomas*, Peeters, Louvain, 2001, pp. 74–90. For the text, see A.F.J. Klijn, *The Acts of Thomas*, E.J. Brill, Leiden, 1962.

[17] See Harold W. Attridge, 'The Original Language of the *Acts of Thomas*', in Harold W. Attridge, John

baptism, which show certain marked differences between the Syriac and Greek versions.

There are five accounts of baptism: of Gundaphorus, of a woman who had been possessed by a devil and healed, of Mygdonia, of Sifur, and of Vizan and certain women. Although there are differences between the Syriac and Greek in all these accounts, there are striking divergences in the first two, in that the Greek versions seem to imply that the rite of initiation consisted of *anointing only*. Thus in the 'baptism' of Gundaphorus, the Greek text reads as follows:

> And they sought after him that they also might henceforth receive the seal of the word, saying to him: 'Seeing that our souls are at leisure and eager toward God, give us the seal; for we have heard you say that the God whom you preach knows his own sheep by his seal.' And the Apostle said unto them: 'I also rejoice and entreat you to receive this seal, and to partake with me in this Eucharist and blessing of the Lord, and to be made perfect therein. For this is the Lord and God of all, even Jesus Christ, whom I preach, and he is the father of truth, in whom I have taught you to believe.' And he commanded them to bring Oil, that they might receive the seal by the oil. They brought the oil therefore, and lighted many lamps; for it was night.
>
> And the Apostle got up and sealed them. And the Lord was revealed unto them by a voice, saying: 'Peace be to you, brothers.' And they heard his voice only, but his likeness they did not see, for they had not yet received the added sealing of the seal. And the Apostle took the oil and poured it upon their heads and anointed and chrismated them, and began to say:
>
> 'Come, holy Name of the Christ that is above every name. Come, power of the Most High, and the compassion that is perfect. Come, gift of the Most High. Come, compassionate mother. Come, communion of the male. Come, she who reveals the hidden mysteries. Come, mother of the seven houses, that your rest may be in the eighth house. Come, elder of the five members, mind, thought, reflection, consideration, reason; communicate with these young men. Come, Holy Spirit, and cleanse their reins and their heart, and give them the added seal, in the name of the Father, and Son, and Holy Spirit.'
>
> And when they were sealed, a youth appeared to them holding a lighted torch, so that their lamps became dim at the approach of that light . And he went forth and was no more seen by them. And the Apostle said unto the Lord: 'Your light, O Lord, is not to be contained by us, and we are not able to bear it, for it is too great for our sight.'
>
> And when the dawn came and it was morning, he broke bread and made them partakers of the Eucharist of the Christ.[18]

No mention is made of water. The Syriac version, however, has the following:

J. Collins and Thomas H. Tobin (eds), *Of Scribes and Scrolls. Studies on the Hebrew Bible, Intertestamental Judaism, and Christian Origins presented to John Strugnell on the Occasion of his Sixtieth Birthday*, University of America Press, Lanham, MD, 1990, pp. 241–50.

[18] E.C. Whitaker, *Documents of the Baptismal Liturgy*, revised and expanded by Maxwell E. Johnson, 3rd edn, Liturgical Press, Collegeville, MN, 2003 (hereafter cited as Whitaker/Johnson, *DBL*), pp. 18–19.

And they begged of him that they might receive the sign, and said to him: 'Our souls are turned to God to receive the sign for we have heard that all the sheep of that God whom you preach are known to him by the sign.' Judas said to them: 'I too rejoice, and I ask of you to partake of the Eucharist and of the blessing of this Messiah whom I preach.' And the king gave orders that the bath should be closed for seven days, and that no man should bathe in it. And when the seven days were done, on the eighth day the three of them into entered the bath by night that Judas might baptize them. And many lamps were lighted in the bath.

And when they had entered into the bath-house, Judas went in before them. And our Lord appeared to them, and said to them: 'Peace be with you, my brothers.' And they heard the voice only, but the form they did not see, whose it was, for until now they had not been baptized. And Judas went up and stood upon the edge of the cistern, and poured oil upon their heads, and said: 'Come, holy name of the Messiah; come, power of grace from on high: come, perfect mercy; come, exalted gift; come, sharer of the blessing; come, revealer of hidden mysteries; come, mother of seven houses, whose rest was in the eighth house; come, messenger of reconciliation, and communicate with the minds of these youths; come: Spirit of holiness, and purify their reins and their hearts.' And he baptized them in the Name of the Father and of the Son and of the Spirit of holiness. And when they had come up out of the water, a youth appeared to them, and he was holding a lighted taper; and the light of the lamps became pale through its light. And when they had departed, he became invisible to them; and the apostle said: 'We were not even able to bear Your light, because it is too great for our vision.' And when dawn came and was morning, he broke the Eucharist.[19]

The Syriac mentions a bath, with baptism on the eighth day (paralleling circumcision), and the fact that baptism is in water is made explicit. It is possible, therefore, that the account in the Greek text both here and in the baptism of the woman possessed by a devil, are earlier than the extant Syriac, and are evidence of some ecclesial groups whose initiation consisted solely in anointing the head or 'sealing' with olive oil.[20] The Syriac text would represent a revision to bring the account into line with other ecclesial groups, or perhaps, at least, the normative ritual of the redactor's church. The ritual outlined in each of the five accounts may be summarized as shown in Table 2.1.

A number of points emerge. First, the anointing is on the head, though in the case of Mygdonia, after the apostle anoints her head, her female nurse anoints her body; in the case of Vizan, the apostle anoints him all over, while Mygdonia anoints the women. Second, in several of the accounts the oil is blessed, though the formula varies. In the first we have an *epiklesis* of the Spirit, and in both Greek and Syriac the feminine of the Syriac is expanded in erotic and maternal imagery. For example, in the baptism of Gundaphorus, the invocation of the Spirit includes, 'Come, compassionate mother. Come, fellowship of the male.' Caroline Johnson observes:

> The metaphors and images which govern this literature create 'verbal icons' for the reader. Each of these images in the *Acts of Thomas* epicleses – dove, mother,

---

[19] Ibid., pp. 16–17.

[20] See Susan Myers, 'Initiation by Anointing in Early Syriac-Speaking Christianity', in *Studia Liturgica* 31 (2001), 150–70.

Table 2.1   Summary of Baptisms in Syriac and Greek Acts of Judas Thomas

	Syriac	Greek
Gundaphorus	Bath closed for seven days Baptism on eighth day Oil on heads – prayer over the oil Baptism in three-fold name Lighted taper mentioned	Receives a seal Oil on heads and anointed/chrismated Prayer over the oil Lighted taper mentioned
Woman possessed by devil	Request for the seal Baptism in three-fold name in a river	Request for the seal Sealing in the three-fold name
Mygdonia	Oil poured on head with formula Nurse anoints her Cloth put on her loins Baptism in three-fold name in the basin of their conduit	Oil on her bare head with formula Nurse unclothes her and puts a linen cloth about her Baptism in three-fold name in a fountain of water
Sifur	Exposition on baptism Oil on the heads with formula Baptism in three-fold name in vat Clothed	Exposition on baptism Oil on heads with formula Baptism in three-fold name in a vessel Clothed
Vizan	Stripped Oil blessed Oil cast on the heads Baptism in water in three-fold name	Unclothed Oil blessed Oil poured on heads Baptism in water in three-fold name

nestlings, fellowship of the male, noble combatant – contains its own set of associations, stories, and meanings for the ancient Syriac audience ... This rich language of symbol and metaphor allows Thomas to invoke the full power of the Holy Spirit, with all of her diverse attributes and activities, into these rituals of initiation and eucharist.[21]

Third, we note that baptism is in the triune formula of Matthew 28:19 and fourth, the word 'seal' (*rusma*; *sphragis*) is used – this is ambiguous, seemingly able to suggest the anointing, the actual baptism in water, or the whole rite.[22]

These accounts of baptism have been central in the extremely influential hypothesis of Professor Gabrielle Winkler. Winkler has argued for grouping the accounts in a chronological development or evolution of the ritual of baptism in East Syria, with the accounts of Mygdonia and Vizan representing a later development than those of Gundaphorus, the woman healed who had been possessed by a demon, and Siphor. According to Winkler, the earlier pattern was water baptism, and then anointing of the head followed by baptism, and then finally anointing of the head, followed by anointing of the body and baptism. At a still later date, a post-baptismal anointing would be added to the developing ritual pattern. The rite was based on the paradigm of Jesus' baptism in the Jordan, particularly the Lukan account.[23]

Rather like the attempts to find a linear development in the baptismal accounts in the canonical Acts of the Apostles, Winkler's quest for chronological layers in these Apocryphal Acts is somewhat arbitrary. To begin with, it would seem that the Greek and Syriac attest to at least two different patterns in what Winkler wants to take as the earliest stratum – namely, initiation with oil alone, and initiation with oil and water. Second, contemporary with the Apocryphal Acts is the *Didascalia*, which attests to anointing with oil on the head, followed by the body, and then baptism. Third, the anointing of the body comes in accounts where a woman is on hand to anoint women, and the apostle anoints the bodies of men, after anointing all on the head. These accounts are akin to the record of the *Didascalia*. Rather than attempting to find linear development here, it may be preferable, as with the canonical Acts, to see in this document witness to a variety of ritual patterns coexisting.

Finally, though Winkler is correct to note the importance of oil in this strand of East Syrian tradition, it is difficult to understand why she fastens on the Synoptic account of the baptism of Jesus as the paradigm for this pattern. There the descent of the Spirit, or messianic declaration, comes after the baptism in water. A better paradigm might be the incarnation of Jesus and then his baptism, where the messianic Spirit hovers at conception to bring forth new birth. The themes of the invocations on the oil combine

---

[21] Caroline Johnson, 'Ritual Epicleses in the Greek *Acts of Thomas*,' in F. Bovan, A.G. Brock and C.R. Matthews (eds), *The Apocryphal Acts of the Apostles*, Harvard Divinity School Studies, Harvard University Press, Cambridge, MA, 1999, pp. 171–204, p. 204.

[22] Simon Jones, 'Womb of the Spirit. The Liturgical Implications of the Doctrine of the Spirit for the Syrian Baptismal Tradition', Ph.D Thesis, University of Cambridge, 1999, p. 78.

[23] Gabriele Winkler, 'The Original Meaning of the Prebaptismal Anointing and its Implications', *Worship* 52 (1978), 24–45.

new birth and fertility, as well as cleansing and remission of sins. Again, there is no need to see any one theme having priority; rather, they are juxtaposed, just as they are in the canon of scripture.

The Gospel of Phillip

Recent scholarship has brought to light the fact that in most large cities and areas, groups which would later be called Gnostic lived side by side with groups who later would regard themselves, or be regarded by later epochs as orthodox and who defined their beliefs over against those who were termed Gnostic. It has long been known that in Syriac Christianity in the first two centuries CE, a strong Semitism combined itself with theologies and ideas which by later doctrinal standards were regarded as heretical. That same picture has now emerged for Egyptian Christianity, and that of Rome. Since early Christian congregations tended to be based either on the house church model or the philosophical school, with the patron of the house or teacher of the school exercising leadership and authority, it was not difficult for groups whose ideas seem syncretistic to have established themselves as quite respectable congregations within the wider collection of churches. While their theology of baptism, and even their practice, may not be regarded as normative, they witness to the variety of views and rites in the early Church. They also show us practices and ideas against which orthodox groups reacted.

There has been some dispute as to whether Gnosticism was a pre-Christian movement, stemming from a combination of Oriental mythology and Hellenistic philosophy, or a movement which grew out of Judaism, or out of Christianity. In his book, *Gnostic Truth and Christian Heresy*, Alastair Logan has argued that at least certain documents, which spring from Valentinus and the Sethians, only make sense if seen as developments from a Christian setting. Logan isolated the earliest forms of the foundational myth in Irenaeus' account and the *Apocryphon of John*, and traced its development until it underwent a Sethian reinterpretation in the early third century CE. He argues that the Gnostics felt themselves to be Christians, true interpreters of the message of the unknown God of love first revealed in Christ, the heavenly Son. He argues that they were the first Christian Platonists, and the first to develop a Trinity – of Father, Mother and Son.[24]

Logan, following a number of other scholars, places the origin of some of the Gnostic documents in the environs of Antioch, to communities of the second century. It might be possible to see these groups as the very opposite of that which produced the *Didache*. The latter is conservative Jewish, with concern for the Torah; the Gnostic groups had no time for the Torah and Judaism, and used Platonist terminology and ideas.

---

[24] Alastair Logan, *Gnostic Truth and Christian Heresy*, T & T Clark, Edinburgh, 1996.

The *Gospel of Phillip* is thought to have originated from one such group either in Edessa or Antioch.[25] It is more of a homily than a Gospel, but it does seem to know a sacramental sequence, and speaks of five mysteries: baptism, chrism, eucharist, salvation and bride-chamber. The author testifies to two prime actions or symbols of initiation: water and chrism. Of these, the latter is the more important. Chapter 22 says 'there is water within water, there is fire within chrism', and Chapter 83 declares:

> Chrism has more authority than baptism. For because of chrism we are called Christians, not because of baptism … Whoever has been anointed has everything: resurrection, light, cross, holy spirit.

In Chapter 23 a stripping-off is mentioned. In 37, God is compared with a dyer, dipping clothes. Thus the image here is of being dyed, echoing the imagery of the Book of Revelation, where verse 51 seems to link the reception of the Spirit with the descent into and ascent out of the water. Chapter 58 stresses the link between chrism and fire. In 67 the distinction is made between the rebirth in the water, and light from the fire, namely, the chrism. Chapter 86 refers to stripping off and putting on, and 90 to the effects of putting on the Lord Jesus. Chapter 94 is again concerned with the perfume of chrism, and 107 returns to the idea of a garment of light.

In terms of ritual, we seem to have a community whose rite involves stripping naked, baptism in water followed by chrism, and possibly putting on a white garment representing light or enlightenment. And its theology? This document is mainly concerned with enlightenment, the process of salvation whereby someone becomes a 'bridegroom's attendant', and putting on the garment of salvation.

Rome and Italy

Rome was, of course, the political centre of the empire, and like most centres, was host to a large immigrant population, many of whom came from Syria, Egypt and North Africa. Amongst these ethnic groups were Christians. The letters of Paul indicate that Christianity was established by the 50s, and he refers to what seem to be various groups meeting in private houses. That situation apparently flourished at Rome well into the third century. Some of what are called 'Tituli churches' in the city of Rome may have been built on the foundations of some of these house churches. But we also know that Justin Martyr in the second century had a school based on the philosophical school model, which seems also to have been an *ekklesia*.

It would seem that the emergence of a monarchical bishop in Rome and Egypt was relatively late, and that in Rome the churches were presided over by presbyter-bishops. In articles in the *Harvard Theological Review* of 1925, George La Piana drew attention to the ethnic diversity in second-century Rome, and noted the Latin-speaking

---

[25] Finn, *ECBC* 1, pp. 122–7.

groups, many of them expatriate North Africans, who eventually dominated the Christian church at Rome; similarly, J.S. Jeffers has noted the different concerns of Hermas and Clement of Rome, each reflecting their different social backgrounds and representing different groups.[26] We will look at some of the writings left behind to see how baptism was being articulated in these communities.

Hermas

In the work entitled *The Shepherd*, there is reference to those being baptized as being dead and then coming out of the font alive, contrasted with the apostles and teachers who go down with them, who are already alive. The emphasis is on salvation. Thus, in the third vision, the Church (the Lady) explains that the tower is built on the water because 'Your life has been saved by water and will be so saved' (11:5). In the ninth parable the Pauline theme from Romans 6 is prominent:

> For a man is dead before he receives the name of the Son of God, but, when he receives the seal, he puts off death and receives life. The seal, therefore, is water. The dead go down into the water and come out living. Therefore, this seal was proclaimed to them and they put it to use to enter the kingdom of God.' (15:3–4)[27]

Here the Pauline teaching has been extended. It is not simply dying and rising, but that the water brings to life those who are already dead, as in Ephesians 2:1.

Justin Martyr

With Justin Martyr we encounter a work from the head of one of the philosophical school models of the church. His school was at the house of Martin near the Tiburtine bath, and one might speculate as to whether the baths might have on occasion been the venue of baptisms. Justin was originally from Samaria, and his famous pupil, Tatian, was Syrian. In his *First Apology* (*c.* 150 CE), addressed to the Emperor Antoninus Pius, his philosopher son Verissimus, and the philosopher Lucius, Justin discloses something of the practice of baptism. However, one must bear in mind that Justin's group may have been of Syrian or Palestinian ethnicity, and his practice of baptism and its rationale should not be interpreted as being that of all the Christian groups in Rome; it is the practice of one group in Rome at this time.

In *First Apology* 61, Justin speaks of 'regeneration' through Christ. Instruction is implied, including guidance in how to pray. As in the *Didache*, candidates and ministers fast and pray. They are led to water, where they are regenerated. This is

---

[26] George La Piana, 'The Roman Church at the End of the Second Century', *Harvard Theological Review* 18 (1925), 214–77; James S. Jeffers, *Conflict at Rome: Social Order and Hierarchy in Early Christianity*, Fortress Press, Minneapolis, MN, 1991.

[27] Thomas M. Finn, *Early Christian Baptism and the Catechumenate – Volume 2: Italy, North Africa and Egypt*, Liturgical Press, Collegeville, MN, 1992 (hereafter, *ECBC* 2), p. 36.

explained with scriptural references as new birth (John 3:3) and washing of sins (Isaiah 1:16–20). Justin adds:

> This washing is called illumination, since they who learn these things become illuminated intellectually. Furthermore, the illuminated one is also baptized in the name of the Jesus Christ, who was crucified under Pontius Pilate, and in the name of the Holy Spirit, who predicted through the prophets everything concerning Jesus.[28]

This latter certainly echoes a credal summary which the candidate might have recited. In Chapter 65 the baptizand is led to the worshipping assembly to join the eucharistic community.

Since the *Apology*, in theory at least, was supposed to be for a non-churched readership, there is little theological reflection. In Justin's *Dialogue with Trypho*, an imaginary dialogue (though probably with some factual basis) between a Christian and a Jew, baptism is called the bath of repentance and knowledge of God, the living water which cleanses penitents. Indeed, the Christian fulfils the cleansing of the leper in Leviticus 14, and in baptism is cleansed from spiritual leprosy. Justin claims that, unlike Jewish lustrations, Christian baptism bestows the Holy Spirit.

E.C. Ratcliff noted that Justin shows concern for the gifts of the Spirit in association with Isaiah 11, which formed the core of the later Roman 'confirmation' prayer. Ratcliff suggested that Justin therefore knew a ritual action which ritualized the imparting of the Spirit.[29] A.H. Couratin, noting the comparison with the cleansed leper in Leviticus 14, where oil is mentioned, proposed that Justin knew an anointing in association with the Spirit.[30] However, this is not at all obvious from the text, and must remain purely conjectural.

Hippolytus and Novatian

Hippolytus, a presbyter or presbyter-bishop of Rome, who was martyred *c*. 235, wrote a commentary on Daniel. In reference to Daniel 3:15 he wrote:

> On that day [Easter] the bath is prepared in the Garden for those who are burning and the Church ... is presented to God as a pure bride; and faith and charity, like her [Susanna's] companions, prepare the oil and the unguents for those being washed. What are the unguents but the commandments of the Word? What is the oil but the power of the Holy Spirit, with which, like perfume, believers are anointed after the bath?[31]

Here there is a strong hint that oil is used and in some manner symbolizes the Holy Spirit.

---

[28] Whitaker/Johnson, *DBL*, p. 3.

[29] E.C. Ratcliff, 'Justin Martyr and Confirmation', *Theology* 51 (1948), 133–9.

[30] A.H. Couratin, 'Justin Martyr and Confirmation – A Note', *Theology* 55 (1953), 458–60.

[31] Gustave Bardy and Maurice Lefévre, *Hippolyte: Commentaire sur Daniel, Sources Chrétiennes* 14 (1947), 100.

Reflection of a somewhat more theological nature is provided by another schismatic, Novatian, a Roman Presbyter writing on the Trinity *c.* 250. In Chapter 29, on the Holy Spirit, he stresses that the Spirit is received in baptism, citing Isaiah 11:2 and 61:1, Psalm 45:8, Romans 8:9 and 2 Cor. 3:17. He affirms:

> He it is who effects from water a second birth, the seed, as it were, of a divine generation. He is also the consecrator of a heavenly birth, 'the pledge' of a promised 'inheritance', a kind of written bond, so to speak, of eternal salvation. He it is who makes us the temple of God and makes us his dwelling place.[32]

Here, what is emphasized is the second birth from above, but since Novatian is writing primarily on the subject of the Holy Spirit, and not on baptism *per se*, we should not conclude that he gave it no other emphasis.

A later idealized pre-Nicene rite? The So-called Apostolic Tradition

This document was, in the 1960s, regarded as crucial for liturgical renewal. It has now become something of an albatross. Found in a variety of redactions in Church Orders associated with Egypt, Syria and, in one instance, Italy, the text was isolated at the beginning of the twentieth century by R.H. Connolly and Eduard Schwarz. The common liturgical material, a sort of liturgical 'Q', was identified as the 'missing' work of Hippolytus, the *Apostolic Tradition*, and dated *c.* 215 to the city of Rome. This identification was made because of a headless statue found in Rome *c.* 1552, on the plinth of which was inscribed a list of theological works, some of which were known to be by Hippolytus. One work listed on the plinth, but of which no copy had survived, was entitled '*Apostolic Tradition*'. This work was then identified as the 'Q' document found in the number of Church Orders. Once this identification was made, it was argued that Hippolytus was a rival pope who went into schism because he felt that Pope Callistus was heretical and liberal. Thus the document was seen as representing a conservative Catholic liturgical use of Rome *c.* 215.

In the late twentieth century, this estimation of the document began to be seriously questioned. Some scholars have argued that the statue was that of a woman, not a man, and that the list of works are a library, not the works of one author. The community from which it stemmed appears to have been a conservative group, perhaps in the last years of the third century, when a monarchical episcopate had clearly emerged in Rome. This community looked back to a time when all churches in Rome had their own presbyter-bishop, and to a particularly influential one named Hippolytus. The liturgical document thus is an attempt to record an ideal past which no longer existed, and perhaps never had. It seems to represent the wishful thinking of a nostalgic dissident group in Rome at the end of the third century, and is in no way representative of all things Roman *c.* 215.[33]

---

[32] Finn, *ECBC* 2, p. 51.

[33] Allen Brent, *Hippolytus and the Roman Church in the Third Century: Communities in Tension before*

Paragraphs 15 and 16 represent a development of the 'two ways' found in the *Didache*. It notes that those wishing to become Christians are asked about their motives and beliefs, and their life-style. Not all life-styles were acceptable: owners of brothels, sculptors and painters of idols, actors, charioteers, gladiators and pagan priests must all change their profession or be rejected. Prostitutes, profligates and eunuchs must be rejected, and soldiers must not kill or take oaths. A slave woman who was a concubine was to behave as though her master/lover were her one husband. Whereas Callistus extended this injunction to include male slaves in relation to free women, the Hippolytus community did not.[34]

The period of instruction was three years. The sexes were kept apart, and after instruction there was prayer and a laying-on of hands. If a candidate was arrested and put to death before baptism, this counted as baptism in blood. There is a further warning about the character of the catechumens. In an article in 1989, Thomas Finn noted the very detailed and extended nature of the catechumenate which lasted three years, far longer than elsewhere. He argued that what we have here is a rite of passage from Roman society into the Christian community. Christians were mainly resident aliens in Rome, and the Hippolytus house church may have been predominantly Syrian or even Egyptian in ethnic background, and thus regarded as outsiders with precarious legal status. This, Finn suggests, would explain the enquiry and the exclusion of untrustworthy groups. The lengthy time of instruction is a time of liminality, with exorcisms to protect the community against Roman society and its evils. Finally, the candidate made the transition by baptism into this house church. Finn notes, 'Survival of Christianity before Constantine depended heavily on the development of an effective catechumenate, a powerful ritual process.'[35]

There were rituals for the days leading up to the baptism. On the Thursday, all were required to bathe, though for menstruating women baptism must be postponed. On the eve of the Saturday and on Saturday, the candidates were to fast. There was an imposition of hands, breathing in the face, and signing of parts of the body – if this signing was with oil, the document does not specify it. Prayer was offered over the water, and then the renunciation was made. All the baptizands undressed, and babies were baptized first. All were anointed with the oil of exorcism as they renounced Satan and his works. A triple immersion followed, with interrogatives based on the three sections of a creed.

Then we encounter ceremonies which seem to have become peculiar to the city of Rome: a post-baptismal anointing with the oil of thanksgiving by a presbyter, then a prayer by the bishop, asking for grace, with hand imposed. The bishop then anointed the candidates and imposed his hand. He kissed each candidate on the forehead, and

---

the Emergence of a Monarch-Bishop, E.J. Brill, Leiden, 1995; Paul F. Bradshaw, Maxwell E. Johnson and L. Edward Phillips, *The Apostolic Tradition*, Augsburg Fortress Press, Minneapolis, MN, 2002.

[34] Finn, *ECBC* 2, pp. 46–51.

[35] Thomas M. Finn, 'The Ritual Process and Survival in Second-Century Rome', *Journal of Ritual Studies* 3 (1989), 69–89, p. 80.

then came the kiss of peace. This dual anointing and hand-laying is not found in other traditions.

There has been much debate over the post-baptismal prayer said by the bishop, which later would become a detached ritual in the Western Church and evolve into the rite of confirmation. In the Latin Verona version of this document, the prayer assumes that the candidate had already received the Holy Spirit, presumably in the ritual in the water. The Egyptian versions phrase the prayer so that the Holy Spirit is being imparted in the laying-on of hands: 'make them worthy to be filled with the Holy Spirit and ... '. Anthony Gelston suggested that the original prayer may have referred to receiving the Spirit in the water and in the hand-laying.[36] However, Geoffrey Cuming's view was that the original had not mentioned the Spirit at all, and that the additions were made differently in the Latin and Egyptian texts, giving different theologies of the Spirit in baptism.[37]

Other explanations of these composite rituals have also been offered. Noting that in the African tradition witnessed by Tertullian there is a hand-laying and a single anointing after baptism, Bouhot has argued that *Apostolic Tradition* represents a fusion of the Roman with the North African tradition; the Roman rites focused on the bishop, whereas the North African tradition focused on the presbyters and deacons.[38] Paul Bradshaw has taken this further, suggesting three strata in the document. The earliest, reflecting the *Didache* and Justin Martyr, described the baptism and confession of faith. A second layer was the development of rites for the bishop, the post-baptismal anointing and hand-laying. A third stratum was the ceremonies of the presbyters and deacons, including the presbyteral post-baptismal unction.[39] However, this theory overlooks the fact that Rome seems to have maintained the polity of each church having a presbyter-bishop much later than most places. It may well be that what we have was a house-church rite with deacons and presbyters, with a sequence of baptism and post-baptismal anointing, to which has been added a 'confirmation' whereby the newly emerged monarchial bishop of Rome showed his central authority by the rite of hand-laying and a further anointing of all candidates from the various house-churches.

Whatever may be the make-up of this document, it witnesses to a community collecting and supplementing traditions about its rites. This community did not have an open font. It set forth qualifications for being a candidate, together with a prolonged period of liminality. Exorcisms were needed to safeguard the progress of the candidates, and to cast out Satan. Oil was used prior to baptism, and the ritual of

---

[36] Anthony Gelston, 'A Note on the Text of the *Apostolic Tradition* of Hippolytus', *Journal of Theological Studies* 39 (1988), 112–17.

[37] G.J. Cuming, 'The Post-baptismal Prayer in the *Apostolic Tradition*: Further Considerations', *Journal of Theological Studies* 39 (1988), 117–19.

[38] Jean-Paul Bouhot, *La confirmation, sacrement de la communion ecclésiale*, du Chalet: Lyons, 1968.

[39] Paul F. Bradshaw, 'Redating the *Apostolic Tradition*: Some Preliminary Steps', in Nathan Mitchell and John Baldovin (eds), *Rule of Prayer, Rule of Faith*, Pueblo Liturgical Press, Collegeville, MN, 1996, pp. 3–17.

baptism was a three-fold immersion with a confession of faith. Further anointings followed, and the bishop in this community played a crucial ritual role. In the document's redactions it is clear that different and later communities using the tradition had differing views as to when the Spirit was ritually imparted.

North Africa

Tertullian

Tertullian was born to pagan parents *c.* 160 CE and lived in Carthage. Trained in rhetoric, he became a Christian in 190 CE, and is the one of the founding fathers of African Latin theology. He later broke from the Catholic Church to be a member of the more rigorist Montanist group. However, his theological writings give us some insight into both the practice of baptism in early third-century North Africa, and also something of how Tertullian understood baptism.

In his work *De Corona* 3, Tertullian notes that there are certain ceremonies and customs which have no specific scriptural warrant, but which are part of the faith. In *De Baptismo*, he refers to instruction, which included frequent prayer, fastings, bending the knee, all-night vigils and confession of sins. *De Corona* reports that at baptism candidates renounce the devil and his pomp and his angels (*contestamur nos renuntiare diabolo et pompae et angelis eius*). There seems to be reference to blessing the water. In *De Baptismo*, Tertullian discusses at some length the waters of creation in Genesis, and notes that the Holy Spirit, or an angel, comes down from heaven and stays upon the waters.

According to *De Spectaculis*, 'we make profession of the Christian faith in the words of its rule', which would seem to be confession of a credal formula. After this, candidates were immersed three times, which in *Adversus Praxean* 26 is explained in reference to Matthew 28:19, 'for not once only, but three times are we baptized into each of the three Persons at each of the several names'. Immediately after the baptism the candidates were anointed, though whether it was the head only or all over we are not told. This was followed by a signing with the cross, and then 'the imposition of the hand in benediction, inviting and welcoming the Holy Spirit'. This was followed by the eucharist, with the reception of milk and honey.

As E. Evans says, Tertullian's doctrinal understanding of baptism is allusive rather than systematic.[40] Tertullian refers to the sins of our original blindness which are washed away, and death being washed away. This seems to echo Romans 6 – and Tertullian believed that Paschal-tide was the preferred time for baptism, 'for then was accomplished our Lord's passion, and into it we are baptized'. He emphasized the

---

[40] Earnest Evans, 'Introduction', *Tertullian's Homily on Baptism*, SPCK: London, 1964, p. xxix <http://www.tertullian.net/articles/evans_bapt/evans_bapt_text_trans.htm>.

theme of cleansing, but rebirth and new birth are also important concepts for Tertullian. In *De Baptismo* he comments how at creation the Spirit of God hovered over the waters, noting that matter, in this case water, is used by God to bring forth living things. He thus observes that God has brought into service in his very own sacraments that same material which he has had at his disposal in all his acts and works. The Holy Spirit is the baptizer, and comes and abides on the water. But here Tertullian seems to become less precise. He argues that the nature of the waters, having received holiness from the Holy, itself conceived power to make holy. Thus:

> Therefore, in consequence of that ancient original privilege, all waters, when God is invoked, acquire the sacred significance of conveying sanctity: for at once the Spirit comes down from heaven and stays upon the waters, sanctifying them from within himself, and when thus sanctified they absorb the power of sanctifying.

It is interesting that Tertullian locates the sanctification of all waters in creation, where others locate it in the baptism of Jesus. However, Tertullian then asserts that the waters acquire healing power by an angel's intervention, and teaches that the water cleanses in order for the Spirit to be received:

> Not that the Holy Spirit is given to us in the water, but that in the water we are made clean by the action of the angel, and made ready for the Holy Spirit.

The anointing for Tertullian is paralleled with the anointing of Aaron by Moses, which was for priesthood, though with the emphasis on unction of the flesh turning to spiritual profit. But it is the imposition of the hands in benediction which he seems to associate with the Holy Spirit, though he is far from clear:

> Human ingenuity has been permitted to summon spirit to combine with water, and by application of a man's hands over the result of their union to animate it with another spirit of excellent clarity … At this point that most Holy Spirit willingly comes down from the Father upon bodies cleansed and blessed, and comes to rest upon the waters of baptism as though revisiting his primal dwelling-place.

Here the example of Noah is invoked.

It would seem that the ritual sequence encouraged Tertullian to give a theological sequence, but he also realized that this is not strictly possible. He affirms the North African conviction that no one may be saved without baptism, and that the rite of baptism is under the presidency of the bishop. As already noted, his preference was for Paschal-tide baptism, though Pentecost is also auspicious. But in the final analysis, every day is the Lord's day, and so any day is suitable.

Cyprian

Cyprian was bishop of Carthage from 249 until his martyrdom in 258. His *Letters* reveal something of his understanding of baptism, though much of what we find in them is in a polemical context urging the invalidity of heretical baptism.[41] We can

---

[41] Finn, *ECBC* 2, pp. 131–40.

glean from the *Letters* an initiatory sequence not unlike that already encountered in Tertullian. Cyprian witnesses to Trinitarian baptism, and to a credal interrogatory, including 'Do you believe in the remission of sins and eternal life through the Church?'. Candidates were anointed, and the bishop laid hands on them; Cyprian, like Tertullian, associated this with the Holy Spirit. He also mentions the *signaculo dominico*, the sign or seal of the Lord. This may mean the sign of the cross, or may simply refer to the hand-laying. Maxwell Johnson has taken it as the former, and suggests that by the time of Cyprian it had moved to a place after the hand-laying, but this may be a too strict reading of Cyprian's passing statement.[42]

Cyprian's baptismal teaching is ecclesiological in its emphasis. Salvation can only come from the Church, and only the Church can give valid baptism. The baptism of heretics bestows nothing at all, because, although they might confess belief in the Church, they actually reject the Church. They might, therefore, administer the rite of baptism, but it gives no remission of sins; the oil they use cannot be sanctified, and the imposition of hands gives nothing. Thus heretics must be baptized when being (re)admitted to the Church, and not simply be admitted with the laying-on of hands. He wrote:

> But if all heretics and schismatics from without do not give the Holy Spirit and, therefore, hands are imposed by us that here he may be received because there he is not and cannot be given, it is clear that the remission of sins cannot be given through those men who, it is certain, do not have the Holy Spirit. And, therefore, that, according to the divine plan and the evangelical truth, they may be able to obtain the remission of sins and to be sanctified and to become the temples of God, all who come from adversaries and antichrists to the church of Christ must, indeed, be baptized in the baptism of the church.[43]

Thus being washed from sin, and receiving the Spirit, can only come from the rites as celebrated by the Church; *extra ecclesia non salus est*.

Egypt

Gnostic Documents

We have already encountered the Gnostic *Gospel of Phillip,* which is thought to have been written in Antioch or Edessa. However, it was well known to some groups in Egypt, where Gnostic forms of Christianity flourished in Alexandria under Basilides and Valentinus. The Nag Hammadi library – a rubbish dump containing many documents first discovered in 1946, and finally all published in 1972 – is a witness to the strength of Christian Gnosticism in this region. The *Gospel of Truth*, which some

---

[42] Maxwell E. Johnson, *The Rites of Christian Initiation*, Collegeville, MN, Liturgical Press, 1999, pp. 66–7.

[43] Finn, *ECBC* 2, p. 135.

think was written by Valentinus, alludes to stripping off clothes and putting on garments. Baptism in water is mentioned once, and is described as belonging to the sphere of cold fragrance.[44] The fragrance of the oil, which follows baptism, is stressed. Alastair Logan has argued that the myth of the five seals outlined in the *Trimorphic Protennoia*, but also mentioned in the *Apocryphon of John* and the *Gospel of the Egyptians*, refers to a post-baptismal anointing of the two eyes, two ears and the mouth.[45] He also argues that baptism was in the name of the Father, Mother and Son.

Elizabeth Leeper notes that the *Excerpta ex Theodoto* (Theodotus being the pupil of Valentinus, and this work compiled by Clement of Alexandria) witnesses to a pre-baptismal exorcism, and understood baptism as death and resurrection in line with Romans 6.[46] Baptism in this document requires fasting, supplication and prayer, and was administered in the name of the Father, Son and Holy Spirit. The *Excerpta* states:

> And the bread and the oil are sanctified by the power of the Name, and they are not the same as they appeared to be when they were received, but they have been transformed by power into spiritual power. Thus, the water, also, both in exorcism and baptism, not only keeps off evil, but gives sanctification as well.

The cumulative Gnostic evidence for Egypt suggests that some form of pre-baptismal exorcism was not unknown, and that anointing with oil came after baptism.

Clement of Alexandria

Clement believed that 'catholic' Christians, or his groups of Christians, were the true Gnostics, and he firmly opposed the teaching of the Gnostic groups under Theodotus. He was a presbyter in Alexandria, though he left Egypt in the early 200s. He died *c.* 215. In his work, *Christ the Tutor*, Clement explained:

> This is what happens with us, whose model the Lord made himself. When we are baptized, we are enlightened; being enlightened, we become adopted sons; becoming adopted sons, we are made perfect; and becoming perfect, we are made divine. 'I have said,' it is written, 'you are gods and all the sons of the most High.'[47]

This ceremony is often called 'free gift', 'enlightenment', 'perfection' and 'cleansing':

> ... 'cleansing' because through it we are completely purified of our sins; 'free gift,' because by it punishments due to our sins are remitted; 'enlightenment,' since by it we behold the wonderful holy light of salvation, that is, it enables us

---

[44] E. Segelberg, 'The Baptismal Rite according to some of the Coptic-Gnostic Texts of Nag Hammadi', *Studia Patristica* 5, Part Three (1962), 117–28.

[45] Alastair H. Logan, 'The Mystery of the Five Seals: Gnostic Initiation Reconsidered', *Vigiliae Christianae* 51 (1997), 188–206.

[46] Elizabeth A. Leeper, 'From Alexandria to Rome: The Valentinian Connection to the Incorporation of Exorcism as a Prebaptismal Rite', *Vigiliae Christianae* 44 (1990), 6–24.

[47] Finn, *ECBC* 2, p. 186.

to see God clearly; finally, we call it 'perfection' as needing nothing further, for what more does he need who possesses the knowledge of God?[48]

Origen

A successor to Clement, Origen was a great Bible teacher, though he and his teaching were later to come under a cloud of suspicion. In his *Homilies* on Exodus and on Joshua, Origen taught that the Red Sea was a type of baptism, and that Christian baptism replaced circumcision.[49] He also took up the Pauline imagery of death and resurrection, though he also uses the model of Jesus' baptism in the Jordan. Perhaps the most disputed aspect of Origen's teaching is whether or not he alludes to a particular ritual pattern of initiation. In his homilies he speaks of 'the Holy Spirit and the water', and 'the unction of chrism and the baptism have continued in you undefiled'. It has been suggested that Origen knew a pattern of initiation like the Syrian, namely anointing and then baptism. However in the same homily he speaks of 'visible water and visible chrism', which could equally be taken as a pattern of baptism, then anointing. It may be wiser to see this as stylistic, and not really intending to express accurately a particular ritual pattern. It is clear, however, that the Gnostic groups knew a post-baptismal anointing and thus both patterns probably coexisted in Egypt.

Concluding Remarks

The early evidence allows us only to document what happened in certain places at certain times, and is not sufficient to build some universal picture. We find different ritual patterns. In some communities perhaps initiation was by anointing only (*Acts of Judas Thomas*) elsewhere we find baptism in water (*Didache*) only. However, most of the documents yield a ritual pattern of initiation with anointing and water. Thus even if oil was not used in New Testament times, it quickly established itself as part of the baptismal ritual. In some places there might have been the use of ritual torches as a sign of illumination (*Acts of Judas Thomas*), and there is reference to Trinitarian baptism, in some places the Matthean 28:19 formula perhaps being the formula associated with the water bath.

In some places the anointing came before the water bath, and others apparently afterwards. The coexistence of these different patterns may perhaps be interpreted as simply reflecting the varied etiquette in the ancient culture, and particularly Romano-Greek bathing customs. It is helpful here to cite the comments of Fikret Yegül on the flexibility of this etiquette:

> To take one example: that anointing was one essential accompaniment to exercise and bathing is clear. However, not so clear is the determination of the exact step

---

[48] Ibid.
[49] Finn, *ECBC* 2, pp. 195–211.

in the sequence in which anointing was undertaken. Pliny anointed before exercise; Alexander Severus, after. In Apuleius's *Metamorphosis*, Milo's guest was first rubbed with oil at home and then taken to the nearest baths. But this might have been done because he was weary after a long trip; normally, one was anointed after bathing (as was Julius Caesar's custom), then one sat down to dinner. The final bathing treat that Homer's heroes enjoyed in the *Odyssey* before they were entertained by their host was the 'fragrant oil'. Galen recommends rubbing of the body with oil after the bath because oil 'hinders the penetration of excess air by closing the pores and protects the skin against a dryness and harmful winds.' Celsus supplied a more critical view: whether the patient should be anointed before or after the hot baths should be decided by the doctor according to each individual case and the state of the patient's recovery ... Anointing was not simply smearing the body with oil: it was a serious and quasi-scientific procedure of massage with oils and unguents of different preparations and qualities in order to obtain a wide range of benefits – protective, preventive, mollifying, and cosmetic.[50]

He also notes that anointing could be before bathing, after bathing, or both.[51] According to Garrett G. Fagan, anointing prior to exercise and bathing was the norm, though he notes that once the bather had dried off, those who could afford it were anointed with perfumes before putting on a fresh set of clothes.[52] The secular pre-bathing unction is illustrated in a mosaic from Piazza Armenia, Sicily, where slave/servant attendants anoint the bather (see Fig. 2.1).[53] Fagan also noted that some benefactors gave free oil.[54] Ralph Jackson observes that it was common to add olive oil to the bath itself.[55] Thus the different ritual patterns found in the early Christian evidences mirror secular bathing customs. While interpreting the anointing as messianic is distinctly Christian, the idea of anointing for protection and healing which we also find, simply spiritualized a commonly accepted secular understanding of the use of oil in bathing. The anointing by deacons and deaconesses mirrors the servant/ slave, the white robe is a counterpart to clean clothes, and the eucharist is the meal. It was the significance, meaning and context which made the Christian ritual distinctive. In terms of theological understanding, we find the themes of forgiveness and cleansing, as well as rebirth, clothing and illumination, all accomplished by undergoing the ritual.

---

[50] Fikret Yegül, *Baths and Bathing in Classical Antiqity*, MIT Press, Cambridge, MA, 1992, pp. 354–5. References are to Apuleius, *Metamorphosis*, 1,23 and 1,7; Galen, *Opera Omnia*, 6,4; Celsus, *De Medicina*, 2,17,8 and Pliny, *Naturalis Historia* 15.5.

[51] Ibid., p. 38.

[52] Garrett G. Fagan, *Bathing in Public in the Roman World*, University of Michigan Press, Ann Arbor, 1999, p. 10.

[53] Fig. in ibid.

[54] Ibid., p. 344 for the Greek inscription and translation.

[55] Ralph Jackson, 'Spas, waters, and Hydrotherapy in the Roman World', in J. DeLaine and D.E. Johnston (eds), *Roman Baths and Bathing*, Portsmouth, RI, 1999, pp. 107–16, p. 112.

Figure 2.1   Anointing of a Patron by Slaves. Plate IV from La Villa Erculia di Piazza Armerina I Mosaici Figurati Gino Vinicio Gentili, Edizioni Mediterranee, Rome 1959

Baptismal Rites, Commentaries and Mystagogical Catecheses: The Fourth and Fifth Centuries

The fourth and fifth centuries were a period of change as well as continuity for the Christian churches. The Church went from being a periodically persecuted dissident religious group in the Roman Empire to being the preferred and official religion of the Empire. This shift brought many more converts into the Church, swelling the size of congregations, which required new buildings large enough to house them. The Church now had a much more public persona than in pre-Nicene times. But the post-Nicene period also saw successive battles between Arians, semi-Arians, Homoiousians and Eunomians, and then Apollinarians, over against the Nicene party. These theological tensions resulted in the final triumph of Nicene Christology at the Council of Constantinople in 381, and a clearer doctrine of the Trinity. But Christological disagreements would lead to the fragmentation of the Church, first at Ephesus in 431, and then at Chalcedon in 451.

These later Christological disputes resulted in the division of the Syriac-speaking churches into the Church of the East or East Syrian, and Syrian Orthodox or West Syrian, both of which rejected Chalcedon but which espoused different Christologies; and the Maronite Church, which accepted Chalcedon. Joining with the Syrian Orthodox on this issue were the Armenian and the Coptic (and Ethiopic) Orthodox Churches. Regional differences in ritual patterns now also became the particular characteristics of particular denominational churches.

For this period, we have relatively few surviving liturgical texts. However, we do have mystagogical or catechetical homilies from some significant churchmen which attest not only to ritual patterns, but also give an insight into how those responsible for teaching the catechumens and neophytes understood the rituals of their respective baptismal traditions.

Jerusalem, Antioch and Cappadocia

Jerusalem

Two sources shed some light on baptism in Jerusalem at this time. First are the homilies of Cyril of Jerusalem, bishop from 349 to 387. We have a Protocatechesis and eighteen pre-baptismal catechetical lectures by him, together with five mystagogical lectures given in Easter week to the newly baptized which are attributed to him. Some have argued that these homilies are really by Cyril's successor bishop, John of Jerusalem, because in some of the manuscripts these are attributed to John, and because of perceived differences in tone and style between these and the catechetical lectures.[1] The view of Edward Yarnold was that they were by Cyril, but at a later date than the pre-baptismal homilies, and that this accounts for the differences.[2] The most recent discussions are by Alexis Doval, who concludes that they were indeed by Cyril, and Juliette Day who reaches the opposite conclusion.[3]

A second, less theological source comes from the travel diary of Egeria, a Spanish nun who recorded the worship in Jerusalem that she witnessed while visiting the holy city sometime towards the end of the fourth century, and possibly when either Cyril or John was bishop. Egeria's information does present at least one problem. According to her diary, the bishop gave a homily every day except Sunday throughout the period of Lent. She also says that the creed was given and explained to the catechumens after five weeks of teaching. Cyril has only eighteen lectures, and the creed is given in the fifth. Maxwell Johnson has suggested that this apparent discrepancy can be reconciled if Cyril was using an earlier calendar which knew only a three-week Lent.[4]

By the time that Cyril was bishop of Jerusalem, the city had been rebuilt in splendid style by Constantine, with buildings constructed over the traditional locations of the passion, death and resurrection of Jesus. This meant that ceremonies could be given a dramatic celebration, linking them with the appropriate places. Important churches were the Eleona, on the Mount of Olives; the Imbomon, or place of the ascension, and the Church of the Holy Sepulchre and Anastasis at Golgotha.

According to Egeria, those catechumens who wished to be baptized had to give their names before Lent began. Then they assembled with their sponsors in the Martyrium for examination and enrolment. Throughout Lent the candidates received exorcism and catechesis. At the paschal vigil on Easter Eve the congregation met in the Martyrium, but the candidates were baptised elsewhere – probably in the cisterns or baths behind the Anastasis. After Easter they received further instruction – the mystagogical lectures – on what they had experienced. Edward Ratcliff wrote:

> When Cyril, consecrated bishop of Jerusalem in AD 348, delivered his five
> memorable Mystagogical Catecheses, or Lectures on the Sacraments of Baptism

---

[1] Conveniently summarized in F.L. Cross (ed.), *St.Cyril of Jerusalem's Lectures on the Christian Sacraments*, SPCK, London, 1966.

[2] E.J. Yarnold, 'The Authorship of the Mystagogic Catecheses Attributed to Cyril of Jerusalem', *Heythrop Journal* 19 (1978), 143–61.

[3] Alexis Doval, *Cyril of Jerusalem, Mystagogue: The Authorship of the Mystagogic Catecheses*, Catholic University of America Press, Washington, DC, 2001; Juliete Day, 'The Mystagogic Catecheses of Jerusalem and their Relationship to the Eastern Baptismal Liturgies of the Fourth and Early Fifth Centuries', Ph.D dissertation, University of London 2003.

[4] Maxwell E. Johnson, 'Reconciling Cyril and Egeria on the Catechetical Process in Fourth Century Jerusalem', in Paul Bradshaw (ed.), *Essays in Early Christian Initiation*, Grove Books, Bramcote, 1988, pp. 18–30.

and Eucharist, to the newly baptized in Easter week of *c.* AD 350, he spoke, not in the old cathedral church of Mount Sion, but in the new colonnaded precinct erected by Constantine to enclose the sacred site of Christ's crucifixion, burial, and resurrection. Prominent to the east of the precinct, with its facade facing eastward, was the Martyrium or Church. To the west of the church, and possibly connected with its south aisle by a stairway, was the Montculus Calvariae, or Golgotha, the site of the crucifixion. Farther to the west of the church, and in line with its apse, stood 'as it were the head of the whole' (so Eusebius describes it) the Holy Sepulchre, in which Christ's body had been buried after the crucifixion, and from which he had risen on the third day. The surrounding ridge of the rock in which the sepulchre was hewn had been cut away; and the Sepulchre itself, now resembling a small house, stood in isolation in the midst of a garden. To the south of the precinct, projecting externally from it and not quite in line with the Sepulchre, was the Baptistery. The candidates for baptism entered the Baptistery by an external western door without passing through the precinct. Baptized, they left the Baptistery by a door opening on to the garden of the sepulchre; and passing between the sacred memorials of the passion and the resurrection, they proceeded to the Martyrium for their first attendance at the eucharistic Liturgy and for their first communion.[5]

The rite of baptism was preceded by a period of catechesis, with enrolment, exorcism and handing-over of the Creed. The rite itself, as described in the mystagogical lectures, consisted of the following:

- The renunciation (*apotaxis*) and credal commitment (*syntaxis*)
- Stripping
- Anointing
- Baptism
- Anointing
- A white garment.

According to Cyril, on the eve of Holy Saturday the candidates entered the antechamber of the baptistery and renounced Satan, facing west and stretching out their hands. This *apotaxis* is likened to the children of Israel fleeing Pharaoh and crossing the Red Sea. Cyril provides the formula which was used, and comments on each part of it: 'I renounce you, Satan, and all your works, and all your pomp, and all your worship.' For Cyril, renouncing 'pomp' included avoiding horse racing! But he commented:

> When you renounce Satan, trampling underfoot every covenant with him, then you annul that ancient 'league with Hell' [Isa. 28:15], and God's paradise opens before you, that Eden, planted in the east, from which for his transgression our first father was banished.[6]

---

[5] E.C. Ratcliff, 'The Old Syrian Baptismal Tradition and its Resettlement under the Influence of Jerusalem in the Fourth Century', in *Liturgical Studies*, A.H. Couratin and D.H. Tripp (eds), SPCK, London, 1976, pp. 135–54, pp. 142–3.

[6] Mystagogic Cateches (hereafter MC) 1:9; Finn *ECBC* 1, p. 46.

Here we have themes of escape from slavery (Red Sea), covenant and paradise regained.

Cyril gives a brief credal formula which the neophytes confessed as they turned from west to east to adhere to Christ, the *syntaxis*. Next they stripped off their clothes, and this was seen as stripping off the old Adam, though Hugh Riley notes that clothing had considerable significance in the ancient world, and so the resonances are more than just biblical.[7] Then the candidates were anointed with 'exorcised olive oil'. Cyril explained:

> Then, when stripped, you were anointed with exorcised olive oil from the topmost hairs of your head to the soles of your feet, and became partakers of the good olive tree, Jesus Christ.[8]

It is interesting that Paul's Letter to the Romans is constantly in the background in Cyril's explanation of the rites. Here it is the olive tree of Romans 11. The anointing is given a Christological meaning, engrafting into Christ, but Cyril also sees it as a purging and cleansing from sin.

The actual baptism followed and was a threefold dipping. Cyril emphasized the concept of dying and rising as in Romans 6 and, being in Jerusalem, he had good reason to do so, as Hugh Riley explained:

> Cyril enjoyed the most advantageous position to capitalize on this mystagogical explanation of the act of baptism as meaning a participation in the sufferings, death and resurrection of Jesus. His mystagogical discourses, delivered in Easter week, were held, it will be remembered, in the *Anastasis*, the rotunda of the resurrection. Listening to Cyril's catecheses, the neophytes had, as he himself points out to them, the holy sepulchre itself before their very eyes. This 'on-the-scene' advantage is the first material from which Cyril draws the interpretation of the baptismal act as a being buried with Christ.[9]

Throughout his catecheses Cyril uses the concepts of *eikon-mimesis* – image and imitation – and he gives an extended treatment here of the imitation of Christ's burial and resurrection. However, the image of new birth is also present in his teaching, if muted.

The post-baptismal anointing is also given extended treatment, with a variety of associations and meanings, though the dominant interpretation is that it is the imparting of the Holy Spirit. The anointing is of the forehead, ears, nostrils and breast. Cyril notes that when Jesus came up from the waters of the Jordan, the Spirit rested on him: 'Similarly for you, after you had ascended from the sacred streams, there was an anointing with chrism, the antitype of that with which Christ was anointed, that is, of the Holy Spirit.'[10] By being anointed, candidates have become 'partakers and fellows of Christ'. The oil is described as holy because the Spirit has been invoked

---

[7] Hugh M. Riley, *Christian Initiation*, Catholic University of America, Washington, DC, 1974, p. 159.

[8] MC2:3; Finn *ECBC* 1, p. 47.

[9] Riley, *Christian Initiation*, p. 228.

[10] MC3.1; Finn, *ECBC* 1, p. 50.

upon it. But Cyril also says that the anointing signifies that the neophytes are 'Christs' or anointed ones. He argues that the oil is prefigured in the Old Testament for priests and kings, and that it will keep the neophytes unsullied and without blame. Although the emphasis is on conveying the gift of the Spirit, Cyril also hints at spiritual protection as well as incorporation into Christ.

Antioch

From the environs of Antioch comes a surviving liturgical text, contained in the *Apostolic Constitutions*. This latter is a Church Order, containing teaching and regulations as well as liturgical material. The compiler is thought to have held a semi-Arian theology, with a Christology which falls short of Nicene standards. He has drawn on previous documents: the *Didache*, the *Didascalia* and the so-called *Apostolic Tradition*, as well as some Hellenistic Jewish prayers. The compiler did not completely harmonize his sources, so there is duplication. This is true of the treatment of baptism. The compiler first discusses baptism in Book 3:16–18, which is an expanded version of the *Didascalia*, witnessing to a pattern of anointing all over, with the deacons anointing only the foreheads of women, leaving the rest to deaconesses. Baptism follows, but there is also an anointing with chrism afterwards. The predominant imagery is death/burial from Romans, though the Holy Spirit is linked with the oil.

In Book 7:22 we have an expansion of the provisions given in the *Didache* (the expansions are in italics):

> Matthew 28:19
> *Anointing with holy oil, a participation of the Holy Spirit.*
> Baptism in water; the water is a sign of death
> *Sealing with chrism (myron), a seal of the covenants.*

The compiler adds that if oil is not available, water alone suffices. However, unlike Cyril, the compiler holds that it is the pre-baptismal anointing which is linked with the Spirit, while the post-baptismal anointing is linked with covenants.

A much more detailed account of baptism is given in Chapters 39–45, and the author may well have been drawing on the practice of his own community at this point. There is instruction and teaching, and this appears to have been ritualized by prayer and the laying-on of hands. The renunciation of Satan is given a full description, with a formula similar to Cyril's. The s*yntaxis* is followed by confession of a creed reflecting the sub-Nicene theology of the compiler. Then comes the first anointing, with oil that has been blessed by the priest:

> ... for the remission of sins, and the first preparation for the confession of baptism, that so the candidate, when he is anointed, may be freed from all ungodliness, and may become worthy of initiation, according to the command of the Only-Begotten.[11]

---

[11] Finn, *ECBC* 1, p. 58.

The water was then blessed with a prayer which apparently was rather like a eucharistic prayer in that it gave thanks for the wonderful works of God. It included a petition for sanctification:

> Look down from heaven and sanctify this water and give it grace and power, that so he that is baptized, according to the command of Christ, may be crucified with him, and may die with him, and may be buried with him, and may rise with him to the adoption which is in him, that he may be dead to sin and live to righteousness.[12]

What is perhaps noteworthy here is that the prayer makes only one reference to the work of the Holy Spirit, while the force of the petition at the end of the prayer is to effect the Pauline imagery of Romans. Baptism is in the name of the Trinity, and is followed by an anointing with myron (perfumed olive oil) and a prayer. The prayer asks that the myron may be efficacious, and is concerned with cleansing rather than linking it to the Spirit, unless the 'sweet odour of Christ' is an allusion to the Spirit. A laying-on of hands is mentioned as necessary; otherwise, only the body is cleansed, and not the soul. The recitation of the Lord's Prayer is mentioned, as is a more general prayer which asks for the influence of the Holy Spirit. All three accounts testify to pre- and post-baptismal anointings.

In addition to this liturgical document from Antioch, we have the homilies of John Chrysostom and Theodore of Mopsuestia. Both John and Theodore were presbyters in Antioch. Chrysostom was to become bishop of Constantinople, and Theodore was to become bishop of Mopsuestia. It may be assumed that their knowledge of the baptismal rites upon which they preached reflect something of the use of Antioch, though Theodore's may well have been on the practice of Mopsuestia.

Three sets of homilies have survived from John Chrysostom, known as the Montfaucon series (two homilies, cited as Mont), the Papadopoulas-Kerameus series (four homilies, one the same as Montfaucon, cited as P-K), and the Stavronikita series (eight homilies, the third being a duplicate of the fourth in the P-K series cited as Stav). Hugh Riley gives the following table:[13]

Stav. 1	10 days after Lent began	390
Stav. 2	Shortly after Easter	390
Stav. 3(=P-K4)	Immediately after baptism	388
Stav. 4	Easter Sunday or Monday	390
Stav. 5	Easter Tuesday	390
Stav. 6	Easter Wednesday	390
Stav. 7	Easter Thursday	390
Stav. 8	Easter Friday	390
P-K 1(=Mont.1)	10 days after Lent began	388

---

[12] Ibid., p. 59.

[13] Riley, *Christian Initiation*, p. 14.

P-K 2	20 days after Lent began	388
P-K 3	Holy Thursday	388
Mont. 2	20 days after Lent began	390(?)

Chrysostom witnesses to the need for candidates to undergo exorcisms, and to the need for sponsors. The formula of the Renunciation as he gives it is 'I renounce you, Satan, your pomp, your worship and your works.' Chrysostom comments:

> There is great power in these few words. For the angels who are present and the invisible powers rejoice at your conversion and, receiving the words from your lips, carry them to the common Master of all things, where they are inscribed in the books of heaven.[14]

The anointing is described as a pledge and making the person a soldier. The forehead was anointed with a simple Trinitarian formula, and there was a stripping-off of clothes, of which Chrystostom made much with regard to wealthy women:

> Strip off your adornment and put it in Christ's hands through the hands of His poor. He will guard all your riches for you against the day when he will raise up your body with great glory. Then He will put on you a better wealth and a richer adornment, since your present wealth and adornment are really paltry and ridiculous.[15]

The whole body was anointed, and Chrysostom interprets this as providing armour and protection. The baptism in water involved a triple immersion, and was likened to a bridal bath, but also to burial, circumcision and the cross. And for Chrysostom, it was in the baptismal action that the Spirit was imparted. He makes no mention of a post-baptismal anointing, though he does mention the kiss given to candidates after they came up from the water.

Theodore, a close friend of Chrysostom, was highly regarded during his lifetime. But he was later seen as a precursor to the Nestorian heresy, and was condemned in 553. His writings were conserved in the East Syrian Church. Theodore left sixteen surviving catechetical homilies. These are in Syriac, though originally in Greek. They may have been given in Mopsuestia where he was bishop from 392 to 428.[16]

Theodore explains that in the ritual known to him candidates stood on sackcloth, and were barefooted. They fell on their knees and stretched out their hands. According to Theodore, the words of renunciation were:

> I renounce Satan, all his angels, all his works, all his service, all his vanity and all his worldly enticements. I pledge myself by vow, I believe, and I am baptized in the name of the Father, of the Son and of the Holy Spirit.[17]

---

[14] Stav. 2.21; Finn *ECBC* 1, p. 78.

[15] Montf. 2:46, cited in Riley, *Christian Initiation*, p. 168.

[16] For a recent discussion, see Frederick G. Mcleod, 'The Christological Ramifications of Theodore of Mopsuestia's Understanding of Baptism and the Eucharist', *Journal of Early Christian Studies* 10 (2002), 37–75.

[17] Finn, *ECBC* 1, p. 83.

However, Theodore in a sense demythologizes the exorcisms and the renunciations, and portrays the rite as a court trial. H. Ansgar Kelly writes:

> [In Theodore's service] the exorcists do not exorcise demons, even ostensibly, but rather play the role of lawyers who plead with God in a suit on behalf of their clients ... Satan is present as defendant, and God is the judge. The exorcists are mentioned as the candidates' counsel or advocates – Theodore uses the technical term *synegoroi* ... They make a long appeal to God in a loud voice and demand that the evil master of the plaintiffs be punished and removed from his position of authority over them.[18]

As in Cyril and Chrysostom, this renunciation was followed by an anointing or sealing on the forehead. Then came the stripping, and anointing all over. Theodore explained the ritual thus:

> After you have taken off your garments, you are rightly anointed all over your body with the oil of anointing, a mark and sign that you will be receiving the covering of immortality, which through baptism you are about to put on. After you have taken off the covering which involves the sign of mortality, you receive through your anointing the sign of the covering of immortality, which you expect to receive through baptism. And you are anointed all over your body as a sign that unlike the covering used as a garment, which does not cover all the parts of the body, because although it may cover all the external limbs, it by no means covers the internal ones – all our nature will put on immortality at the time of the resurrection, and all that is seen in us, whether internal or external, will undoubtedly be changed into incorruptibility according to the working of the Holy Spirit which shall then be with us.[19]

In the act of baptism in the water, according to Theodore, 'the one baptized settles in the water as in a kind of womb, like a seed showing no sign of an immortal nature'. He refers to a threefold immersion, the donning of a white garment, and post-baptismal anointing on the forehead. The latter is explained in light of the fact that after Jesus was baptized, he received the grace of the Holy Spirit who descended like a dove. Theodore seems to suggest that this anointing symbolizes the gift of the Spirit but, unlike Cyril, he does not explicitly teach that the gift of the Spirit is given in this anointing.

A number of things are striking about the explanations given by Cyril, Chrysostom and Theodore. First, they do not work with a theology of baptism as though there existed a generic rite called baptism. Each inherited a ritual pattern, and their theology develops from the ritual pattern. It is precisely because of this that they give different interpretations and different emphases to the various stages of the ritual. Thus, for example, we find a difference in interpretation over the significance of the anointings. Cyril sees in the post-baptismal anointing a ritual action explicitly imparting the gift

---

[18] Henry Ansgar Kelly, *The Devil at Baptism. Ritual, Theology, and Drama*, Cornell University Press, Ithaca, NY and London, 1985, p. 149.

[19] Here I have preferred to use the translation in A. Mingana (ed.), *Woodbrooke Studies* VI, Heffers, Cambridge 1933, p. 54.

of the Spirit, whereas Theodore sees it more as symbolic of what is given as a result of baptism. John Chrysostom is silent on this point, because the rite known to him does not appear to have had a rite of anointing after the water baptism at all. A number of explanations have been given for this.

One explanation was proposed by Edward Ratcliff, who classed Jerusalem and Antioch together as 'Syrian' Christianity, even if not Syriac-speaking. Observing that the earlier evidence gives the pattern as anointing-baptism, or, eventually, an anointing after the renunciations, and then a further pre-baptismal anointing, Ratcliff argued that Cyril of Jerusalem was an innovator in many things, and being concerned with the life of Jesus, reshaped the Jerusalem ritual pattern so that the anointing followed baptism.[20] It then reflected the Spirit alighting on Jesus after his baptism. Cyril also abandoned the use of plain olive oil and substituted chrism or myron. He introduced the Pauline imagery from Romans 6 in place of rebirth imagery. The importance of Jerusalem as a place of pilgrimage meant that the new pattern was copied elsewhere. John Chrysostom had not yet copied Jerusalem; *Apostolic Constitutions* had.

Another explanation is Gabriele Winkler's, who, extending her argument regarding the *Acts of Judas Thomas*, suggested that we can see a developmental pattern of 'moving the Spirit' taking place. First, the Spirit was associated with messianic adoption in the single anointing of the head. Later, this was duplicated with the body also being anointed, signifying protection. As a result, the 'giving' of the Spirit was shifted temporarily to the water (Chrysostom), and then to a post-baptismal anointing.[21]

Finally, Sebastian Brock has built upon the foundations of both Ratcliff and Winkler. In his examination of the texts he finds some confusion and fluidity over the meaning of the two pre-baptismal anointings. He suggests that the older Syrian ritual pattern of anointing-baptism was modelled on the Jewish ritual for converts of circumcision-ritual bath. Later, under the impact of a strict linear interpretation of the baptism of Jesus, and the revival of Pauline imagery of dying and rising, the themes of the older pre-baptismal anointing were transferred to a post-baptismal anointing, and the pre-baptismal anointings were given an exorcistic and protective interpretation.[22]

The problem with Ratcliff's view is that, as reasonable as it may seem, we have no evidence that Cyril made these innovations, and the evidence from the *Gospel of Phillip* is an early witness to the ritual pattern of baptism-anointing. Winkler's view rests not only on her particular reading of the evidence in the *Acts of Judas Thomas*,

---

[20] See Edward Ratcliff, 'The Old Syrian Baptismal Tradition and its Resettlement under the Influence of Jerusalem in the Fourth Century'.

[21] Gabriele Winkler, 'The Original Meaning of the Pre-baptismal Anointing and Its Implication', *Worship* 52 (1978), 24–45.

[22] Sebastian Brock, 'The Transition to a Post-baptisal Anointing in the Antiochene Rite', in Bryan D. Spinks (ed.), *The Sacrifice of Praise. Studies on the themes of thanksgiving and redemption in the central prayers of the Eucharistic and baptismal liturgies*, Edizioni Liturgiche, Rome, 1981, pp. 214–25.

but also on regarding John Chrysostom as a passing, temporary theology defending an older pattern. Brock's appeal to the Jewish ritual pattern founders because the Jewish practice may well post-date the Christian pattern. It may be that what we have is what is already found in the pre-Nicene evidence, namely, local variations in ritual patterns giving rise to varying theological interpretations.

This is suggested by the compiler of *Apostolic Constitutions*, who in one document gives different patterns. It is further suggested by the early Syriac baptismal commentaries published by Sebastian Brock.[23] Brock edited three West Syrian baptismal commentaries which share a basic text in common. He dated the common text as mid-fifth century. Although West Syrian, it was also used by East Syrians. In what Brock thinks is the earliest text we find a renunciation of Satan, a confession of Christ, an exorcism and mention of a sponsor. There is anointing of the forehead, the baptism, crowns or linen placed on the head, white garments and lighted tapers. However, in the other two texts we find an expansion with a further anointing before the baptism, and after the baptism, an anointing which is explained thus: 'The myron after he has been baptized: because he receives a sweet and spiritual scent by means of the imprint; and it is the perfecter of the divine gifts.'[24]

What we have is two ritual traditions using a common text, but altered to suit the different ritual patterns. It is the ritual pattern which generates a theology or exegesis. We also note in the fourth/fifth-century explanations the increasing use of the Pauline ideas about baptism in Romans, particularly of dying and rising, and the font as a tomb. The womb/new birth imagery is still present, but becomes less prominent.

Cappadocia

No early rite of Cappadocia has survived. Paul Bradshaw has speculated that when Origen spoke of 'Holy Spirit and water', he was referring to the early Egyptian ritual sequence, and when he spoke of visible water and visible chrism, he might have been referring to the Caesarean ritual sequence.[25] However, we do not have anything to corroborate this, and we have already suggested that Origen is probably not giving a strict ritual sequence attributable to Egypt or elsewhere. Furthermore, as will be suggested in Chapter 5, the early Armenian evidence, which shows a sequence of anointing and baptism, may well reflect pre-Nicene Caesarean usage. Despite the lack of concrete evidence of a rite, we do however have the post-Nicene teaching on baptism in the writings of the three great Cappadocian fathers, Basil, Gregory of Nyssa and Gregory of Nazianzus.

---

[23] Sebastian Brock, 'Some Early Syriac Baptismal Commentaries', *Orientalia Christiana Periodica* 46 (1980), 20–61.

[24] Ibid., p. 43; Syriac text is on p. 42.

[25] Paul Bradshaw, 'Baptismal Practice in the Alexandrian Tradition: Eastern or Western,' in Paul Bradshaw (ed.), *Essays in Early Christianity*, Alcuin/GROW Liturgical Study, Grove Books, Bramcote, 1988, pp. 5–17, p. 15.

Basil's teachings are outlined in *Concerning Baptism* (DB) and *Concerning the Holy Spirit* (DSS).[26] He teaches that instruction is necessary if baptism is to be received worthily (DB 2, 349), and that it certainly involves freeing ourselves from the tyranny of the devil, and renouncing the world and its concupiscence (DB1, 347). Since Basil was writing in the continuing Christological struggles after Nicaea, and at a time leading up to the formulation of Trinitarian doctrine of Constantinople in 381, he puts an emphasis on the names of the three persons of the Trinity. In DSS, XI.27, Basil speaks of 'belief in the Father and in the Son and in the Holy Spirit, when they renounced the devil and his angels'. Again:

> Faith and baptism are two kindred and inseparable ways of salvation: faith is perfected through baptism, baptism is established through faith, and both are completed by the same names. For as we believe in the Father and the Son and the Holy Ghost, so are we also baptized in the name of the Father and of the Son and of the Holy Ghost; first comes the confession, introducing us to salvation, and baptism follows, setting the seal upon our assent. (DSS, XII.28)

Further, defending the threefold name, Basil says, 'For the naming of Christ is the confession of the whole, showing forth as it does the God who gave, the Son who received, and the Spirit who is, unction' (DSS, XII.28). This may be an allusion to an anointing with oil in the rite, but it is by no means clear. Basil does allude more obviously to the instruction, renunciation, confession of faith, and baptism in the threefold name. He writes that the effect of baptism is 'like the change of colour which occurs in wool when it is dipped into dye – or rather, that we may enkindle the light of knowledge unto the comprehension of the great Light' (DB2, 361). One is crucified with Christ in baptism, and the water is an image of the Cross and death (DB2, 371); through baptism one is crucified, dead, buried and planted and raised again (DB2, 376). Again, baptism 'is a type of the cross and of the death, burial, and resurrection from the dead' (DB2, 384). In DSS, XV.35 death and burial again seem to be Basil's favourite motives, and in DSS, XV.35 he explains that 'the water receiving the body as in a tomb figures death, while the Spirit pours in the quickening power, renewing our souls from the deadness of sin unto their original life'. Those who have been baptized have been 'born anew' and undergo 'a change of abode, habits, and associates, so that, walking by the Spirit we may merit to be baptized in the Name of the Son and to put on Christ' (DB2, 385).

In his homily, *On the Baptism of Christ*, Gregory of Nyssa explained the salvific nature of Jesus' baptism thus:

> Today he is baptized by John that he might cleanse him who was defiled, that he might bring the Spirit from above, and exalt man to heaven, that he who had fallen might be raised up, and he who had cast him down might be put to shame.[27]

---

[26] 'Concerning Baptism' in *Saint Basil. Ascetical Works*, Fathers of the Church, New York, 1950, pp. 339–430; Concerning the Holy Spirit, online text: <http://www.ccel.org/fathers 2/NPNF/F2-08>.

[27] Finn, *ECBC* 1, pp. 62–70, p. 63.

For Gregory, baptism is for the 'purification of sins, a remission of trespasses, a cause of renovation and regeneration'. The water serves to express cleansing, but it is not the water which bestows, but the command of God and the visitation of the Spirit which come sacramentally. Yet Gregory shortly speaks of the sacramental oil and the water, which 'after the sanctification bestowed by the Spirit, has its several functions'. This seems to allude to pouring consecrated oil into the water, together with the invocation of the Spirit over the water. Later still he speaks of the threefold immersions by which

> ... we represent for ourselves that grace of the resurrection which was wrought in three days: and this we do, not receiving the sacrament in silence, but while there are spoken over us the Names of the Three sacred Persons on whom we believed, in whom we also hope, from whom comes to us both the fact of our present and the fact of our future existence.[28]

The result is a recalling to paradise where we may join the angels' song, offering the worship of their praise to God.

Both G. Kretschmar and J. Danielou suggested that there is evidence in Gregory's writings to show that he knew of the use of oil and chrism, and that both were pre-baptismal anointings.[29] In his work *On the Holy Spirit, Against the Followers of Macedonius*, Gregory was concerned to stress that the Spirit is of the same rank as the Father and the Son; if he is in any way inferior, then 'He is quite disconnected.'[30] Gregory proceeds to demonstrate that the Spirit is very much connected with the Father and the Son, and remarks, 'For how can one who does not think of the unction along with the Anointed be said to believe in the Anointed?'[31] He then argues that unction is a symbol of Kingship:

> If, then, the Son is in His very nature a king, and the unction is the symbol of His kingship, what, in the way of a consequence, does your reason demonstrate? Why, that the unction is not a thing alien to that Kingship, and so that the Spirit is not to be ranked in the Trinity as anything strange and foreign either. For the Son is King, and His living, realized, and personified Kingship is found in the Holy Spirit, who anoints the Only-begotten, and so makes Him the Anointed, and the King of all things that exist. If, then, the Father is King, and the Only-begotten is King, and the Holy Ghost is the Kingship, one and the same definition of Kingship must prevail throughout this Trinity, and the thought of 'unction' conveys the hidden meaning that there is no interval of separation between the Son and the Holy Spirit. For as between the body's surface and the unction of the oil (*tes tou elaiou chriseos*) nothing intervening can be detected, either in reason or in

---

[28] Ibid., p. 66.

[29] G. Kretschmar, 'Die Geschichte des Taufgottesdienstes in der alten Kirche' in (eds) Karl Ferdinand Muller and Walter Blakenburg, *Leiturgia, Handbuch des evangelischen Gottesdienstes*, Kassel-Wilhennshohe, J. Stauda-Verlag, 1970; Jean Danielou, 'Chrismation Prebaptismale et Divinité de l'Esprit chez Gregoire de Nysse', in *Recherches de Science Religieuse* 56 (1968), 177–98.

[30] *On the Holy Spirit*, NPNF, <http://www.ccel.org/fathers2/NPNF2-05/Npnf2-05-26.htm#P2435#1676104>, p. 1.

[31] Ibid., p. 6.

perception, so inseparable is the union of the Spirit with the Son; and the result
is that whosoever is to touch the Son by faith must needs first encounter the oil
(*to muro*) in the very act of touching; there is not a part of Him devoid of the Holy
Spirit.[32]

Kretschmar and Danielou suggest that this alludes to the pre-baptismal anointing
before the confession of faith and baptism, and was regarded as imparting the Spirit,
as in the Syrian tradition. Later Gregory says:

> Is that life-giving power in the water itself which is employed to convey the grace
> of Baptism? Or is it not rather clear to everyone that this element is employed as
> a means in the external ministry, and of itself contributes nothing towards the
> sanctification, unless it be first transformed by the sanctification; and that which
> gives life to the baptized is the Spirit.[33]

Though there is some ambiguity here, it could well be that Kretschmar and Danielou
are correct.

Gregory of Nazianzus, in his *Oration on Holy Baptism*, explains that we call
baptism 'the Gift, the Grace, Baptism, Unction, Illumination, the Clothing of
Immortality, the Laver of Regeneration, the Seal, and everything that is honourable'.[34]
He calls on Christians to 'defend themselves with the water; defend yourselves with
the Spirit', for baptism is 'a covenant with God for a second life and a purer
conversation'.[35] He is content to use dying and rising imagery, as well as the image
of putting on Christ. Alluding to Exodus 12:22 he says:

> But if you would fortify yourself beforehand with the Seal, and secure yourself
> for the future with the best and strongest of all aids, being signed both in body
> and in soul with the unction, as Israel was of old with that blood and unction of
> the first born at night that guarded him, what then can happen to you, and what
> has been wrought out of you?[36]

This seems to be a reference to a pre-baptismal anointing, since Gregory seems to use
the term 'seal' in this homily to mean baptism. He also alludes to a baptismal garment
– 'for it is base to say, "Where is my offering for my baptism, and where is my
baptismal robe, in which I shall be made bright?"' – though arguing that they should
clothe themselves with Christ. He speaks of the laver being not only for the body, but
for the image of God in us, and likens cleansing to the cleansing of lepers. He likewise
says that baptism is in the triune name, and quotes a creed in the context of baptismal
faith. For Gregory, cleansing and illumination seem to be the main consequences of
baptism.

Thus, although we have no rite for Cappadocia, the three great Cappadocians
witness to elements found elsewhere: instruction, renunciation, anointing, and baptism

---

[32] Ibid.

[33] Ibid., p. 7.

[34] NPNF VII (1894), p. 360 <http://www.ccel.org/fathers2/NPNF2-07/Npnf2-07-52.htm#TopOfPage>.

[35] Ibid., p. 362.

[36] Ibid., p. 364.

in the triune name, and the baptismal robe. It may be that Gregory of Nyssa witnesses to only a pre-baptismal anointing, associated with the Spirit, and Gregory of Nazianzus may also imply this when he speaks of unction before the seal.

East Syria: Aphraat, Ephrem and the *History of John*

Aphraat

Aphraat, the Persian sage, is thought to have lived *c.* 270–360, though his exact dates are unknown. He seems to have belonged to the ascetic group of ecclesiasts in East Syria known as the B'nai Qy'ama, who took a vow of celibacy which at some stage in East Syria had been seen as necessary for baptism. He lived on the edge of the Persian Empire, and is regarded as being one of the least hellenized of the Syrian theologians. Though he did not treat baptism directly, some hints of the rite he knew and his understanding of it can be gleaned from his *Demonstrations*. This has been treated at length by Edward Duncan, though at times in his study some ambiguous statements of Aphraat are interpreted by reference to other writers, and the result is to say more than Aphraat actually tells us. It may well be the case that Aphraat knew a ritual pattern which corresponded to that in the early baptismal commentary mentioned earlier.

Finn and Gabriele Winkler both assert that Aphraat knew a renunciation of Satan, but in fact, although this is likely, there is no explicit reference. Duncan points out that, in the reference in 'On the Pasch' to 'and the giving of the sign, and baptism according to its due observance', the Syriac word for sign, *rushma*, quite frequently does refer to the anointing. In Demonstration 23.3 Aphraat writes:

> When the door was opened to ask for peace, the darkness fled from the minds of many and there arose the light of intelligence and the fruitfulness of the shining olive in which is the sign (*rushma*) of the mystery of life and by which Christians and priests and kings and prophets were made perfect.[37]

While this indeed suggests a reference to a pre-baptismal anointing, there is no obvious association with the Holy Spirit. In fact, rather like the *Didascalia*, it has a Christological/messianic connotation. However, Aphraat does associate the Holy Spirit with the consecration of the water, on which he is quite explicit:

> Through baptism we have received the Spirit of Christ; for at the very hour the priests call on the Spirit heaven opens, and she descends, moves the waters, and those who are baptized put her on. For the Spirit is absent from all born from the body, until they come to rebirth from the waters; then they receive the Spirit. For in the first birth they were born, endowed with the animal Spirit created in man;

---

[37] Cites in Edward J. Duncan, 'The Administration of Baptism in the Demonstrations of Aphraates', in Jacob Vellian (ed.), *Studies in Syrian Baptismal Rites, Vol. 6 (Syrian Church Series)*, Kottayam, Kerala, CMS, 1973, pp. 16–36, p. 21.

nor will it ever die, as it is written, 'I made man into a living spirit.' But in the
second birth, namely, baptism, they receive the Holy Spirit immortal from divinity
himself. When, therefore, people die, the animal spirit is hidden, with the body
sensation taken away. However, the heavenly Spirit, whom they received according
to her nature, returns to Christ.[38]

As Simon Jones has observed, new birth within the context of the second Adam is one
of Aphraat's central themes.[39] Behind this is a favourite theme of the Syriac theological
tradition, of Adam having lost the robe of glory and his nudity being covered by
Christ's robe of glory.[40] The Spirit is invoked to come upon the waters to accomplish
this.

In Demonstration 11, 'On Circumcision', Aphraat turns to consider the concept of
covenants, and the relation of these to baptism. He compares Joshua, son of Nun with
Joshua (Jesus), Son of God. Thus he writes:

Blest, therefore, are those who are circumcised in the foreskins of their hearts and
are reborn from the water of the second circumcision; they receive inheritance
with Abraham, the head of the believers and the father of all Gentiles, for his faith
was reckoned for him as righteousness.[41]

In Demonstration 12 Aphraat interprets baptism within the context of Christ's passion
and death:

Moreover, Israel was baptized in the middle of the sea on Passover night, the day
of salvation; likewise, our Saviour washed the feet of his disciples on Passover
night, which is the mystery of baptism. For you know, Beloved, that the Saviour
gave the true baptism on this night. As long as he travelled about with his disciples,
they were baptized in the baptism of the law with which the priests were baptizing,
the baptism about which John had said: 'Repent of your sins.' But in that night
he disclosed to them the mystery, the baptism of his suffering death, of which the
apostle spoke: 'You were buried with him in baptism for death, and you rose with
him through the power of God.' Understand, then, friend, that the baptism of John
had no value for the remission of sins, but only for repentance.[42]

Thus Aphraat seems to witness to the ritual pattern of anointing, blessing of the
water and baptism. It has been conjectured that he also knew a rite of foot-washing
as part of the baptismal liturgy. Although this possibility cannot be entirely ruled
out, the text seems simply to be giving the foot-washing in John a clear baptismal
meaning.[43] In addition, we have a number of theological themes, including clothing
in the glorious body as a restoration of Paradise, together with new birth and death/

---

[38] *Dem.* 6.14. Finn, *ECBC* 1, p. 137.

[39] Simon Jones, 'Womb of the Spirit. The Liturgical Implications of the Doctrine of the Spirit for the
Syrian Baptismal Tradition', Ph.D Thesis, University of Cambridge, 1999.

[40] See Sebastian Brock, *The Luminous Eye*, Placid Lectures,CIIS, Rome, 1985.

[41] *Dem.*11.12. Finn, *ECBC* 1, p. 141, adapted.

[42] *Dem.* 12.10. Finn, *ECBC* 1, p. 148.

[43] See Gabriele Winkler, *Das Armenische Initiationsrituale*, *Orientalia Christiana Analecta* 217,
Pontifical Oriental Institute, Rome (1981), 156.

resurrection typology. We also find an analogy drawn between circumcision/covenant and baptism/covenant.

Ephrem

Ephrem is the great poet-theologian shared by the Syriac traditions of East and West Syria. He lived from the beginning of the fourth century until 373. Most of his life was spent at Nisibis until that city fell to the Persians, and he then moved to Edessa. He accepted the conclusions of the Council of Nicaea, but still wrote theology in poetry, using the earlier Syriac traditions. Thus in Hymn on the Nativity 23 he describes the incarnation in terms of the Merciful One stripping off glory and putting on a body, and Christ being baptized for Adam's sin.

Hymn on Virginity 7 alludes to the importance of oil, not only to the ancient Semitic cultures, but also its religious associations with Christ and baptism. The hymn stresses the need for repentance, and considers the months of October and April: October has rain when the fruit is on the tree, fruit is gathered, and oil is pressed in this month. April is the month when fasting stops, anointing, baptism and clothing in white take place. He writes:

> A royal portrait is painted with visible colours,
> and with oil that all can see is the hidden portrait of our hidden King portrayed
> on those who have been signed: on them baptism, that is in travail with them in its womb,
> depicts the new portrait, to replace the image of the former Adam who was corrupted;
> it gives birth to them with triple pangs,
> accompanied by the three glorious names, of Father, Son and Holy Spirit.
> This oil is the dear friend of the Holy Spirit, it serves him, following him like a disciple.
> With it the Spirit signed priests and anointed kings;
> for with the oil the Holy Spirit imprints his mark on his sheep.
> Like a signet ring whose impression is left on wax, so the hidden seal of the Spirit
> is imprinted by oil on the bodies of those who are anointed in baptism;
> thus are they marked in the baptismal mystery.[44]

The Hymn explains that oil forgives sins, that baptism is a second womb, that anointing precedes the bath, and that the Holy Spirit hovers over the water. Interestingly, although Ephrem says that the oil is a 'dear friend' of the Holy Spirit, with which the Holy Spirit marks people, and that it is a seal of the Spirit, in this hymn he seems more concerned with its ability to give repentance and freedom from sin. In Hymn 36 Ephrem links the baptism of Christ with the incarnation, and Jordan's womb becomes the fountainhead of Christian baptism. Here the theme of rebirth dominates; just as Mary's womb gave birth to Jesus, so too the womb of the Jordan gives birth to

---

[44] Finn, *ECBC* 1, pp. 154–5.

Christians. Hymn on the Faith 10 links fire and Spirit in the incarnation with fire and Spirit given at baptism.

The Hymns on the Epiphany are regarded as the work of a 'Pseudo-Ephrem', one of his disciples. In Hymn 1 candidates for baptism are likened to lepers. The baptisms take place during Epiphany, January 6th, the great festival which commemorated in Ephrem's day both the birth of Christ and his baptism. Thus we have birth imagery. Hymn 6 is concerned with the blessing of the water, and only this water can truly cleanse. The hymn also mentions marking, stripping and robing. In Verse 7:

> Angels and watchers rejoice at the birth effected by Spirit and water:
> beings of fire and spirit rejoice since those in the body have now become spiritual;
> the seraphs who cry 'holy' rejoice
> because the number of those who sing 'holy' is increased.[45]

The hymn affirms that baptism sanctifies and cleanses, and the candidate is reclothed with the glorious robe lost by Adam. It also mentions that the candidates are clothed in white, like sheep. What is interesting in this hymn – as in the *History of John the Son of Zebedee* – is that baptism is regarded as taking place in the presence of angels and watchers.

The History of John the Son of Zebedee

As with the *Acts of Thomas*, the dating of this document is disputed, as is whether its original language was Syriac or Greek. A fourth-century date is likely. In the account of the baptism of Tyrannus we find a detailed ritual in which the Trinity was invoked, and then a sign of the cross made over oil, fire blazed over the oil, and angels spread their wings over the oil and chanted 'holy, holy, holy'. The water, too, was signed and, it is assumed, consecrated by invocation of the triune name, while two angels hovered over it and sang the *sanctus*. The candidate stripped, and was anointed on the forehead and then all over, being likened to a new firstling lamb with a new fleece. A Trinitarian confession of faith was followed by a threefold immersion with the triune formula. A white garment was placed upon the candidate, and he was given the kiss of peace. The Pax formula describes the candidate as a new bridegroom, an old person who has become a youth, and someone whose name is written in heaven: 'Peace be to you, new bride-groom, who had grown old and effete in sin, and lo, today have become a youth, and your name has been written in heaven.'[46]

In the account of the baptism of the priests of Artemis, John gives glory to the Trinity and prays over the oil and water the following prayer:

> Lord God Almighty, let your Spirit of holiness come, and rest, and dwell upon the oil and upon the water; and let them be bathed and purified from uncleanness;

[45] Finn, *ECBC* 1, p. 167.
[46] Whitaker/Johnson, *DBL*, p. 25.

and let them receive the Spirit of holiness through baptism; and henceforth let them call you 'Our Father who art in heaven.' Yes, Lord, sanctify this water with your voice, which resounded over the Jordan and pointed out our Lord Jesus as with the finger, saying, 'This is my beloved Son, in whom I am well pleased, hear him.' You are here who was on the Jordan. Yes, I beseech you, Lord, manifest yourself here before this assembly who has believed on you with simplicity, and let the nations of the earth hear that the city of Ephesus was the first to receive your gospel before all cities, and became a second sister to Urhai [Edessa] of the Parthians.[47]

The account says that fire blazed over the oil, and the wings of angels were spread over the oil, as the assembly chanted the *sanctus*. The priests made a trinitarian confession of faith, and were anointed and baptized with the triune formula 'for the forgiveness of debts and the pardon of sins'.

This tradition laid considerable emphasis on the blessing of the oil and water and, as in Ephrem, saw this blessing as confirmed in the heavenly realms by the angelic beings being present and joining in the ritual. The ritual pattern presupposed here reflects the earliest text of the commentaries edited by Sebastian Brock discussed earlier. In this part of the Syrian tradition, which was probably known to Aphraat and Ephrem, there was apparently no post-baptismal anointing.

Egypt, Italy and North Africa

Sarapion, Hippolytus and Didymus

For Egypt during this period we have two liturgical texts as well as gleanings from Didymus the Blind. The first liturgical evidence is the euchology, or collection of prayers, attributed to Sarapion, bishop of Thmuis in the Nile Delta 339–360. Sarapion was a friend of St Anthony and of Athanasius. The collection of prayers which bear his name is preserved in an eleventh-century manuscript, Ms Lavra 149, which was first published in 1894. There are no rubrics, but amongst the prayers are ones for a baptism, for catechumens and for oil. There has been a dispute as to whether these prayers can be attributed to Sarapion. Catholic liturgists Bernard Capelle and Bernard Botte have argued that some of the prayers show traces of Arianism, and that a close friend of Athanasius could not have authored them. However, we must bear in mind first of all that this is a collection; not all the prayers were necessarily written by Sarapion. Furthermore, there is no reason why Sarapion could not have been both a friend of Athanasius and used dyhypostatic prayers. Finally, Geoffrey Cuming contested the evidence presented by Botte, and concluded that there was no good reason for not ascribing the collection to Sarapion.[48]

---

[47] Ibid.

[48] B. Capelle, 'L'Anahore de Serapion: Essai d'exégèse', *Le Muséon* 59 (1964), 425–43; B. Botte, 'L'Eucologe de Serapion est-il authentique?', *Oriens Christianus* 48 (1964), 50–57; Geoffrey J. Cuming,

In an important study Maxwell Johnson made a close examination of the prayers and identified four different hands, confirming that this was indeed a collection.[49] According to Johnson, Prayers 7–11, which are concerned with baptism, together with Prayers 21 and 28 for catechumens, all come from the same hand; the prayers for oil, 15 and 16, come from another, and Prayer 20 for catechumens comes from a third author. Johnson worked with the conviction that the earliest Eygptian evidence, particularly that found in Origen, attests a ritual pattern of anointing-baptism, as in much of the Syrian evidence. He therefore suggests that since Prayers 15 and 16 are for protection and post-baptismal chrism, they represent a later stage of development than Prayers 7–11. However, we have already seen that many so-called Gnostic documents, including the *Gospel of Phillip*, circulated not only on the fringes but within the Egyptian Church at this time. Thus, the pattern of a post-baptismal anointing in Egypt pre-dates Sarapion, and there is consequently no absolute necessity to conclude that the prayers concerning oil in Sarapion are compositions later than other prayers. They may be, but if Sarapion compiled the baptismal Prayers 7–11 himself, yet borrowed the oil prayers 15 and 16 from an existing source, they would obviously pre-date Prayers 7–11 in composition. However, any attempt to date these is purely conjectural. It seems a safer interpretation of the ritual to say that, at least when Sarapion compiled his prayers, he felt that an adequate rite for Thmuis required prayers for catechumens, a pre-baptismal anointing with exorcism, and after baptism, an anointing with chrism.

What is the theology presented in this collection? The prayer for the catechumens [21] gives thanks for the call of these catechumens, and asks that they may be confirmed in their faith, guarded in what they have learnt, so that they may be worthy of regeneration. The prayer for the pre-baptismal anointing asks that their body, soul and spirit be healed of every mark of sin and lawlessness or Satanic fault, so that in baptism they may be washed and have victory over the energies and conceits of the world. The prayer for those being baptized asks that they might be regenerated, and a prayer of renunciation petitions God to seal the adhesion of the candidate. A prayer of acceptance asks that the regeneration they will receive will be honoured. The blessing of the water requests that the ineffable Logos and Spirit come upon the waters and cause them to be regenerative so that the candidates will be made holy and spiritual and able to worship God. The prayer after baptism asks that now the candidates be given fellowship with angelic powers and be named no longer flesh but spiritual, while the prayer over the chrism asks that by this seal the candidates be made secure, steadfast, unmovable, unhurt and inviolate in the Christian life ahead.

'Thmuis Revisited: Another Look at the Prayers of Bishop Serapion', *Theological Studies* 41 (1980), 568–75.

[49] Maxwell E. Johnson, *The Prayers of Serapion of Thmuis: A Literary, Liturgical, and Theological Analysis*, *Orientalia Christiana Analecta* 249, Pontifical Oriental Institute, Rome, 1995. See pp. 46–81 for the text of these prayers.

A second important document which circulated is called the *Canons of Hippolytus*, also dated *c*. 360. This writing claims to follow precepts of Hippolytus, and is one of the documents which make up the psuedo-Hippolytus corpus. Insisting on the Nicene faith over against Arianism, the *Canons* teach that a candidate for baptism must be rigorously examined to ensure that false gods had been abandoned, and be instructed to renounce Satan. People in certain professions were excluded from baptism. Baptism took place at cockcrow on Easter Day. There was a pre-baptismal anointing, and then the baptism itself, a threefold immersion with credal interrogatories. There was also a post-baptismal anointing, followed by an imposition of hands, and then a final anointing by the bishop. The prayer accompanying the imposition asked:

> We bless you, Lord God almighty, for that you have made these worthy of being born again, that you pour out your Holy Spirit on them, and to be one in the body of the Church not being excluded by alien works; but, just as you have granted them forgiveness for their sins, grant them also the pledge of your kingdom. Through our Lord Jesus Christ, through whom be glory to you, with him and the Holy Spirit, to ages of ages. Amen.[50]

This version of the *Apostolic Tradition* prayer is a neat summary of what baptism is believed to achieve. A good summary of the understanding of baptism as taught in the Egyptian church is also given by Didymus the Blind (313–398). In his work *On the Trinity*, Didymus says that the Holy Spirit as God renovates us in baptism and, with the Father and Son, brings us back from a state of deformity to our pristine beauty. The Spirit conforms us to the image of the Son of God, and 'in the divine waters of the baptismal pool extinguishes the inextinguishable fire of hell':

> For when we are immersed in the baptismal pool, we are, by the goodness of God the Father and through the grace of his Holy Spirit, stripped of our sins as we lay aside the old man, are regenerated, and sealed by his own kingly power. But when we come up out of the pool, we put on Christ our Saviour as an incorruptible garment, worthy of the same honour as the Holy Spirit who regenerated us and marked us with his seal.[51]

Zeno of Verona

Zeno was bishop of Verona from *c*. 362 until *c*. 370. A considerable number of his homilies have survived, and a good many of these seem to allude to baptism, though it is difficult to be too precise about the occasion and sequence of these sermons. The most obvious reference is in I.23, when, after Psalm 41 is chanted, Zeno says:

> Hurry, hurry for a good wash, brothers! The water, living with the Holy Spirit and warmed with the sweetest fire now invites you with its soft murmur. Now the bath attendant is girded up and waiting for you, ready to provide the necessary anointing and washing, and also a golden denarius signed with the union of the triple seal.

---

[50] Whitaker/Johnson, *DBL*, p. 131.
[51] *On the Holy Trinity*, Finn, *ECBC* 2, p. 218.

> So rejoice! You will indeed go down naked into the font, but soon you will rise
> from there robed in white, dressed in heavenly vesture. Whoever does not defile
> it will possess the heavenly kingdoms, through our Lord Jesus Christ.[52]

A further homily tells us:

> After the chaste fast of holy expiation has been most devoutly accomplished, after
> the sweet vigils of a night dazzling with its own sun, after your souls grew to the
> hope of immortality by the life-giving bath of the milky font from which you who
> differed in age and race have come up suddenly as full brothers, suddenly as
> infants born together, I urge you to celebrate the feast of such a great birth with a
> joyful banquet.[53]

According to Gordon Jeanes, it is possible to reconstruct from the extant homilies the
baptismal rite at Verona at the time of Zeno. He suggests the following sequence:
anointing, renunciation, entry to the baptistery, stripping, immersion, anointing and
sealing, clothing with a white garment, all followed by the paschal eucharist. He
suggests, for example, that in Homily I.37, with reference to the parable of the Good
Samaritan, we have an allusion to the renunciations: 'The inn-keeper ... receives the
person who suffered the attack by the devil and his angels and this world into the inn,
that is by the revered mysteries into the Church.'[54] The formula at Verona might have
been:

> *Abrenuntias diabolo? Abrenuntio*
> *Abrenuntias pompis eius? Abrenuntio*
> *Abrenuntias seaculo? Abrenuntio.*[55]

Although Zeno provides no discussion of the blessing of the font, Homily I.23
describes the water as 'living with the Holy Spirit', and I.61 speaks of water being
purged by the wood of the cross. Zeno also associates oil with the Holy Spirit.

What of Zeno's theology? Jeanes notes that he was an able, though not outstanding
theologian, who nevertheless made a distinctive contribution through use of baptismal
imagery. He exhorts his audience to exult, and to wash and be clean. Jeanes writes:

> For Zeno, dirt and foul smell are symbolic of sin. The filth of the first birth, of
> prison, of the worldly life and of punishment for sin are, at least in these sermons,
> brought together and identified one with another. The sweet smell of oil, bread,
> and wine communicate freedom and new life in the Church, filled with the grace
> of the Holy Spirit.[56]

Zeno contrasted the winter of sin with the Easter/springtime of growth.[57] But the theme
that Jeanes finds running throughout the homilies is the contrast between *imago* and

---

[52] Gordon Jeanes, *The Day has Come. Easter and Baptism in Zeno of Verona*, Liturgical Press,
Collegeville, MN, 1995, p. 62.

[53] Ibid., p. 63.

[54] Ibid., p. 171.

[55] Ibid., p. 173.

[56] Ibid., p. 223.

[57] Ibid., p. 226.

veritas, where the partial and worldly *imago* is contrasted with the spiritual *veritas*, the full and eternal revelation of God. Thus Zeno wrote:

> So we must believe that the image of God is not this fleshly garment but the spiritual image of the heavenly person which of his abundance he lavishes on us from the sacred font. Paul clearly shows forth this matter when he says, 'Just as we have borne the image of the man of dust, so we shall bear the image of the man of heaven.' Those who bear it in holiness, as did the apostles and all the just, will bear not only the image, but even God himself, as it is written, 'You are the temple of God, and the spirit of God dwells in you.'[58]

This is not too dissimilar to the focus in Ephrem of the robe of glory, but, as Jeanes notes, Zeno does not articulate how being the temple of God and having the Holy Spirit in the heavenly fulfilment differs from being the *imago* and possessing the Spirit on earth.[59] Other concerns for Zeno are guilt, sin and forgiveness (the latter associated in part with the first anointing), as well as the theme of martyrdom and new birth.

The so-called *Leonine Sacramentary* is neither by Pope Leo nor is it a sacramentary.[60] Rather it is a collection of mass texts compiled at Verona in the sixth century. But some of the texts are thought to date from the late fourth century, and thus possibly from the time of Zeno. The mass texts are grouped by month, starting from January, and damage to the manuscript has resulted in loss of the texts for Lent and Easter, where the baptismal material would have been located. However, baptismal material is preserved in the mass for Pentecost. The collect of the day speaks of 'the children of adoption whom your Holy Spirit has called to himself'. In the canon of the mass, the oblation is offered 'for these who have been regenerated by water and the Holy Spirit'. There is a blessing of water, honey and milk, which was given to the neophytes. There is also a blessing of the font which quotes from Genesis 1:3, mentions the baptism of John, and asks that 'your hand may be laid upon this water that you may cleanse and purify the lesser man who shall be baptized therefrom, and that he ... may be reborn and brought to life again through the new man reborn in Christ Jesus.' The emphasis seems to be on cleansing and renewing the old Adam through the new.

Ambrose of Milan

Ambrose was bishop of Milan between 373 and 397. In addition to being an outstanding leader and teacher, he is also credited with converting Augustine of Hippo to Christianity. His teaching on baptism is outlined in his homilies explaining the rites in use at Milan. In one place Ambrose stresses that, for most of the rites, Milan follows Rome, but he notes one or two differences.

In Milan during Ambrose's time, the baptismal candidates assembled on Saturday night at Paschal-tide, and Ambrose says that the bishop touched their ears and nostrils,

---

[58] Ibid., p. 234.

[59] Ibid., p. 235.

[60] Finn, *ECBC* 2, pp. 90–91.

ritualizing the *effeta* miracle of the Gospels, where Jesus touched the ears and mouth of the deaf and dumb man. Ambrose explains that the nostrils are substituted for the mouth 'out of respect', because amongst the candidates are women. The bishop 'touches the nostrils so that you may receive the sweet fragrance of eternal goodness; so that you can say as the holy apostle said: "We are the aroma of Christ to God"'.[61] In the baptistery the candidates were anointed as athletes, and to give protection for the earthly wrestling match with Satan. They renounced the devil and his works, and the world and its pleasures. Ambrose presents these renunciations as twofold rather than threefold as elsewhere, but this may be a conflation for homiletic purposes.

The water of the font is likened to the water in which Naaman the Syrian was cleansed. However Ambrose here notes that in the account of the baptism of Jesus, both Christ and the Holy Spirit came down. This seems to be linked with his explanation of the fact that the bishop first exorcises the water, and then, secondly, 'utters invocation and prayer that the water may be sanctified and that the eternal Trinity may dwell there'. He explains this as being 'in order that the Lord Jesus might not appear to have need of this mystery of sanctification, but that he himself might sanctify, and that the Spirit might also sanctify'. In fact, though, Ambrose sees the Trinity as present.[62] It seems that during this blessing, a wooden cross was thrown or placed in the water.[63] Ambrose sees baptism prefigured in the flood which was a remedy for sin:

> So the Lord, when he saw the sins of men multiplying, preserved the righteous man alone with his progeny, and commanded the waters to flow even above the level of the mountain-tops. In the flood, then, all the corruption of the flesh perished, and only the race and the likeness of the righteous remained. Is not this flood baptism, by which all sins are wiped out and only the spirit and the grace of the righteous are revived?[64]

Thus the font is a means of dealing with sin. It heals human sickness (that is, sin) just as Jesus commanded the paralysed man to go into the pool for healing. In fact Ambrose gives considerable emphasis to the cleansing of sin in baptism:

> In the beginning our Lord made man so that he would never die, so long as he never tasted sin. But he committed sin; he became subject to death; he was cast out of paradise. But the Lord, who wished his gifts to last for ever and to destroy all the wiles of the serpent and to cancel out all harm it had done, first passed sentence on man: 'You are dust and to dust you shall return', and so he made man subject to death. The sentence was divine, and could not be remitted by humankind. The remedy was found. It was that man should die and rise again.[65]

---

[61] Edward Yarnold, *The Awe Inspiring Rites of Initiation*, St Paul Publications, Slough, 1971, p. 100.

[62] Ibid., pp. 106, 112.

[63] See William Ledwich, 'Baptism, Sacrament of the Cross: Looking behind St. Ambrose', in Bryan D. Spinks (ed.), *The Sacrifice of Praise. Studies on the themes of thanksgiving and redemption in the central prayers of the Eucharistic and baptismal liturgies. In honour of Arthur Hubert Couratin*, CLV, Rome, 1981; Gordon Jeanes, *The Day has Come!*, p. 177; Edward Yarnold, *The Awe Inspiring Rites*, p. 113.

[64] Yarnold, *The Awe Inspiring Rites*, p. 109.

[65] Ibid., p. 115.

Thus, baptism is a means of breaking the hold of the devil.

Ambrose attests a threefold immersion, which symbolizes death and resurrection:

> This is a death, then, not in the reality of bodily death, but in likeness. When you are immersed, you receive the likeness of death and burial, you receive the sacrament of his cross ...[66]

The font for Ambrose is tomb rather than womb. Indeed, regeneration is linked to new life and resurrection.

The baptism was followed by an anointing with a formula which combines the themes of new birth with forgiveness of sin. It is made with chrism, on the head.[67] After this Ambrose describes a ceremony of foot-washing, which washes away the serpent's poison since the heel is mentioned in the curse of Genesis 3:15:

> The Lord answered him [Peter], after he had spoken of hands and head: 'He who has washed, does not need to wash again, except his feet only.' Why? Because in baptism all guilt is washed away. The guilt has disappeared; but Adam was tripped and thrown by the devil, so that the devil's poison infected his feet; so you have your feet washed, in order to receive the special help of sanctification in the place where the serpent lay in ambush so that he cannot trip you up again. You have your feet washed to wash away the serpent's poison.[68]

In this ritual, Ambrose notes, Milan differed from Rome.

Finally Ambrose mentions a sealing:

> This happens when the Holy Spirit is infused at the priest's invocation: 'the Spirit of wisdom and understanding, the Spirit of counsel and strength, the Spirit of knowledge and piety, the Spirit of holy fear.' These might be called the seven 'virtues' of the Spirit.[69]

This begs the question: was this sealing rite accomplished by a laying-on of hands? How did it relate to the Roman practice which knew of a presbyteral post-baptismal anointing, followed by an episcopal hand-laying with a prayer for the seven-fold gifts of the Spirit and a signing with chrism which is Christic in meaning?[70] The later Milanese rite lacks any 'sealing'. Therefore, does Ambrose give us the Milanese usage, or does he here reflect Roman usage of his day, 'attempting to make the Milanese rite sound as "Roman" as possible by using his episcopal freedom to cite a Roman prayer for the sevenfold-Spirit as a concluding prayer for the rite'?[71] And if the latter is so, did the Roman rite of his day lack the episcopal anointing? By the time of Innocent I's letter to Decentius, the episcopal anointing is justified by appealing to Acts 8:14–17. Innocent wrote:

---

[66] Ibid., p. 118.

[67] Ibid., p. 120.

[68] Ibid., p. 123.

[69] Ibid., p. 125.

[70] See Maxwell E. Johnson, 'The Postchrismational Structure of Apostolic Tradition 21, the Witness of Ambrose of Milan, and a Tentative Hypothesis Regarding the Current Reform of Confirmation in the Roman Rite', *Worship* 70 (1996), 16–34.

[71] Ibid., p. 26.

> Regarding the signing of infants (*infantibus*), this clearly cannot be done validly by anyone other than the Bishop. For even though presbyters and priests, none of them holds the office of pontiff. For not only is it ecclesiastical custom that shows this should be done only by pontiffs – in other words, that they alone would sign or give the comforting Spirit – but there is also that reading in the Acts of the Apostles that describes Peter and John being ordered to give the Holy Spirit to those who had already been baptized. For whether the Bishop is present or not, presbyters are allowed to anoint the baptized with chrism. But they are not allowed to sign the forehead with the same oil consecrated by the bishop, for that is used by the bishops only when they give the Spirit, the Paraclete. I cannot reveal the words themselves, lest I seem to betray more than is needed to respond to your inquiry.[72]

Here is evidence of the Roman post-baptismal presbyteral and episcopal anointing, though whether the citation of Acts 8 allows us to infer also an episcopal hand-laying is less clear. But it shows that, at least for Innocent, the episcopal anointing is associated with the giving of the Spirit. These are tantalizing questions for addressing the issue of how and why the rite called 'Confirmation' became a separate rite with its own theologies in the later Western tradition.

After citing the sealing, Ambrose speaks of the neophytes being priests and being the sweet fragrance of Christ, both of which might hint at an anointing. He alludes to the putting-on of white garments by way of reference to Song of Solomon 8:5, in order to stress once more that those who were until recently soiled with the gloom and squalor of sin suddenly shine out brilliantly.[73] Whatever the text of the liturgy at Milan at this time might have been, Ambrose tends to place a considerable emphasis on the rite as cathartic. It washes and cleanses from sin. The wrestle with the devil, the death to sin in the flood of the water, and even the white garment, are all, according to Ambrose, about being freed from sin. Furthermore, while the idea of birth and growth are not absent, the concept of dying and rising in relation to sin is the dominant model here.

Gaul and Spain

Information on baptismal practice is sparse for Gaul and Spain.[74] The First Council of Arles, 314, in Canon 8 or 9 makes reference to Africans who rebaptize (Donatists?), and in this context mentions baptism in the name of Father, Son and Holy Spirit. The First Council of Orange, 441, Canon 2 mentions that baptisms must not take place without chrism, and that in *confirmatione* 'the *sacerdos*' (bishop) will remind those who were not chrismated. The Canon is obscure, and may be prohibiting more than one chrismation – given by the bishop if not given at baptism, but if given at baptism, not repeated by the bishop.

---

[72] Martin F. Connell, *Church Worship in Fifth-Century Rome: The Letter of Innocent I to Decentius of Gubio*, Grove Books, Cambridge, 2002, p. 28.

[73] Yarnold, *Awe Inspiring Rites of Initiation*, p. 129.

[74] Texts of the Councils cited in Whitaker/Johnson, *DBL*: Gaul, pp. 255–6; Spain, pp. 154–5.

We also have an account of the baptism of King Clovis by Remigius, bishop of Reims, on Christmas Day, but opinion is split over which Christmas it was, though we know it was between 496 and 506.[75] The account is given by Gregory of Tours around the end of the sixth century, but is believed to be based on a lost *vita* of Remigius, as well as on Gregory's knowledge of how baptisms were performed in Frankish Gaul. The account, of course, is of a bishop baptizing a king, and therefore not necessarily normative. We are told that the bishop called the king in private and 'began to instil into him faith in the true God, Maker of heaven and earth', and told him to forsake other gods.[76] The king was hesitant over the reaction of his people, but because of the divine power, the people agreed that they too would give up their false gods:

> The streets were overshadowed with coloured hangings, the churches adorned with white hangings, the baptistery was set in order, smoke of incense spread in clouds, perfumed tapers gleamed, the whole church about the place of baptism was filled with the divine fragrance.[77]

The king moved towards the water 'to blot out the former leprosy, to wash away in this new stream the foul stains borne from old days'. He confessed Almighty God, three in one, and was baptized and anointed with holy chrism with the sign of the cross. One of the king's sisters, Lanthechild, was apparently an Arian, and she received the chrism having confessed the Son and Spirit equal to the Father. Here we have no reference to anointing before baptism, and only a single anointing after baptism – which was also needed for heretics received into the Church.

For Spain we have three Canons from the Council of Elvira, 305, which mention the catechumenate, prohibit the washing of the feet of the baptized by priests and clerics (was this practiced in some places as it was in Milan?), and the need for a bishop to perfect (*perficere*) a baptism administered by a deacon without a presbyter or bishop present. Canon 20 of the First Council of Toledo, 398, restricted the blessing of chrism to bishops (apparently in some places presbyters blessed chrism) and restricted the use of chrism to bishops and presbyters. The evidence suggests a variety of uses and customs in Spain, and these canons attempted some uniformity of practice.

The Doctrinal Legacies of St Augustine in North Africa

Augustine was converted to Christianity through the preaching of Ambrose of Milan. Rejecting his early espousal of Manichaeism, he was eventually to be elected bishop of Hippo in North Africa, and was one of the great Latin theologians. He wrote a treatise on catechizing, stressing the need for sincere motives and right behaviour in

---

[75] See Mark Spencer, 'Dating the Baptism of Clovis, 1886–1993', in *Early Medieval Europe* 3 (1994), 97–116.

[76] Saint Gregory of Tours, *The History of the Franks*, translated by O.M. Dalton, Volume 2, Clarendon Press, Oxford 1927, pp. 69–70.

[77] Ibid., p. 69.

candidates for baptism. In his writings he mentions various aspects of the rite known to him in Hippo. He speaks of the use of salt in exorcism of the catechumens, and of the sign of the cross on the forehead. He refers to the handing-over of the Creed to the candidates, and of men and women being separated for decency. He alludes to the renunciation:

> 'Look how wide the east is from the west, so far has [God] set our sins from us.' Those who know the sacraments know this. Nevertheless, I only say what all may hear. When sin is remitted, your sins fall, your grace rises. Your sins are, as it were, on the decline; your grace which frees you, on the rise ... You should look to the rising, and turn away from the setting.[78]

Augustine alludes to the triple immersion, and also to anointing:

> Without fire, bread does not exist. What then does the fire signify? The chrism. For the sacrament of the Holy Spirit is [the oil of] our fire.[79]

However, Augustine is remembered not for detailed commentary on the baptismal rites of North Africa, but for his teaching on the efficacy and validity of sacraments, and baptism as the necessary means for the overcoming of original sin and guilt. In Sermon 213 on the Creed, Augustine turns to examine the words 'I believe in the forgiveness of sins':

> If this power were not in the Church, there would be no hope; if there were no remission of sins in the Church, there would be no hope of future life and eternal salvation. We give thanks to God who gave this gift to His Church. Behold, you are about to come to the sacred font; you will be washed in baptism; you will be renewed in the saving laver of regeneration; when you rise from the waters, you will be without sin. All the sins which in the past haunted you will be wiped out. Your sins will be like the Egyptians following the Israelites, pursuing only up to the Red Sea. What does 'up to the Red Sea' mean? Up to the font consecrated by the cross and blood of Christ. For, because that font is red, it reddens. Do you not see how the member of Christ becomes red? Question the eyes of faith. If you see the cross, see the blood, too. If you see what hangs on the cross, see what drips down from it. The side of Christ was pierced with a lance and our purchase price flowed forth.[80]

Augustine's emphasis on the salvific dimension of baptism in terms of forgiveness was underpinned by his teaching on grace in his anti-Pelagian writings. Pelagius was troubled by the remark in Augustine's *Confessions*, 'Give what you command, and command what you will', which seemed to suggest an excuse for avoiding spiritual responsibility.[81] An uneasy truce seems to have lasted between the two between 405 and 411. However,

---

[78] *Enarrationes in psalmos* 102.19, cited in William Harmless, *Augustine and the Catechumenate*, Pueblo Liturgical Press, Collegeville, MN, 1995, p. 308.

[79] *Sermo* 227, cited in ibid., p. 320.

[80] Saint Augustine, *Sermons on the Liturgical Seasons*, translated by Mary Sarah Muldowney, The Fathers of the Church, New York, 1959, p. 128.

[81] G. Bonner, *St. Augustine of Hippo. Life and Controversies*, Westminster Press, Philadelphia, PA, 1963, Chapters 8 and 9.

in his *De Peccatorum Meritis et Remissione et de Baptismo Parvulorum*, Augustine set out to refute what he thought were the pastoral and theological implications of the teachings of Pelagius. In this work Augustine insisted that sin passes on to all humanity by natural descent, and not merely by imitation as Pelagius' supporters seemed to imply. 'No doubt,' said Augustine, 'all they imitate Adam who by disobedience transgress the commandment of God; but he is one thing as an example to those who sin because they choose; and another thing as the progenitor of all who are born with sin.'[82] He wrote, 'The apostle, however, has declared concerning the first man, that "in him all have sinned"; and yet there is still a contest about the propagation of sin, and men oppose to it. I know not what nebulous theory of "imitation".'[83]

Augustine taught that there is seminal identity of the human race with Adam. Since all future generations were in one sense present in Adam's sperm at the time of the Fall, so all humanity participated in the sin, and so participate in the punishment. He appealed to the Latin translation of Romans 5:12, where the Greek words *eph ho pantes hemarton*, 'because all have sinned', were rendered as in *quo omnes peccaverunt*, 'in whom (Adam) all sinned'. Gerald Bonner has noted that Augustine was following Ambrosiaster in referring to all sinning in Adam as a lump (*massa*).[84] He further notes that the theory of seminal identity, while buttressed by a false reading of Romans 5:12, is not dependent on it. 'What it demands,' says Bonner,

> ... is a belief that the biblical account of the Fall is literal history combined with the ability to ignore the problem of how moral responsibility can be incurred by a being which exists, as yet, only in potentiality – a belief which, as we have noticed, could be readily accorded in the ancient world, accustomed to the idea of divine retribution to the third and fourth generations.[85]

Russell J. De Simone concluded that the sources of Augustine's teaching were Scripture – particularly the writings of St Paul, the baptism of infants – the fact that the Church baptized them, tradition – he drew on Jerome, and also his own experience and reflection.[86]

What is at issue here is not the legitimacy or otherwise of Augustine's doctrine of grace and original sin, but rather their implications and effects for a later Western understanding of baptism. Whereas his opponents seemed to imply that infants of Christians are in some way already saved by being born of baptized parents, Augustine argued that baptism was necessary to salvation, and that infants who die unbaptized are not saved. They may have only a light penalty in the hereafter, but they will be penalized. Furthermore, in arguing this point, he appealed to the rites of baptism, in particular the exorcisms:

---

[82] *De Peccatorum*, Book 1, Chapter 10, text at <http://www.newadvent.org/fathers>.

[83] Ibid., Book 1, Chapter 11.

[84] Bonner, *St. Augustine of Hippo*, p. 373.

[85] Ibid.

[86] Russell J. De Simone, 'Modern Research on the Sources of Saint Augustine's Doctrine of Original Sin', *Augustinian Studies* 11 (1980), 205–27.

What shall I say of the actual form of this sacrament? I only wish some one of those who espouse the contrary side would bring me an infant to be baptized. What does my exorcism work in that babe, if he be not held in the devil's family? The man who brought the infant would certainly have had to act as sponsor for him, for he could not answer for himself. How would it be possible then for him to declare that he renounced the devil, if there was no devil in him? that he was converted to God, if he had never been averted from Him? that he believed, besides other articles, in the forgiveness of sins, if no sins were attributable to him? For my part, indeed, if I thought that his opinions were opposed to this faith, I could not permit him to bring the infant to the sacraments. Nor can I imagine with what countenance before men, or what mind before God, he can conduct himself in this. But I do not wish to say anything too severe. That a false or fallacious form of baptism should be administered to infants, in which there might be the sound and semblance of something being done, but yet no remission of sins actually ensue, has been seen by some amongst them to be as abominable and hateful a thing as it was possible to mention or conceive. Then, again, in respect of the necessity of baptism to infants, they admit that even infants stand in need of redemption, – a concession which is made in a short treatise written by one of their party, – but yet there is not found in this work any open admission of the forgiveness of a single sin.[87]

As Augustine's work and reputation established itself in the West, so the remission of sins and reception of grace became important theological keys in understanding baptism, for both churchmen and laity. It would become canon law that infants must be baptized within eight days of birth, lest they should die unbaptized. Imputation of righteousness and infusion of grace, as an insurance policy or protection against eternal punishment, tended to be in the foreground of clerical and popular understanding of the rite.

Augustine's other legacy came from his teaching about the validity of sacraments in relation to the Donatist split in the African Church. Following the Diocletian persecution of 311, Bishop Secundus and others, who regarded the newly elected bishop of Carthage as unworthy because of his alleged neglect and compromise during the persecution, elected and ordained Majorinus as bishop of Carthage, and so a split occured. Majorinus was succeeded by Donatus. The Donatists argued that the Church and its ministers were supposed to be pure, and unworthy ministers could not celebrate valid sacraments. The schism was still in existence at the time of Augustine.

Against the Donatists Augustine argued that, since Christ himself was the real minister of baptism, the worthiness of the minister was not a factor in validating or invalidating a sacrament. Providing the right element (water) was used, and the proper words (formula of baptism) were spoken, Donatist sacraments would be regarded as valid, and Donatists being reconciled did not need to be rebaptized. Augustine's teaching was set forth as an answer for a specific pastoral situation. Once divorced

---

[87] *De Peccatorum*, Book 1, Chapter 63. See also Daniel van Slyke, 'Augustine and Catechumenal "Exsufflatio": An Integral Element of Christian Initiation', *Ephemerides Liturgicae* 118 (2004), 175–208.

from that pastoral circumstance, the later theological temptation would be to regard sacraments as consisting of certain correct formulae and elements, presided over by a validly ordained minister, with the conclusion that, providing these minimum requirements were met, it was a valid sacrament – almost *ex opere operato*, an automatic obligation on God. Long after Augustine, this teaching would become the focus of understanding sacraments rather than the study of the rituals and prayers themselves. The stress on baptism for remission of original sin, and certain basic requirements for valid sacraments, would be legacies that Augustine would pass on to the later Western Church.[88]

Concluding Remarks

In the baptismal homilies and catecheses of the fourth and fifth centuries the writers inherited a ritual pattern of baptism, and their theologies develop from the ritual pattern. There appears to have been considerable diversity within a basic pattern, particularly with regard to the placing and meaning of anointing. This is particularly true as regards the difference between East Syria where the anointing continued to be before baptism, and West Syria where an anointing comes before and after baptism. In at least the Milanese tradition there was a washing of the feet (and perhaps in Aphraat's churches), and in Rome a double post-baptismal anointing, one by the presbyter, and another by the bishop. In Rome there was also a hand-laying by the bishop. There is a tendency to develop the theme of dying/rising and the font as a tomb, though alongside and never entirely in place of new birth and font as womb. The commentators begin to develop a theology of the various stages of the rite, with a tendency amongst several to link the gift of the Spirit with the anointing with chrism/ myron. In the West the teaching of St Augustine of Hippo became increasingly influential, whereby baptism was seen as primarily the means of washing of original sin. Though cleansing from sin was part of the meaning of the rite from the baptism of John, it was Augustine who underpinned the sinful state of humanity, and promoted baptism as the means of sacramental salvation from that state. Here baptism came to be a baptism from something (original sin) more than a baptism into something (the eschatological community of God). Though not mutually exclusive, the Western Church would in time give more emphasis to the first of these.

---

[88] See G.M. Lukken, *Original Sin in the Roman Liturgy*, E.J. Brill, Leiden, 1973.

PART II
THE DEEP RIVERS OF
TRADITION

The Formation and Theology of the Eastern Rites of Baptism: I The Syrian Traditions

The Christian East was divided forever by the Christological controversies of the fifth century which resulted from the struggle between Cyril of Alexandria and Nestorius of Constantinople. As a result of the Council of Chalcedon in 451, many of those churches loosely described in the Nicene period as East Syrian refused to condemn Nestorius, and would become the Church of the East. Opponents would describe them as 'Nestorian.' In contrast, large areas of the Syriac-speaking Church in the region of Antioch, together with the Egyptian Church and the Armenian Church, refused to accept Chalcedon, and espoused the theology of Cyril of Alexandria. They would become known as the Oriental Orthodox Churches. Opponents would call them 'monophysites'. One Syriac-speaking group which remained Chalcedonian was the Maronites. In this chapter we turn to consider the rites of the Church of the East, the Syrian Orthodox Church and the Maronite Church.

The Church of the East, or East Syrian Rite

The liturgical inheritance of this Church seems to have been the ritual pattern found in the *Acts of Judas Thomas* and the *Didascalia*, with the theological interests of Aphrahat and Ephrem. It also espoused the teachings of Theodore of Mopsuestia, and his catechetical homilies formed the basis for a similar genre in this Church, the first being the homilies of Narsai.

Narsai

Narsai was a teacher at the school of theology at Edessa from 437. In 457 the followers of Ibas were expelled for refusing to condemn Nestorius, and Narsai founded a new school at Nisibis. He wrote a number of metrical homilies and some liturgical homilies, though some believe that the latter have been expanded by a later hand.

In Homilies 22 and 21 (for some reason they seem to have been reversed), we have explanations of the rite of baptism and the eucharist. In Homily 22 there is a reference to the renunciation of Satan, and the ceremony seems to have included the use of sackcloth. Sponsors are also mentioned. Narsai wrote:

> With feeble waters He was pleased to confirm feeble bodies; and with the power
> of the Spirit He would strengthen the wavering faculties (of the soul). The furnace
> of the waters His purpose prepared mystically; and instead of fire He has heated
> it with the Spirit of the power of His will.[1]

Of the oil he says:

> The iron of the oil the priest holds on the tip of his fingers; and he signs the body
> and the senses of the soul with its sharp [edge].[2]

The images Narsai uses here centre around the refashioning and rebirth of the
candidate. Narsai is particularly interested in the oil, which appears to have been
consecrated by an invocation which included the triune names. The anointing is prior
to baptism. Narsai wrote:

> The cause of the signing on the forehead is (that it may be) for the confusion of
> the devils; that when they discern (it) on the head of a man they may be overcome
> by him (or it). On account of these (the devils) are performed the mysteries of the
> oil and water, that they may be an armour against their warfare and attacks. An
> armour is the oil with which the earth-born are anointed, that they may not be
> captured by the (evil) spirits in the hidden warfare.[3]

Narsai then uses military images to describe the wrestling with evil, but also refers to
the candidates as athletes. In Homily 21 he continues with the blessing of the water:

> With the Name of the Divinity, the three Names, he consecrated the water, that it
> may suffice to accomplish the cleansing of the defiled.[4]

Narsai uses imagery of the grave for the font, but combines it with the imagery of
birth from the womb:

> As a babe from the midst of the womb he looks forth from the water; and instead
> of garments the priest receives him and embraces him. He resembles a babe when
> he is lifted up from the midst of the water; and as a babe everyone embraces and
> kisses him.[5]

The eucharist follows, and there is no mention of any post-baptismal anointing.

In his metrical homilies Narsai is concerned to draw out the soteriological
implications of Christ's baptism, contrasting him with Adam – and thus continues the
theological emphasis found in Ephrem. Narsai places the following words on the lips
of John the Baptist:

> In a womb of water, he will generate men in a spiritual way,
> as they are enrolled with a new name [as] first-born of the Spirit.[6]

---

[1] R.H. Connolly, *The Liturgical Homilies of Narsai, with an Appendix by Edmund Bishop*, Cambridge
University Press, Cambridge, 1909, p. 41.

[2] Ibid.

[3] Ibid., p. 43.

[4] Ibid., p. 50.

[5] Ibid., p. 52.

[6] Finn, *ECBC* 1, p. 176.

Jesus announces to John:

> Let it be so! I will be baptized by you in water as in a grave;
> and I will bring mortality down with me and up [again].
> I shall now be baptized as one who is in need of purification;
> and after a while, I will show my power by purifying those unclean.[7]

The homily continues:

> The high priest descended into the water and bathed and sanctified it
> and conferred upon it the power of the spirit to give life.
> The holy one drew near to the weak and inanimate element
> and made it a womb which begets men spiritually.
> He descended and was plunged into the womb of water as in a grave;
> and he rose and was raised [to life] and raised Adam in mystery.[8]

The homily then says that he ascended from the womb of a new mother, and was anointed by the Spirit as an athlete to engage in wrestling. Narsai interprets this as recapitulating Adam, thereby opening up renewal for humanity. Here there is a very real and obvious continuity with Ephrem, both in genre and in imagery.

From Cyrus of Edessa to the Present Ordo

The sixth-century theologian Cyrus of Edessa who trained at Nisibis and taught at Seleucia-Ctesiphon, offers one or two pieces of information in his homilies.[9] He attests the baptism of infants who were too young to fast. Cyrus regarded baptism as wiping out sin. Macomber has argued that Cyrus presents us with two distinct views of original sin which he left unresolved: one not unlike the classic Augustinian view, with a definitive restoration in Christ of the old order disrupted by Adam's sin, and another which sees redemption as the culminating act in the long history of divine pedagogy, a process which will only end with the final resurrection.[10] Macomber believes that Cyrus alludes to the formal renunciation of Satan and the demons, though this is too general to be certain.[11]

The early seventh-century commentator, Gabriel Qatraya, is unfortunately silent on the rites of baptism. The next commentators of any substance are the Anonymous Author (attributed wrongly to George of Arbel), and 'Ammar Al-Basri, both of the ninth century, the latter being one of the first theologians writing in Arabic. However, both commentaries are thought to post-date the traditional compilation date of the present East Syrian *Ordo*. The Chronicle of Se'ert attributes the latter along with other

---

[7] Ibid., p. 180.

[8] Ibid., p. 181.

[9] W.F. Macomber (ed.), *Six Explanations of the Liturgical Feasts* (CSCO 356), Corpus Scriptorum Christianorum Orientalium, Louvain, 1974.

[10] W.F. Macomber, 'The Theological Synthesis of Cyrus of Edessa, an East Syrian Theologian of the Mid Sixth Century', in *Orientalia Christiana Periodica* (1964), 1–38; 363–84, 150.

[11] Macomber, *Six Explanations*, p. 150.

liturgical rites to Iso'yabh III, Catholicos of Seleucia-Ctesiphon *c.* 649–59, and the title ascribed it to him. If this ascription is taken at face value, Iso'yabh drew up the rite which presupposes infant baptism. Yet, later commentators still discuss rites which assume adult baptism, and it may be that the present rite was the result of additions and alterations made by Elias III (1176–90) and Yahballah III (1281–1317).

The present *Ordo* is structured as follows:[12]

1 *Introductory Rites:* Invocation, *Gloria*, Lord's Prayer, prayer, Psalm 84, prayer.
2 *Imposition of Hands and First Signing:* Three prayers and signing of the forehead.
3 *Entry to Baptistery:* Psalms 45, 110, 132, interspersed with diaconal biddings.
4 *Preparation of the Font:* Prayer, *Laku-Mara* and pouring of water, prayer and *Trisagion.*
5 *The Liturgy of the Word:* Epistle, Gospel, litany and imposition of hands.
6 *The Disposition of the Oil: Onita d'Raze* and Creed.
7 *The Consecration of the Oil:* 'Eucharistic' Prayer with *Sanctus*, Lord's Prayer.
8 *Consecration of the Baptismal Water:* Salutation, invocation, pouring-in of oil, anthem.
9 *Pre-baptismal Anointing and Baptism.*
10 *Post-baptismal Signing and Hand-laying:* Introductory prayer, Psalm 95:1–7, two prayers of imposition, signing (with oil), crowning and prayer.
11 *Concluding rites:* anthems, prayer, *huttama* and release of baptismal water from consecration.

It is perhaps helpful to look at some of the ways in which biblical and theological themes are articulated in this rite. The first striking difference between this rite and that presupposed by Narsai is that there is no ritualized renunciation of Satan and the devil, and no exorcisms. This should not be interpreted as some semi-Pelagian interest, since the rite certainly does not jettison the idea of sin. Rather, it seems to have been a practical response to infant baptism. The baptism of infants is defended on the grounds of the largesse of God's mercy: 'Thy grace has caught them in the life-giving net and has laid them in the holy vessel of absolving baptism.' An opening prayer speaks of the 'holy mysteries of absolving baptism, given for the renewal and for the salvation of our nature in the mercies of Thy grace'. Another prayer uses imagery of the lost and found. The initial prayer during the imposition of hands attributes ignorance to infants but, though it seems to affirm that their bodies are unspotted with the pollution of sin, it asks that 'they may receive a cleansing that changes not'. One of the *Karuzuta* prays:

> Let us all therefore, being beloved children of holy baptism, pray for these our
> sons and daughters, who are about to receive the sign of life, denying Satan and

---

[12] The text is from *The Liturgy of the Holy Apostles Addai and Mari, and the Order of Baptism*, SPCK, London, 1893, reprinted by Georgias Press, Piscataway, NJ, 2002, pp. 63–82.

all his works, and being perfected and fulfilled in the true faith of the Father and of the Son and of the Holy Spirit, that they may be made worthy to receive this great and wonderful gift of grace, and to put off in absolving Baptism the old man who was corrupt in the lusts of error.[13]

A prayer said by the priest while the deacon says the *karuzuta* speaks of oil being poured into wounds (the 'salving' by the Good Samaritan) and the Holy Spirit like a sponge cleansing us from the taint of sin. Later, in a prayer of imposition of hands, we find 'May ... the armour of righteousness which you have put on, keep you from the Evil One and his hosts.' The *Ordo* certainly recognizes the sinful nature of humanity, and baptism is seen as a remedy against Satan and corruption.

Deliverance through Christ and the presence of the Trinity are other important themes in the *Ordo*. The first *karuzuta* tells of how Christ, being God and taking the likeness of a servant, offered this headship of humanity in the Jordan. Christ showed the meaning of baptism, and gave it to his apostles, and this token of his salvific work is now to be received. The condescension of God in Christ is again stressed in the second *karazuta*:

> With medicine of His sayings He bound up our stripes and healed our sickness and raised up our fall ... Let us confess him who stooped to be baptized by John.[14]

When water is poured into the font, a cross and the Gospels are laid on top of it. After the consecration of the water in the name of the Father, the Son and the Holy Spirit, the priest says, 'The holy [Thing] is meet and right, unto one divine nature.' The people reply, 'One Holy Father, one Holy Son, one Holy Spirit, for ever and ever. Amen'. All these, together with other prayers which call upon the grace of the Spirit, reinforce the Trinitarian dimension of the ritual.

Narsai, following the tradition found in Ephrem, and before that, in the *Acts of Judas Thomas*, puts great importance on the oil. Yet, though important, it is not so forcefully expressed in the *Ordo*. The first anointing, which may be a remnant of the anointing after the renunciations, is concerned with bringing the candidates into the fold.[15] The formula for the second anointing immediately before baptism is as simple as the first. However, it follows an elaborate blessing of oil and water. The oil in the flagon is consecrated by prayer and by adding to it oil from the *qarna* (horn). According to tradition, this latter consisted of water from Christ's baptism and water from his pierced side, to which oil was added after Pentecost, and each apostle took a horn of oil with this mixture in it. The *ghanta,* which is an epiklesis, asks that by the will of the Father and the will of the Son, grace from the gift of the Holy Spirit may come and 'mingle in this oil'. The prayer states that the oil has been entrusted to

---

[13] Ibid., p. 69.

[14] Ibid., p. 67.

[15] Cf. Jones, 'Womb of the Spirit', p. 207, 'if the Patriarch's rite grew from an adult liturgy, it is perhaps not surprising that some of the characteristic features of the more ancient liturgy have been preserved'.

the priests of the Church to be a parable of things heavenly; the soul is to be circumcised with the circumcision not of hands. Sebastian Brock has made the suggestion that the pre-baptismal anointing and baptism of the early and East Syrian tradition was patterned on the Jewish ritual for proselyte men, that of circumcision followed by ritual bath.[16] The text, however, may be too late a composition to indicate such continuity of thought.

After the recitation of the *Sanctus,* the grace from the gift of the Spirit is again requested, so that those anointed may be given 'full and true holiness and the exalted communion of the Kingdom of heaven'.[17] The water, too, is consecrated, and God is asked that the Spirit come upon the water. However, oil is also poured into the font, in order that 'it may become a new womb bringing forth spiritually in absolving baptism'.[18] Thus, though the formula is simply '*N.* is signed in the Name of the Father and of the Son and of the Holy Spirit for ever', the implication is that the oil conveys considerable salvific power, for not only is it linked directly with Christ (the legend of the *qarna*) but the grace of the Spirit has touched it.

The baptism is with the passive formula of the Eastern churches: '*N.* is baptized in the name of the Father and of the Son and of the Holy Spirit', suggesting baptism as a divine act or, at the least, an objective act. But since the water too is understood to impart the grace of the Spirit, it is a womb which gives new birth. The laying-on of hands after baptism makes it clear that the Holy Spirit has been received, and the prayer at that point asks for protection and sanctification. The signing or sealing (which seems often to be made with oil, though the rubrics do not mention it, and some commentators do not refer to it) is linked with the crowns.

The commentary of the Anonymous Author still assumes adult baptism. He explains that, although Christ was baptized at Epiphany, Christians are baptized at Easter because they partake in the dying and rising of Christ. In baptism we conquer both Satan and death.[19] He makes mention of the renunciation of Satan and confession of God.[20] The use of the *qarna* is explained. He outlines what he regards as the important ritual moments in the rite: the first signing, the *rushma,* which he links with the sign given to Abraham (circumcision?); the unction, making candidates children of Aaron and kings, and baptism, the baptism of John for the remission of sins. The final obsignation is explained as the baptism of Christ and being perfected in the Holy Spirit.[21]

---

[16] Brock, 'The Transition to a Post-baptismal Anointing in the Antiochene Rite', in Bryan D. Spinks (ed.), *The Sacrifice of Praise*, Edizioni Liturgiche, Rome, 1981.

[17] Ibid., p. 74.

[18] Ibid., p. 76.

[19] R.H. Connolly, *Anonymi Auctoris Expositio Officiorum Ecclesiae Georgio Arbelensi vulgo adscripta. Accedit Abrahae Bar Lipheh Interpretatio Officiorum,* 4 vols, Corpus Scriptorum Christianorum Orientalium, 2nd edn, Louvain, 1953–61, vol. 2, p. 88. See Sebastian Brock, 'The Baptismal Anointings According to the Anonymous Expositio Officiorum', *Journal of Syriac Studies* 1 (1998), pp. 1–9.

[20] Ibid., p. 89.

[21] Ibid., p. 96.

The commentary of 'Ammar Al-Basri includes a defence of the rite of baptism against a Muslim critic.[22] In his writing, baptism symbolizes the resurrection from the dead, and is a symbol of life. The Messiah died and rose for us, and will raise us from the tomb. But it is also a new birth, in which the creature is remodelled in the water – a concept found in Narsai.

The tenth-century poem on baptism by Emmanuel bar Shahhare gives a clear reference to the renunciations. Apparently commenting on the second *karuzuta* of the deacon where it mentions 'putting off the old man', bar Shahhare explains that the candidate renounces Satan and all his powers and his rule. The candidate faces west, and renounces Satan standing barefoot and naked, as captives of the Evil One, and like Adam, devoid of glory.[23]

The *Mimra on the Interpretation of the Divine Mysteries,* by the thirteenth-century writer Johannan bar Zobi, is mainly concerned with the eucharist. In a small section on baptism he asserts that 'Baptism which has been established in the Church represents the Resurrection of the body and renewal of the soul in endless life.' He writes:

> In the glorious name of the Father and of the Son and of the Holy Spirit the waters of baptism consecrate the children of the Church. He bestowed upon them the adoption of sons in the new birth, and the baptized become co-heirs of the Hidden Father.[24]

The thirteenth/fourteenth-century writer, Abdisho, in *The Pearl*, briefly explains the meaning of baptism. He lists five types of baptism, from utilitarian washing of the body, through the washing according to the law, the traditions of the elders, to that of John the Baptist, and then of Jesus 'which is received through the Holy Spirit, for the gift of adoption of sons, for the resurrection from the dead, and for everlasting life; which is "the circumcision made without hands, in putting off the body of the sins of the flesh by the circumcision of Christ"'.[25] Influenced by Western thought, he speaks of the 'matter' of baptism as pure water, and the form as the triune formula.

An important commentary is that of Timothy II, *The Mystery of Baptism*. Though writing in the fourteenth century, Timothy speaks of exorcists and exorcisms, as well as other rites having to do with the catechumenate. W. de Vries suggested that this reaches back none too accurately to a time before Iso'yabh's reforms.[26] However,

---

[22]   Michel Hayek, *Ammar Al-Basri, Apologie et Controverses,* Beirut, 1977; P. Khalil Chalfoun, 'Baptême et Eucharistie chez 'Ammar Al-Basri', *Parole de l'Orient* 27 (2002), 321–34.

[23]   J. Isaac (ed.), 'Emmanuel Bar Shahhare, Memra on the Explanation of Baptism', *Bayn al-Nahrayn* 11 (1983), 26–66.

[24]   W. de Vries, 'Die Erklärung aller Göttlichen Geheimnisse des Nestorianers Johannan Bar Zo'bi (13. Jahrh.)', *Orientalia Christiana Periodica* 96 (1943), 191–203; D. Webb, 'The Mimra on the Interpretation of the Mysteries by Rabban Johannam Bar Zo'bi and its symbolism', *Le Muséon* 88 (1975), 297–326, p. 306.

[25]   *The Book of Marganitha on the Truth of Christianity,* translated by His Holiness Nar Eshai Shimun XXIII, Mar Themotheus Memorial Printing House, Ernakuluam, Kerala, 1965, pp. 51–2.

[26]   W. de Vries, 'Zur Liturgie der Erwachsenentaufe bei den Nestorianern', *Orientalia Christiana Periodica* 96 (1943), 460–73.

Timothy also drew on the writings of the Syrian Orthodox writers bar Hebraeus and Moses bar Kepha, and it may be that his inaccuracies are simply the result of his misusing their tradition and adding it to his own.

According to Timothy, baptism, which is friendship with God through conversion from a sinful life and corrupting passions of the flesh, has three names: *immersio* and baptism, enlightenment, and birth.[27] Baptism is by water and the Spirit, and the latter is the purifier of the soul's uncleanness through the renunciation of Satan and his works. But certain things are necessary for a baptism: water, oil, priest and priestly prayer, without which baptism is not effected. According to Timothy, oil represents the male seed, whereas the water resembles the maternal womb. He notes that, although the water is consecrated using the old oil (the *qarna*), the new oil is just as good, since both are sanctified by the Spirit, and the oil is necessary to symbolize the Spirit. He explains that the old oil is handed down from generation to generation because the Spirit too is handed down from generation to generation. Timothy adds:

> Although after the oil and the water have been consecrated they have the same power, we sign them with the oil of the horn; for the Holy Spirit, the sanctifier of both (the new and the old oil) is one and the same in the descent of grace. It makes known the firmness of our faith and the genuineness of our birth in Christian tradition. (It is also meant) for symbolizing the descent of the grace of the Spirit, who by his descent, sanctifies the (sacramental) generation, and the mystery of our communion and participation in heavenly things.[28]

Timothy also notes that the oil of the horn is a type of the Holy and operative Spirit,[29] and embarks on its family tree, tracing it back to David, Solomon and the prophet Samuel. By means of the oil and water, birth by the Spirit is signified. Timothy adds that the Spirit raised Jesus from the dead, and that the threefold dipping delineates the mystery of death and resurrection. Womb/birth rather than tomb/resurrection is the focus of his commentary.

The commentary explains that only olive oil is blessed for anointing and signing, and not other oils. Here Timothy is implicitly noting that chrism/myron is not used. The signings are described in some detail – the first on the forehead with the forefinger, the second on the breast, and a third, the sealing after baptism, on the forehead with the thumb. These are given further allegorical meanings.

As already noted, Timothy also expounds the task of sponsors and exorcists, and describes a signing, the stripping, and then, in this section, baptism as tomb. This is followed by an explanation of the baptismal garments. Like the Anonymous Author, Timothy also expounds on why the priest wears a white hood. But he immediately returns to the signings and the oil. Here, as in the Anonymous Author, the first signing is described as indicating Abraham's seed, the second, priests and kings, and the third,

---

[27]   Paul B. Kadicheeni (ed.), *The Mystery of Baptism ... Timothy II*, Dharmaram Publications, Bangalore, 1980.

[28]   Ibid., p. 21.

[29]   Ibid.

the Holy Spirit perfecting the baptism, as he did at the baptism of Jesus. In one sense, Timothy represents an expansion on the previous commentaries, as well as additional insights from Syrian Orthodox commentators. However, his main focus is the anointing, and particularly those signings made with oil and the associations with the Spirit.

If Timothy takes us to the fourteenth century, a twenty-first-century view is provided by the discussion of Chorbishop Michael J. Birnie.[30] According to Birnie, the East Syrian *Ordo* baptism,

> ... effects the onset of a new creation, the renewal of the person who, according to the words of our Lord, is in need of such renewal in order to enter the kingdom of God. This new creation is begun in response to faith and is culminated in baptism through the operation of the Holy Spirit, whose power is the effective agent of that renewal. In baptism the Church teaches that one is freed from sin and reborn as a son of God through adoption, and made into Christ's likeness; he becomes a member of Christ, is incorporated into the Church, and made a sharer in her ministry to the world. This sacrament makes new our 'worn out constitution' and endows us with immortality through 'water and the renewing Spirit,' for it signifies and actually brings about the rebirth, without which no one can enter the kingdom of God.[31]

This is an admirable summary of the theology of the rite. However, Birnie emphasizes that the East Syrian structure is anointing and baptism, quoting Theophilus to Autolycus and Babai, the seventh-century theologian of the Church of the East. He argues that the pre-baptismal anointing of the head, followed by the body, is retained, but that its meaning has changed. The text implies that now its meaning is that the Trinity is fixed in the heart, and that we put on Christ: 'Confirmation, or "completion," is removed to a post-baptismal anointing, aligning the Persian practice with that of the Church of the West.'[32]

It should be noted that Birnie's discussion is in the context of dialogue with other Syrian Churches, and with the Roman Catholic Church. Certainly it confirms (!) that the post-baptismal signing is now made with oil, perhaps in imitation of the Syrian Orthodox/West Syrian tradition. Whether this action, together with all the Eastern rites' post-baptismal signing, should be seen as being the same as 'Confirmation', or even called that, is dubious. In this rite it follows the imposition of hands, which itself seals what has already taken place in the water consecrated with the *qarna*. It does not, as in the Western Catholic tradition, suggest a moment of imparting the Spirit. As Simon Jones remarks:

> It seems incredible that, even in the last decade of the second millennium, liturgists still try to find an equivalent to confirmation in the Syrian baptismal tradition!

---

[30] *'Baptism, Confirmation and the Eucharist in the Church of the East'*, Syriac Commission Study Seminar, Holy Apostolic Catholic Assyrian Church of the East Commission on Inter-Church Relations and Education Development, Feb./March 2000 <http://www.cired.org/east/0402_initiation_rites.pdf>.

[31] Ibid., pp. 5–6.

[32] Ibid., p. 4.

> The fruitless search for the seventh sacrament will not be helped by interpreting
> Syrian texts through the lens of Western sacramental theology.[33]

Even if other rites might suggest that the Spirit is imparted after baptism, *pace* Birnie,
it is not so of the *Ordo* of the Church of the East.

The Syrian Orthodox or Antiochene Tradition

It has already been noted that the homilies of St John Chrysostom, perhaps those of
Theodore of Mopsuestia, and the Church Order called *Apostolic Constitutions* witness
to baptismal usage in the area of Antioch in the fourth century. It has also been noted
that, whereas Chrysostom refers to two pre-baptismal anointings, *Apostolic
Constitutions* and Theodore both witness to an additional, post-baptismal, anointing.
The two branches of the baptismal commentary edited by Sebastian Brock suggest a
divergence between the two Syrian traditions regarding post-baptismal anointing,
together with some duplication or development as regards a single or double anointing
before baptism. These trends are found in more developed form in the two Syrian
Orthodox *Ordos*, and in the later commentaries.

The Syrian Orthodox tradition knows two baptismal *Ordos*. One of these is attributed
to Timothy of Alexandria (Aelurus?), and is no longer used. The other is attributed to
Severus of Antioch. Brock's view is that the former could date from the sixth century
or the seventh; the earliest manuscript of the latter seems to be dated to the eighth
century, but he thought the rite was not inconsistent with a sixth-century date.[34] The
manuscripts of Severus show some considerable variation in the content of the prayers,
and especially in the blessing of the water, but on the whole the structure of the rite
seems to have been stable.[35] The rite has been expanded to include material from the
eucharistic rite, resulting in a complex *Ordo*. In the later manuscripts of Severus, the
rite is divided into two parts, Part 1 and Part 2, the former having once been separated
in time from the latter. In the modern rite the two are entitled First and Second Service.
In addition to these *Ordos*, there are commentaries by Jacob (James) of Edessa, George
of the Arabs, and Moses bar Kepha. Later commentaries by bar Hebraeus and
Dionysios bar Salibi tend to be expansions of these earlier commentaries.

The *Ordo* of Timothy has the following outline:

1   *Rite of Renunciation*: with *Sedro*, prayer, renunciation, reception, prayer, signing,
    adjuring of the devil, Creed, prayer and consignation.

---

[33] Jones, 'Womb of the Spirit', p. 220.

[34] Sebastian Brock, 'A New Syriac Baptismal *Ordo* attributed to Timothy of Alexandria', *Le Muséon*
83 (1970), 367–431; *The Sacrament of Holy Baptism according to the Ancient Rite of the Syrian Orthodox
Church of Antioch*, by Metropolitan Mar Athanasius Yeshue Samuel, Hackensack, NJ, 1974.

[35] Sebastian Brock, 'The Consecration of the Water in the Oldest Manuscripts of the Syrian Orthodox
Baptismal Liturgy', *Orientalia Christiana Periodica* 37 (1971), 317–31.

2 *Consecration of the Water*: Incense and prayer of incense, responses, Creed, diaconal litany, *Gloria patri*, statement of remembrance, short exhortation, prayer, prayer over the water, including *sanctus*, blowing on the water, and a succession of prayers, exorcism of the water, *epiklesis*, pouring of oil into the font, pronouncement that the water is blessed.
3 *Consecration of the Myron*: Prayer over the myron, anointing of head and body.
4 *Baptism*: Threefold baptism, with passive formula.
5 *Prayer over the Myron*, consignation with formula, Lord's Prayer, prayer.
6 *Eucharist*, with post-communion prayer and dismissal.

The actual words of renunciation are in one single formula:

> I, *N*, renounce you, Satan, and all your angels and all your powers, and all your works, and all services of yours, and all worship of you, and all your pomp and all your festivals.[36]

After the renunciation the candidate greets Christ as God. However, this is followed by a signing and sealing (the hand is placed on the person) in order to keep back all demons and evil spirits, and is followed by a very lengthy adjuration – 31 units are listed by Brock. Only then comes the Creed. The prayer which follows asks that the Spirit be sent to deliver the candidate from the tyranny of evil, seal him and form him into the likeness of Christ. The signing (*rusma*) follows.

The prayer for consecrating the water asks for the holy angels to gather over the water, and after the recitation of the *sanctus* (cf. *Acts of John*), asks the Trinity to drive away unclean spirits, and for the Father to send the Holy Spirit to sanctify the water so that it becomes 'the womb of the Spirit that gives rebirth anew to humanity baptized in it'. Later there is a distinct *epiklesis* reminiscent of the East Syrian anaphoras:

> And may your living and holy Spirit come, O Lord, and dwell and rest upon this water, and sanctify it and make it like the water which flowed from the side of your only-begotten one on the cross.[37]

The declaration of the blessing of the water brings together the two themes prominent here: rebirth and atonement. The prayer which precedes baptism speaks of signing and anointing, 'that being anointed and baptized, they may be partakers in your beloved Son, through your holy Spirit, and be united to your true flock'. One wonders whether this prayer is a remnant of a tradition which envisaged the ritual pattern to be anointing-baptism. The triple immersion is followed by a prayer which once again speaks of the font as the spiritual womb. The blessing of the myron links the use of oil to the function of the priesthood. The actual anointing speaks of the imprint (*tabah*) and perfecting of the Holy Spirit. As noted, this rite is no longer in use, and may witness to various regional rites.

---

[36] Brock, 'A New Syriac *Ordo*', pp. 372–3, modernized English translation.
[37] Ibid., pp. 386–7.

The rite attributed to Severus has become the standard rite. Both the first and second services have elaborate introductions, including *promion*, *Sedro*, *qolo*, *etro*, and in the first service, a liturgy of the Word in imitation of the eucharist. These have baptismal themes, but seem to be later elaborations. The older stratum seems to be very similar in outline to that found in Timothy. The Syro-Malankara usage, the *Pampakuda Ordo*, has its own variants, though these do not significantly alter the overall theology of the rite.[38] Juan Mateos drew attention to the variants in the manuscripts relating to the signing/ unction of the body before baptism. He noted two usages: one, which is the most common in the formularies of the ninth to eleventh centuries, which begins the unction by a consignation with a formula; and the other, represented by a tenth-century manuscript – and apparently followed by the Syrian commentaries on baptism – where there is neither a consignation nor formula, but the unction of the body is made without any preamble.[39] The service in the modern printed text may be summarized as follows:

First Service

1   *Introductory material*: *Gloria*, diaconal response, opening prayer, Psalm 51, hymn (Christ's baptism has sanctified the baptistery), Psalm 29:1, 3, 4, Prayer, *Gloria*, *eqbo*, *hosoyo*, *promion*, *sedro*, *qolo*, *etro*.
2   *The Liturgy of the Word*: Romans 6:1–8, Galatians 3:23–9, John 3:1–8 (John 3:22–7 for females).
3   *Renunciation*: Prayer, signing, prayer, exorcism and adjurations, shorter exorcism, renunciation, adherence, Creed, prayer of thanksgiving.

Second Service

4   *Introduction and Consignation*: *Gloria*, diaconal response, prayers (private and aloud), anointing, *eqbo*, *hosoyo*, *promion*, *sedro*, hymn.
5   *Consecration of the Water*: Breathing on the water, invocation, pouring of chrism, prayers and anointing.
6   *Baptism*, chrismation and laying-on of hands, white clothes, prayers, crowning and final prayers.

This rite has been the subject of a major study by Sebastian Brock, noting particularly the terminology and imagery surrounding the consignations, as well as the prayer for

---

[38] Philip Tovey, *Essays in West Syrian Liturgy*, Oriental Institute of Religious Studies, 199, Kottayam Kerala, India, 1998 who also discusses the Mar Thoma version. For the text see James Hough, *The History of Christianity in India*, Vol. 2, Nisbet, London, 1845, pp. 645–50, <http://www.nd.edu/~afreddos/translat/biel.htm>.

[39] Juan Mateos, 'Théologie du Baptême dans le formulaire de Severe D'Antioche', *Symposium Syriacum 1972*, Pontifical Oriental Institute, Rome, 1974, 135–61, p. 160. Mateos argues that we have a synthesis between signing with the cross and unction with oil, and he suggests, citing F.J. Dolger, that anointing the whole body was imported from Graeco-Roman culture, since public nudity was not acceptable in Semitic culture. This latter suggestion seems to ignore the *Acts of Judas Thomas* and *Didascalia*.

consecration of the water and its *epiklesis*.[40] Brock notes that a number of prayers found in earlier manuscripts seem to be rearranged in later ones. For example, in early manuscripts the prayer before the first consignation, the *tloyto*, appears in the later manuscripts and printed texts, but is relocated to before the second consignation. Noting the different terminology used, Brock writes:

> To summarize the whole situation for S, as attested in the earliest texts available: the four consignations are neatly provided with different technical terms in the formulae for the action: *htm*, *ršm*, *mšh*, and *tb'* respectively. The accompanying prayers suggest that the first consignation concerns the inscription of the candidates into the church, linked with the idea of Christ's ownership. The second consignation, as the preceding prayer shows, is clearly the original Antiochene pre-baptismal anointing associated with the Holy Spirit, while the formula adds the theme of υἱοθεσία. The third consignation, which has no introductory prayer, is the protective anointing of candidates, presumably regarded as athletes, in preparation for their contest with the devil, i.e. the baptism proper. To this the formula also adds the theme of grafting, from Romans xi. The final consignation is, of course, the post-baptismal anointing conferring the gift of the Holy Spirit, introduced into the Antiochene area about 400, and thus doubling, to some extent, with the second consignation.[41]

The instability of some of the prayers in the manuscript tradition led Brock to suggest that the second and third consignations were duplications:

> Such a duplication of an originally single anointing would have been helped by the fact that the action accompanying the anointing was twofold: the priest anointing the head, the deacons the rest of the body ... What has happened in S and the other (western) Antiochene *ordines* is that the first of the two actions has been allocated to the consignation in position 2, while the two together (since the second alone was unlikely to be kept alone) have been allocated to the consignation in position 3.[42]

In a previous chapter we noted that Brock builds on Ratcliff and Winkler for his conviction that the post-baptismal anointing is a later development, and we stressed that this is far from proven. His conjectures about the duplications are on firmer ground, but perhaps are better nuanced as being the result of liturgical synthesis, where originally different rituals from different communities are brought together and amalgamated, and then duplicated.

Although the theme of resurrection occurs in the many prayers, hymns and chants, the main focus of this rite, as with Timothy, is forgiveness of sins, together with Jesus' baptism in the Jordan. The condescension of God is described, 'who had no need of baptism, but came to be baptized that He might sanctify the waters of the River Jordan by His holy Baptism'.[43] The renunciation and abjuration is akin to that in Timothy,

---

[40] Sebastian Brock, 'Studies in the Early History of the Syrian Baptismal Liturgy', *Journal of Theological Studies* 23 (1972), 16–64.

[41] Ibid., p. 33.

[42] Ibid., p. 37.

[43] *The Sacrament of Holy Baptism*, p. 20.

and the prayer after the Creed asks for the Holy Spirit to be sent to rest on the candidate to cleanse and sanctify him/her. The opening prayer of the second service speaks of the water being 'a garment of incorruptibility', and the anointing formula is concerned with the confrontation of the satanic influence.

The blessing of the font is based upon or derived from the Egyptian anaphora of St Mark,[44] but also has sections in common with the Byzantine rite. Brock divides the prayer in the manuscript tradition a–o, though some of these letters represent acclamations and rubrics.[45]

a   This is a preparation prayer, asking God to fill this water with the power bestowed on the Son at his passion

(b   Doxological conclusion to the prayer a.)

(c   Peace)

d   God is addressed as the creator in language found in the anaphora of St Mark

e   God is asked to 'look' upon the water and grant it the blessing of the River Jordan

f   (Rubric for blowing on the water)

g   Casting out of monsters/evil spirits from the waters, as in the Byzantine prayer, termed there by Miguel Arranz as 'Negative epikleses'[46]

h   God is asked to send the Holy Spirit upon the water and sanctify it and appoint it the waters of repose. This has a parallel in the Byzantine prayer

i   A second epiklesis asking God to send 'from your dwelling that is prepared, from your infinite womb' the Holy Spirit. There are parallels here to the anaphora of St Mark

j   (Kyrie eleison)

k   Request that those baptized may be changed, and put off the old Adam and put on the new – as also in the Byzantine prayer

l   Asking that those so baptized may become partakers of the resurrection and receive crowns of victory

m   (Rubric for pouring oil on water)

n   Requesting that the Holy Spirit may rest upon those being baptized, and appoint them associates of Christ

o   Doxology.

The main concern of the prayer is that the baptism should cleanse and be a laver of regeneration. The womb theme is not prominent, but in the opening prayer the request

---

[44] Cf. Bryan D. Spinks, 'The Anaphora attributed to Severus of Antioch: a note on its character and theology', in J. Getcha and A. Lossky (eds), Θυσία αἰνέσες. *Mélanges liturgiques offerts à la mémoire de l'archevêque George Wagner*, Presses Saint-Serge, Paris, 2005, pp. 345–51.

[45] Brock, 'The Consecration of the Water in the Oldest Syriac Manuscripts'.

[46] M. Arranz, 'Les Sacrements de l'ancien Euchologe constantinopolitain', *Orientalia Christiana Periodica* 52 (1986), 145–78, p. 162.

is made that the water be mixed with the Holy Spirit so it may become a spiritual womb (*karso*). The pre-baptismal anointing is accompanied by a diaconal chant highlighting the *rushmo* being the mark of a lamb. The post-baptismal hand-laying, and myron formula as seal and perfection, seem to look back to the actual baptism as the time of regeneration and giving of the Spirit. *Pace* Brock, Simon Jones concluded:

> The relationship between the descent of the Spirit and Jesus' immersion in the Jordan does not provide a model for the performance of the liturgical rite in any of the descriptions considered in this study: There is no evidence to support the descent of the Spirit upon Jesus having an exact parallel or mimesis in either pre-immersion anointing or epiclesis.[47]

That is also true of the post-baptismal formula.

Is there any link beyond honorific between this rite and that of Severus of Antioch? Severus was at one time patriarch of Antioch during the reign of an anti-Chalcedonian emperor, and he was exiled in Egypt. So, in theory, he would have been in a position to use, or draw upon, pre-Chalcedonian Antiochene and Constantinopolitan material, and to use Egyptian material. But such a possibility cannot be proven. In terms of Severus' rite of baptism and his understanding of it, some ideas can be gleaned from his homilies and other writings. Addressing catechumens, Severus says:

> Look and turn towards the setting sun, and thus renounce Satan and the troop of demons ... Having done that, turn towards the East and make these covenants with Christ.[48]

In Homily 70 he speaks of stretching out the right hand during the renunciation. In Letter 24 he notes that the sign of the cross is used at the consecration of the water.[49] He sees Christ's baptism as consecrating all waters:

> For look, when you enter the sanctuary and see the source of the Jordan, fully formidable and powerful; for all the waters which are consecrated in the name of Jesus are the Jordan – he who first placed the origin of divine baptism into the Jordan, Thus we also pray that the grace of the Jordan be given to the waters.[50]

In Homily 23 Severus ties the triple immersion with the Pauline theme of putting off the old Adam:

> Then you go to the source of the Jordan, full of the Holy Spirit, and of purification and of divine fire, in which you will be buried with Christ at the same time as you are burying the old man in the waters. For because of that, by the triple immersion we also understand the three day burial and resurrection from this world.[51]

---

[47] Jones, 'Womb of the Spirit', p. 231.

[48] *Homily 42*, M. Briere and F. Graffin, *Patrologia Orientalis* (hereafter *PO*) 36.1 (1971), p. 63, cited by Jones, 'Womb of the Spirit', p. 184.

[49] *PO* 12.221.

[50] *PO* 36.1, 66, cited Jones, 'Womb of the Spirit', p. 189.

[51] *PO* 23.1,160, cited Jones, ibid., p. 190.

In *Letters*, Book VI, he states that in the cities it is the custom for deaconesses to minister to women candidates.[52] In other letters he mentions that the word of the anointer is mingled with the myron, and the post-baptismal anointing.[53] In his letter to John the Soldier he explains the latter rite more fully:

> Now concerning the imprint of myron with which those baptized are imprinted after the baptism of rebirth, the holy bishop Proclus made a very fine reply that is not far removed from the truth; for he said that 'this is the giver of spiritual gifts.' I would simply say that it is the completer of the gifts, for the Holy Spirit possesses many categories of gifts, just as the apostle said ...

> Thus, then, we imprint with the imprint of the myron those who have been spiritually reborn after the divine washing of rebirth as well, (doing this) to show by gradual increase the fulfilment of the multiple and immeasurable gifts of God, and (to show that) through the coming of the Paraclete the light of the knowledge of the Holy Trinity has been fully marked upon us ...

> By means of all these things that have been examined by everyone, it is clear that this imprint is the perfecter of sonship and grace and of all the other things which (are to be found) in holy baptism.[54]

The commentary of George of the Arabs gives a very brief explanation of the Syrian Orthodox rite.[55] He taught that baptism cleanses from sin and makes 'a new form and a new creature, as it were in the womb'.[56] Of the renunciation, George explained that 'The exorcism of the priest is a battle with Satan, and a supplication to the Judge that he who is being baptized may be set free from the capacity and subjection of the dominion of evil.'[57] The signing of the cross is given a salvific meaning. The first anointing is for combat: 'the oil is an invincible armour against the demons'.[58] In other imagery, George combines tomb and womb:

> The font represents the tomb of Christ; and the water that is in it, the womb that brings forth children, spiritual and immortal and incorruptible, as by a resurrection of the dead. The baptism of him who is baptized is a re-birth. That he is dipped three times, is a mystery of the three days our Lord was in the tomb. The right hand of the priest is a sign of the secret re-formation of him who is baptized.[59]

George does not give the post-baptismal anointing any particular association with the Spirit; it simply 'completes the divine gifts'.[60] George mentions the white garments

---

[52] E. Brooks, *Letters*, Book VI, Text and Translation Society, Vol. 2, Part 1, London, 1903, p. 194.

[53] Ibid., Part II, 1905, p. 354, p. 418.

[54] Sebastian Brock, 'Severos' letter to John the Soldier', in G.Wiessner (ed.), *Erkenntnisse und Meinungen II*, Otto Harrassowitz, Wiesbaden, 1978, pp. 53–75, pp. 71–4.

[55] R.H. Connolly and H.W. Codrington, *Two Commentaries on the Jacobite Liturgy*, Williams and Norgate, London, 1913.

[56] Ibid., p. 12.

[57] Ibid.

[58] Ibid., p. 14.

[59] Ibid.

[60] Ibid.

signifying that they become 'sons of the heavenly light', and says the crowns represent freedom which Christ brings.[61] In George's day, the eucharist followed.

The *Commentary* of Moses bar Kepha is a little more sophisticated. It knows baptism by three titles – baptism, illumination and regeneration – used by Timothy II for the Church of the East. The divesture of the baptized and the removal of ornaments and shoes signifies their putting off the old Adam, escaping their adversary naked, and taking the lowest place. The anointing represents the salvific work of the cross and the Trinity, and:

> It is as when a painter comes to an image which is already old and has the paint rubbed off. First he scours it and cleans it from the marks of its age, and after that he puts paint on it and adorns it. Because if he put paint on it before he had cleaned and scoured it, he would ruin the paints. Likewise, also, when the priest comes to the baptized, who is old and sullied with sin, he first seals him with the cross without oil, thus cleaning off his [marks of] age, and afterwards he seals him with oil, restoring him to his pristine beauty.[62]

The anointing after the renunciation and adherence is interpreted as preparation for a wrestling match, and being made a wild olive. The pouring of myron into the font represents the incarnation of the Word and the Holy Spirit brooding over the waters.

In explaining the actual baptism, bar Kepha uses Romans 6:1–3, and Matthew 6:9. He considers why Christ constituted baptism by water and the Spirit and not oil and the Spirit (was he aware of the usage in the *Acts of Judas Thomas*?). Water, he explains, is easily accessible in all places to rich and poor alike. He goes on to give biblical citations – the firmament in the midst of the waters, Namaan the Syrian, the torrent of Ezekiel, amongst others – and also quotes from Basil that the water symbolises mortality and the Spirit renewing us in the resurrection. He assigns a number of meanings to the sealing with myron: a sweetness, perfection and reception of the Spirit, a token of Christ, that demons may fear, that his organs are sealed from evil, that it is a mark like that of Passover, that the heart is sealed, and that his joints may be instruments of righteousness.[63]

What is interesting is that reception of the Spirit is not made more significant than the other meanings, and this may be because bar Kepha envisaged this grace as having taken place in the water, since myron was mixed with the water.

Again, the white robes are given six meanings – the light of baptism, putting on the new Adam, that the body acquires form and beauty, that it is the robe Adam lost (cf. Ephrem), that at the resurrection he will dwell as a luminary, and he will shine in the Kingdom.[64] The crowning, as in George, is regarded as freedom, but for bar Kepha it is freedom from Satan.

---

[61] Ibid.

[62] K.A. Aytoun, 'The Mysteries of Baptism by Moses bar Kepha Compared with the Odes of Solomon', in J. Vellian (ed.), *The Syrian Church Series 6*, CMS Press, Kottayam, Kerala, 1973, pp. 1–15, p. 9.

[63] Ibid., pp. 13–14.

[64] Ibid., p. 14.

In summary, the Syrian Orthodox rite tends to stress the themes of forgiveness and recapitulation of the baptism of Jesus in the Jordan. Resurrection is emphasized, but as part of regeneration and new life following the drama of rejecting evil. Both tomb and womb are implicit, womb only slightly more so than tomb. The variety of consignations suggests that no particular ceremony was specifically singled out as imparting the Spirit, but in the actual texts the post-baptismal myron seals and perfects what has taken place in the water, which was blessed and mixed with myron. The association of the Spirit with the myron is indisputable; at what stage in the unfolding ritual the myron symbolized the imparting of the Spirit is ambiguous, and perhaps deliberately so. It is summed up in a sermon on the Baptism of Christ by Patriarch Ignatius Zakka in 1994:

> We believe what happened at the river Jordan when the Lord Jesus was baptized is happening in an unseen and unheard way to every believer when they are baptized in the name of the Holy Trinity by the hand of a legal priest, even to the children who are baptized according to the faith of their parents and god parents … Christ has made us one in the spiritual family when we all were born of one mother that is baptism and he granted us to be living members in his holy sacramental body, the Church.[65]

The Maronite *Ordo*

The Maronite rite, named after Jacob of Serugh, is closely related to that of the Syrian Orthodox both in structure and content. Sebastian Brock published an *Ordo* found in BL Add.14518, which stands directly between the Maronite rite and Severus. The question is whether this *Ordo* is the one from which *Jacob of Serugh* is derived (that is, Severus in transition), or simply a hybrid rite which drew on both the Maronite and Syrian Orthodox rites.[66] The oldest manuscript of the Maronite rite is Vatican Syriac 313, dated fifteenth/sixteenth century. The manuscripts have been studied by Augustin Mouhanna, who divided them into two broad groups.[67] The text used today, however, dates from 1942, and its English translation from 1987.[68]

The structure of the rites may be tabulated as follows:

1 *Introductory material: Gloria patri*, prayer, Psalm 51, *Hosoyo, promion, sedro, qolo, etro, trisagion.*

---

[65] Ignatius Zakka, 'The Baptism of the Lord Jesus', *The Patriarchal Journal* 32 (131–2) (1994), pp. 2–7, trans. 1996 <http://www.syrianorthodoxchurch.org/library/sermons/baptism.htm>

[66] Sebastian Brock, 'A Remarkable Syriac Baptismal Ordo', *Parole de l'Orient* 2 (1971), 365–78.

[67] Augustin Mouhanna, *Les Rites de l'initiation dans l'Église Maronite*, Orientalia Christiana Analecta 212, Rome, 1980.

[68] *Mysteries of Initiation. Baptism, Confirmation, Communion According to the Maronite Antiochene Church*, Diocesan Office of Liturgy, Washington DC, 1987.

2　*The Liturgy of the Word*: *Mazmuro* (Psalmodic hymn), Epistle (Titus), *Hullolo*, *Petgomo*, Gospel (John 3:1–7), *koruzuto*.

3　*Preparatory rites*: Diaconal proclamation, *qolo*, prayer.

4　*Renunciation*: Exorcisms, renunciation, adherence, Creed, with pre-baptismal anointing, prayer of thanksgiving.

5　*Consecration of the Water*, including *sanctus*, insufflation, exorcism of water, invocation of the Spirit and pouring in chrism.

6　*Baptism*: Pre-baptismal anointing, baptism by threefold dipping/immersing, post-baptismal putting-on of white garments, anointing and 'crowning' with head bands.

Within this complexity, certain themes come to the fore. First, the theme of forgiveness and purification. The *promion* speaks of Jesus the High Priest 'who showed us the way of purification, by first purifying himself in the waters of the Jordan, and led us on the path of life to redeem us from our sins'.[69] The diaconal proclamation prays for 'pardon of our faults' and exhorts:

> Let us implore the purifying hyssop to remove and strip from us the old man, –
> the one corrupted and ruined, and clothe us with the new one, –
> rejuvenated, perfected and sanctified by the baptism of forgiveness.[70]

The theme of the condescension of Christ and the new Adam are also important. The *Sedro* proclaims:

> You fashioned children in their mother's wombs, yet you willingly became a child,
> in order to renew the image of Adam, aged and corrupted by sin.[71]

The theme of Adam and the robe, found in Ephrem, occurs in a number of places in the rite. The same *Sedro* proclaims, 'You have clothed us, through your baptism, with the robe of glory.' In the elaborate blessing of the waters the celebrant prays:

> May those who enter them and are baptized,
> be cleansed, purified, and clothed in the robe of justice.[72]

The words for the 'crowning' include, 'you have put on the Holy Spirit, and you have been given the robe of glory, which Adam laid aside'.[73]

This rite declares that Jesus' baptism in the Jordan sanctified the baptismal waters for us, and in the diaconal proclamation after the lections Christ is addressed with these words, 'through your holy baptism, you sanctify the waters of the Jordan and all waters' (a theme later taken up by Luther!). Jesus is described as a shepherd, and the consignations utilize the metaphor of the marking or branding of lambs. Prior to

---

69　Ibid., p. 13.

70　Ibid., p. 28.

71　Ibid., p. 14.

72　Ibid., p. 35.

73　Ibid., p. 48.

the renunciation, the priest says, 'I sign and seal this lamb against the army of the devils'.[74] God is asked in a silent prayer of the celebrant to 'sign your flock with the sign of the glorious Trinity. Protect this flock from the ravenous wolf in your glorious name'.[75] Immediately prior to baptism we have 'May *N.* be signed as an innocent lamb of your flock. With your seal may he/she be numbered among your spiritual sheepfold, enter into your flock, and mingle with your sheep.'[76] The text at the anointing is '*N.* is anointed as a member of the flock of Christ', and the Trinitarian baptismal formula is prefaced by the words, '*N.* is baptized a lamb in the flock of Christ in the name of … .'[77]

In this rite the theme of womb predominates. The celebrant, praying silently at the blessing of the waters, says:

> Though he had no need, he received baptism in the River Jordan and sanctified for us this font of baptism, a salvific and fruitful womb. By your will, Father, Son and Holy Spirit, he abided in the world in three places: in the womb of flesh, in the womb of baptism, and in the dark mansions of Sheol.[78]

Later he blesses God because the waters, 'became a new womb, giving birth to spiritual children'.[79] All these themes seem held together in the invocation of the Spirit upon the waters:

> As the womb of our mother, Eve, gave birth to mortal and corruptible children, so may the womb of this baptismal font give birth to heavenly and incorruptible children. And as the Holy Spirit hovered over the waters at the work of creation, and gave birth to living creatures and animals of all kinds, may (s)he hover over this baptismal font which is a spiritual womb. May (s)he dwell in it and sanctify it. Instead of an earthly Adam, may it give birth to a heavenly Adam. May those who enter it to be baptized be permanently changed and receive a spiritual nature, instead of a corporal one, a participation in the invisible reality, instead of the visible one, and instead of the weakness of their spirit, may the Holy Spirit abide in them.[80]

The post-baptismal anointing with myron, as in the rite of Severus, simply is the seal, the plenitude and grace of the Holy Spirit. Furthermore, this element is absent from the oldest manuscript, and a rubric and first line are added in a later hand. In other words, it may just be that the oldest manuscript witnesses to a tradition known in some Maronite communities which did not have a post-baptismal anointing. Adding to this the concern for marking or branding in the consignations, it seems that this mature rite does not link the Spirit with the myron in the same direct manner as does Severus. Rather it sees the Spirit filling the water and imparting grace in the water.

---

[74] Ibid., p. 24.

[75] Ibid., p. 39.

[76] Ibid., p. 44.

[77] Ibid., pp. 45 and 46.

[78] Ibid., p. 33.

[79] Ibid., p. 37.

[80] Ibid., p. 34.

Of course it is difficult to argue from a late, mature rite back to the fourth century, but is it feasible to think that the Maronite rite may have preserved a ritual pattern of the Antiochene tradition which was akin to that described by Chrysostom, lacking a post-baptismal anointing? The pattern developed in the rites of Timothy and Severus is more akin to that pattern described by Theodore of Mopseustia and found in *Apostolic Constitutions* VIII. We would thus have two West Syrian or Antiochene patterns.

It has been noted that the Maronite baptismal rite was named after Jacob of Serugh (*c.* 451–521). Jacob was trained at Edessa and was to become bishop of Batnae in 519. It is clear from his writings that in his Christology he supported the non-Chalcedonian Syrian churches, though this seems not to have been so pronounced as to cause the Maronites problems with the attribution. In a very fine study, Sebastian Brock examined the baptismal themes found in the writings of Jacob.[81] What is quite remarkable is how Jacob's main themes reflect the emphases found in the Maronite rite. It raises the question of whether Jacob knew a rite with texts articulating themes very close to the Maronite baptismal tradition, or whether perhaps the rite was named after him because he was thought to have been closely involved in its development. For example, the 'three wombs' are found in Jacob:

> He completed his whole course by three staging posts:
> he resided in the virgin and came to birth, though he was God;
> again baptism received him, and yet he was God;
> and he descended to Sheol, and the world recognized that he was God.[82]

For Jacob, Christ's descent into the Jordan affects not only that river's waters, but all waters:

> The Son trod the great highway of baptism, causing his *shekhina* to reside in fountains and rivers, so that all water might receive the power to be healed,

and,

> the entire nature of the waters perceived that you had visited them – seas, deeps, rivers, springs and pools all thronged together to receive the blessing from your footsteps.[83]

Jacob describes Christ's baptism as a descent into Sheol to recover the lost Adam. Christ explains to John the Baptist: 'I am trying to find the lost Adam; let me go down and look for Adam, the fair image.'[84] At his baptism, Jesus 'placed the robe of glory in the womb of the baptismal water; he sent the bride to go down and put it on from the water'; and again, 'Christ came to baptism, he went down and placed in the

---

[81] Sebastian Brock, 'Baptismal Themes in the Writings of Jacob of Serugh', *Symposium Syriacum 1976*, Pontifical Oriental Institute, Rome, 1978, pp. 325–47.

[82] Jacob of Serugh, *Homiliae Selectae Mar-Jacobi Sarugensis*, P. Bedjan (ed.), 5 vols, Harrossowitz, Paris, 1905–10, Vol. 3, p. 593; Brock, 'Baptismal Themes', p. 326, note 4.

[83] Ibid. Vol. 4, p. 707 and Vol. 1, p. 188, cited by Brock, p. 327, and note 10.

[84] Ibid., Vol. 1, p. 177, cited by Brock, p. 328.

baptismal water the robe of glory so that the one Adam had lost might be there for him.'[85]

Other important themes found in Jacob include baptism as betrothal of Christ and the Church, and the piercing of Christ's side as the source of baptism (reversing the Gospel text of blood and water). He wrote:

> The crucifiers cast a lance at the Fair One
> and pierced his side; from it flowed water and blood.
> A new well was opened on Golgotha;
> this is that blessed fountain of Eden,
> which divided itself up as a great river (flowing) towards the four quarters,
> so that the whole of afflicted creation might drink of it.[86]

Jacob contrasts Eve's birth from Adam's side with the Church being given birth to from Christ's side. Christian baptism can be described as protective armour, and as akin to circumcision, and as a stamp or image, and a mark of ownership, so that 'The Lord of the sheep made the *rushma* of oil for his flocks.'[87] However, Brock could find only one occasion when Jacob refers to baptism as 'grave of water'.[88] Though Jacob mentions marking the forehead, he makes no mention of the anointing of the whole body; he also alludes to oil being made sweet by the addition of herbs, suggesting myron. However, Brock concluded that Jacob knew no post-baptismal anointing, but only the traditional Syrian pre-baptismal *rushma*.[89] He also decided that 'Jacob lends support to the view that the older strata of the West Syrian baptismal tradition are best preserved in the Maronite and now disused Syrian Orthodox formularies.'[90] Though any direct link between Jacob and the Maronite baptismal rite is impossible to demonstrate, the ascription of the rite to Jacob is certainly appropriate.

Concluding remarks

We have observed that in the early Syriac evidence for baptism, there appears to have been a diversity of usage. Apparently some groups used only oil, while others had anointing followed by baptism. Perhaps the anointing was separated out between bishop and deacons or deaconesses, and so may have appeared as two anointings. Other groups seem to have known a post-baptismal anointing. The diversity can be seen clearly when comparing Cyril of Jerusalem with St John Chrysostom, Theodore of Mopsuestia and *Apostolic Constitutions*. Such a diversity might still be seen in the manuscript tradition of the Maronites with Vat. Syr. 313, and in the East Syrian rite

---

[85] Ibid., Vol. 1, p. 197 and Vol. 3, p. 593, cited Brock, p. 336, note 60.

[86] Ibid., Vol. 2, pp. 588–9, cited Brock, p. 331.

[87] Ibid., Vol. 4, p. 801, cited Brock, p. 338, note 74.

[88] Brock, ibid., p. 335.

[89] Ibid., p. 339.

[90] Ibid., p. 346.

at the time when Narsai was commenting upon it. But on the whole a ritual osmosis seems to have been under way, with all the mature Syriac *Ordos* finally having a post-baptismal consignation with oil. The main theme of baptism in the Syriac tradition would seem to be forgiveness and regeneration, or restoration of the old Adam in Christ, and baptism as regeneration or rebirth from the spiritual womb. The Maronite rite exemplifies these themes.

CHAPTER 5

The Formation and Theology of the Eastern Rites of Baptism: II The Byzantine, Armenian, Coptic and Ethiopic Rites

The rites described in the previous chapter are linked by socio-linguistic culture. Links between the rites discussed in this chapter are more tenuous. The Byzantine rite has its origins in the rites of Caesarea, Antioch, Jerusalem and Constantinople. Armenia received Christianity from Caesarea and Syria (probably Edessa), and was later influenced by the Byzantine rite and the Latin rite. The Coptic rite has links with the canons of Hippolytus and Sarapion, and the Ethiopic rite is derived from the Coptic.

The Byzantine Rite

The earliest liturgical text of the baptismal rite of Constantinople appears in the Barberini 336 *Euchologion* of the eighth century. The rite shows considerable continuity to the usage of Antioch as witnessed both in *Apostolic Constitutions* 8 and in the homilies of John Chrysostom and Theodore of Mopsuetsia. However, an equally important source for how the rite was developing and how it was understood is found in *The Ecclesiastical Hierarchy* of the Pseudo-Dionysius. The writer is thought to have been Syrian, perhaps writing in the later fifth century after the issue of the *Henotikon*, which was an attempt to win back the pro-Cyrilline non-Chalcedonian churches. Whatever may have been the Christological sympathies of the writer, his works were widely read and, as Thomas Campbell observes, by the sixth century the Eastern Church saw in his writings a theological *summa* for the interpretation of its best writers.[1] Such writers include Maximus the Confessor, Theodore Studites and John Damascene. For Pseudo-Dionysius, the key term for baptism was illumination or regeneration, as a step in the process of divinization, or 'paradise regained'. Here he both articulated and established one of the reasons why the Eastern emphasis on baptism has no real counterpart to Augustine in the West. For the East, it is the effects of the fall that are inherited, not original guilt,

---

[1] *Dionysius the Pseudo-Areopagite*, Thomas L. Campbell, trans., University of America Press, Lanham, MD, 1981, p. 13.

and thus the Eastern churches have had a more ambiguous approach to the problem of babies dying without baptism.[2]

Pseudo-Dionysius describes how candidates for the catechumenate seek out a sponsor who will bring him or her before the bishop.[3] The candidate prostrates himself, and the bishop lays hands on him and seals him. The renunciations are made facing west, and the threefold adherence facing east, and there is an imposition of hands by the bishop. The candidate is stripped, and the bishop begins the anointing which is completed by the priests. Meanwhile the bishop 'proceeds to the mother of filial adoption, sanctifies its water by sacred invocations, and consecrates it by a triple effusion of the most holy oil in the sign of the cross'.[4] Pseudo-Dionysius describes the baptism with threefold immersion and in the name of the Trinity, putting on the appropriate clothing, and the sealing 'with the oil that produces most divine effects', followed by the eucharist. In his section on contemplation, he explains the renunciation as renouncing that which is opposed to deification, adding:

> I think it is quite evident to those learned in hierarchical matters that those who are spiritual possess the constancy of the godlike state through unbroken and vehement striving towards one thing, and by the eradication and annihilation of what is opposed to this.[5]

The pre-baptismal anointing is likened to one entering a contest and being an athlete engaged in a struggle to overthrow 'the energies and powers opposed to his deification by struggles modelled on God's; to speak mystically, he will die with Christ to sin through baptism'.[6] Pseudo-Dionysius uses the image of tomb and death/resurrection for the actual baptism. The garment is 'as white as light', indicating a life full of light. And of the post-baptismal anointing he writes:

> The most perfective anointing with oil makes the one initiated of sweet odor, since the holy perfection of divine regeneration unifies the initiated with the supremely divine Spirit.[7]

In Chapter 4 he expounds his understanding of the sacred oil, noting that 'the tradition of the sacred symbols puts the Seraphim near the divine oil when it is being consecrated'.[8] This recalls the references in the fourth-century *Acts of John*, and may well account for the trend in later consecration prayers to include the *sanctus*.[9] Pouring oil into the font is seen as representing the whole of Christ's saving work – his own

---

[2] See the essay by Jane Baun, 'The Fate of Babies Dying Before Baptism in Byzantium', in Diana Wood (ed.), *The Church and Childhood, Studies in Church History 31*, Blackwell, Oxford, 1994, pp. 113–25.

[3] Ibid., Chapter 2.1ff., pp. 23ff.

[4] Ibid., p. 26.

[5] Ibid., p. 30.

[6] Ibid., p. 31.

[7] Ibid., p. 32.

[8] Ibid., p. 58.

[9] See Gabriele Winkler, 'Nochmals zu den Anfängen der Epiklese und des Sanctus im Eucharistischen Hochgebet', *Theologische Quartalschrift* 174 (1994), 214–31.

'most sublime and divine humility to death itself on the cross for our regeneration in God' to his 'effecting a renewal in a godly and eternal existence'.[10] Of the post-baptismal oil he explains, 'The perfecting unction with the oil grants the descent of the supremely divine Spirit to Him who has been initiated in the most sacred mystery of divine regeneration' – here echoing Cyril of Jerusalem.[11]

The *Barberini* contains two texts, the second of which is older, but it is incomplete and is a rite for the making of catechumens.[12] The older text was for use on Good Friday. In it the candidates removed their clothes and shoes and turned to the West with raised hands and renounced Satan; they also 'blow upon him'. They then turned to the East for the adherence, and after an exhortation and brief intercessions, dressed and entered the sanctuary for the laying-on of hands.

The second rite shows that already by the eighth century adaptations for infant baptism have been made. We find the following ritual pattern:

1   *Prayer for making a catechumen*, with three exorcisms.
2   *Prayer after the making of a catechumen* 'as the hour of baptism approaches', exsufflation, renunciation, blowing, adherence to Christ with Creed, and prayer.

The baptism comes on the 'Holy Sabbath':

1   *Diaconal litany* with biddings for the blessing of the font, with private prayer by the priest.
2   *Blessing of the water*, 'for you sanctified the waves of the Jordan, you sent down your Holy Spirit from heaven and crushed down the heads of the serpents that lurked there. Therefore do you, our loving King, be present now in the visitation of your Holy Spirit and sanctify this water'. Oil is poured into the water.
3   *The candidate is anointed* with olive oil, first by the priest on the forehead, breast and back; and then by the deacon all over the body.
4   *The candidate is baptized*, and Psalm 32 is chanted.
5   *The priest prays a prayer for the candidate* which speaks of the epiphany of Christ and declares that the baptism has conferred new birth and the forgiveness of sins. The priest says 'As many as are baptized in Christ have put on Christ', which may have accompanied the white garment which is indicated in later texts.
6   *The baptized are anointed* on the forehead, eyes, nostrils, mouth and ears with the words 'the seal of the gift of the Holy Spirit'.

The rite also provides for an eighth-day ablution rite and tonsure.

---

[10]   Campbell, *Dionysus*, p. 59.

[11]   Ibid., p. 59, cf. Cyril, *St. Cyril of Jerusalem's Lectures*, Chapter 3.

[12]   Stefano Parenti and Elena Velkovska, *L'Eucologio Barberini gr. 336*, Centro Liturgico Vincenziano, Rome, 1995; Whitaker/Johnson, *DBL*, pp. 109ff.

The *Barberini* text, which was for presbyters, was largely conserved in subsequent manuscripts and printed texts, and still forms the heart of the Eastern Orthodox baptismal rite. A little more information regarding its development as celebrated in Constantinople is found in the *Typicon of the Great Church* and in the eleventh-century manuscript, *Grottaferrata G.b.I.* In the later fifteenth-century manuscripts we find that the ceremonies are telescoped into one service.[13] Miguel Arranz has subjected the manuscript tradition to a careful comparison and study.[14] He notes that the diaconal litany varies in its number of petitions in some of the manuscripts, and it is in fact the baptismal *synapte*.[15] The private prayer of the priest, on the other hand, shows no variations between the manuscripts, and is also found in the Coptic rite and a version in the Syrian Orthodox rite. Arranz draws particular attention to the structure of the blessing of the water, noting how the first part is addressed to the Creator, but the second part is addressed to Christ:

> For thou that art God, being without bounds, whose beginning is past the power of human telling, didst yet come upon earth, taking the form of a servant and was made in the likeness of men.[16]

Though the text would make the *sanctus* appropriate, it is not included in this rite. Arranz points out that there is a duplication of *epikleses* – 'be present now in the visitation of thy Holy Spirit and sanctify this water' and then later:

> But, maker of all things, declare this water to be a water of rest, water of redemption, water of sanctification, a cleansing of the pollution of the body and soul, a loosening of chains, forgiveness of sins, enlightenment of souls, washing of rebirth, grace of adoption, raiment of immortality, renewal of spirit, fount of life.[17]

In addition, Arranz notes what he calls a series of 'negative *epikleses*' for the casting-out of enemy powers.[18] The lack of interest in the post-Constantinople 381 doctrine of the Trinity and the treatment of the Holy Spirit in this prayer leads Arranz to suggest with Brock that the substance of this blessing is pre-381. According to Arranz, the structure is of a *todah* (Jewish thank-offering) with *epiklesis*.[19]

The oil is blessed using a prayer of *Kephaloklisia*, or inclining of the head, and its petition for the Holy Spirit – 'Do thou bless even this oil with the power and operation

---

[13] See K.W. Stevenson, 'The Byzantine Liturgy of Baptism', *Studia Liturgica* 17 (1987), 176–90.

[14] M. Arranz, 'Les Sacrements de l'ancien Euchologe Constantinopolitan', 145–78. Articles on other components of the initiation rites are found in *Orientalia Christiana Periodica* 48 (1982), 284–335; 49 (1983), 42–90; 49 (1983), 284–302; 50 (1984), 43–64; 50 (1984), 372–97; 51 (1985), 60–86; 87 (1987), 59–106.

[15] The *synapte* is a short litany found in the Eucharistic liturgy.

[16] Arranz, 'Les Sacrements', pp. 153–5.

[17] Whitaker/Johnson, *DBL*, p. 121.

[18] Arranz, 'Les Sacrements', p. 162.

[19] *Todah*, sacrifice of praise, is argued by some scholars to be the Jewish prayer genre underlying the eucharistic prayer.

and indwelling of your Holy Spirit' – is regarded as an archaic form.[20] Arranz observes that the rubric for anointing after baptism varies in a number of manuscripts, and notes the duplication of Galatians 3:27. He also notes that Psalm 32:1 was originally the entrance chant coming from the baptistery into the Great Church. The appropriate times of baptism in the *Typicon* were Epiphany, Lazarus Saturday, Holy Saturday and Pentecost.[21]

It is difficult to discern the main theological emphasis of this rite. Washing, cleansing, putting off the old Adam, putting on the new Adam, and death/resurrection seem to be the most prominent. The post-baptismal prayer seems to imply that the cleansing and sanctification have taken place in the water into which chrism was poured, and Arranz suggests that the rite is theologically in line with that of St John Chrysostom – the Spirit is given in the water by virtue of pouring the consecrated oil into the font.[22]

Beyond the rite itself, the exposition by Nicholas Cabasilas gives us an idea of how the rites were understood as the process of telescoping several rites into one was in progress in the fourteenth century. He does not suggest that the ceremonies were separated in time. He begins with considering baptism as new birth in Christ:

> 'New birth' and 'new creation' mean nothing else than that those who are born and created have been previously and have lost their original form, but now return to it by a second birth. It is as when the material of a statue has lost its shape and a sculptor restores and refashions the image, since it is a form and shape effected in us by Baptism. It engraves an image and imparts a form to our souls by conforming them to the death and resurrection of the Saviour. It is thus called a 'seal', since it conforms us to the image of the King and to His blessed form. Since the form clothes the material and puts an end to its formlessness we also call the Mystery 'clothing' and 'baptism.'[23]

But he also says:

> Baptism is called 'anointing' because on those who are initiated it engraves Christ, who was anointed for us. It is a 'seal' which imprints the Saviour Himself. As the anointing is actually applied to the whole form of the body of him who is anointed, so it imprints on him the Anointed One and displays His form and is really a sealing.[24]

Given the reference to anointing the whole body, he seems here to be referring to the pre-baptismal anointing.

Cabasilas commented on the rites of exorcism, the insufflation, stripping, the renunciation and the recitation of the Creed. Of the renunciation, he says, 'He stretches

---

[20] Arranz, 'Les Sacrements', p. 172.

[21] Arranz, *OCP* 53 (1987), p. 104.

[22] Arranz, *OCP* 52 (1986), p. 177.

[23] Nicholas Cabasilas, *The Life in Christ*, trans. Carmino J. de Catanzaro, St.Vladimir's Seminary Press, Crestwood, NY, 1974, p. 67.

[24] Ibid., p. 69.

forth his hands and repels the evil one as though he were present and pressing upon him.'[25] He understands the pre-baptismal anointing in the light of anointing kings and priests, and the baptism as a journey from dark to light and death to life. Later he treats baptism as deliverance from sin, and employs the old Adam/new Adam typology. But he notes, 'It is Christ who bestows birth and we who are born; and as for him who is being born, it is quite clear that He who generates confers His own life on him.'[26] Here we see the same interest in divinizaton as in Pseudo-Dionysius. Like Pseudo-Dionysius, Cabasilis identifies the reception of the Spirit with the laying-on of hands and anointing:

> It would be fitting, then, that those who are thus spiritually created and begotten should obtain an energy suitable to such a birth, and a corresponding animation. This the sacred rite of the most divine chrism accomplishes for us. It activates the spiritual energies, one in one man, another in another, or even several at the same time, depending on how each man is prepared for this Mystery.[27]

Again,

> The cross released us from sin. Since Baptism then has the efficacy of His cross and death, we go forward to the chrism, the participation in the Spirit.[28]

The chrism imparts the energies of the Holy Spirit, and brings forth gifts of godliness, prayer, love and sobriety. What is interesting is that the theology *vis-à-vis* the Spirit which Cabasilis imparts regarding the post-baptismal anointing is hardly suggested by the simple short Byzantine formula for the sealing. Some manuscripts do show expansion at this point, and even incorporation of the Western prayer for the sevenfold gift of the Spirit, but these variants did not survive into the *textus receptus* which forms the modern rite.[29] It would suggest that this short formula was established at an early date, and that subsequent theologizing did not lead to its universal reformulation , and thus the more ancient formula won out. The result, however, is a theology which is not explicit in the words of the liturgical rite. A modern writer such as Ene Braniste can call this part of the rite 'Confirmation' and explain that 'the holy chrism symbolizes the multiplicity and the diversity of gifts and powers of the Holy Spirit, which bring about the different Christian virtues'.[30] As Jones commented on the Syrian rites, so too here, it is not helpful to use the term 'Confirmation' for this part of the Eastern baptismal rites.

The modern rite has the clothing with a formula before the post-baptismal prayer and anointing. After these the rite continues with an Epistle reading from Romans

---

[25] Ibid., p. 71.

[26] Ibid., p. 81.

[27] Ibid., p. 103.

[28] Ibid., p. 105.

[29] See Stevenson, 'The Byzantine Liturgy'.

[30] Ene Braniste, 'Le déroulement de l'Office de l'Initiation dans les Églises de Rite Byzantin et son Interprétation', in *Ostkirchliche Studien* 20 (1971), 115–29, p. 124.

6:3–11, and a Gospel reading, Matthew 28:16–20, with provision for a litany and blessing, but a rubric which says these are 'usually omitted'.[31] These may be a remnant of the baptismal eucharist.

The Armenian Rite

Christianity in Armenia may be traced back to the end of the third and early fourth centuries. Its great missionary was St Gregory the Illuminator (= the Baptizer), who baptized King Trdat, as a result of which Armenia became a Christian kingdom. Gregory was from Caesarea and returned there to be made bishop. However, Armenia was also evangelized from Edessa, and so both Syrian and Hellenistic strains of Christianity were to be found there. Later influences include East Syrian, Byzantine, and through Crusaders in Cilicia, the Latin rite.

Furthermore, given that the Armenian language was heavily influenced by Iranian/ Parthian, many words reflect a Semitic and Syriac background. Thus geo-linguistic factors play an important role in the formation of the liturgical rites of Armenia. The tendency of the Armenians to conserve their older traditions even when integrating newer influences is another important factor. For example, this Church alone of the Oriental churches preserves the celebration of the Nativity on 6 January, and it was thanks to the Armenians that the early Jerusalem lectionary was conserved.

Caesarean liturgical influence is indicated in the preservation of an early version of the eucharistic prayer of St Basil, though it is no longer in use.[32] This may suggest that Caesarea was also the source of the early baptismal rites. However, in her magisterial study of the Armenian rites of initiation, Gabriele Winkler argued that the accounts of baptism preserved in the *History of the Armenians* by Agathangelos, and another version found in the *Life of Gregory*, dated to the early fifth century, indicate a Syrian origin.[33] Agathangelos and the *Life* were both authored in Armenian, though the latter is now only known in translation. The accounts seem to be different recensions or versions of the same events, which Robert Thomson describes as 'a curious mixture of remembered tradition and invented legend; it also exists in several languages and different recensions, not all of which derive from the text extant in Armenian'.[34] Thus we have fifth-century tradition about third-century events. In Agathangelos we find Gregory the Illuminator giving instruction, with fasting and prayer, leading up to 'a new and wonderful birth in fatherly fashion, by his holy and liberal right hand; to give birth once again to everyone by baptism from water and the

---

[31] Isabel Hapgood, *Service Book of the Holy Orthodox-Catholic Apostolic Church*, Association Press, New York, 1922, pp. 271–83.

[32] H. Engberding, 'Das eucharistische Hochgebet der Basileiosliturgie. Textgeschichtliche Untersuchengen und kritische Ausgabe' (Inaugural Dissertation), no publisher, Münster, 1931.

[33] Gabriele Winkler, *Das Armenische Initiationsrituale*.

[34] Robert Thomson, *Agathangelos History of the Armenians*, SUNY, Albany, NY, 1976, p. vii.

womb of the Spirit'.[35] We read that he baptized the king and the people in the River Euphrates, and that the water stopped flowing:

> And a bright light appeared in the likeness of a shining pillar, and it stood over the waters of the river; and above it was the likeness of the Lord's cross. And the light shone out so brightly that it obscured and weakened the rays of the sun. And the oil of anointing which Gregory poured over the people, floated around them in the river. Everyone was amazed and raised blessings to God's glory. In the evening the sign disappeared, and they returned to the town. And those who were baptized on that day were more than one hundred and fifty thousand persons from the royal army.
>
> They went forth in great joy, in white garments, with psalms and blessings and lighted lamps and burning candles and blazing torches, with great rejoicing and happiness, illuminated and become like the angels. They had received the title of God's adoption, had entered the heritage of the holy gospel, and being joined to the rank of the saints were flowing with sweet odor in Christ. So they went forth and returned to the Lord's house. There he offered the blessed sacrifice and communicated them all with the blessed sacrament, distributing to all the holy body and precious blood of Christ the Savior of all, who vivifies and gives life to all men, the creator and fashioner of all creatures; and he liberally administered to all the divinely-given grace.[36]

What is significant in the ritual sequence here is the mention of pre-baptismal oil of anointing, and lack of a post-baptismal anointing.

The version in the *Life* has a more detailed account of the ritual pattern. First to be baptized were Trdat and three other kings. They disrobed and Gregory signed them with myron and the sign of the cross. Gregory took myron and oil, and poured them into the river and perfected a cross (*staurou tupon ektelesas*). Then they descended into the water, and Gregory laid his hand upon them, and then, with his right hand, immersed them three times, baptizing them in the name of the Father, and of the Son and of the Holy Spirit.[37]

Of additional importance is the teaching found in the section of Agathangelos identified as *The Teaching of Gregory*. On the baptism of Jesus, the *Teaching* explains that Jesus submitted to the baptism of repentance, not the baptism of the divine mark of illumination of eternal life (that is, John's baptism, not 'Christian' baptism), though John at one point is described as the 'seal-giver'.[38] Christian baptism for Gregory is centered in Christ's baptism: 'At his baptism He vivifies all baptized by having Himself received baptism, and He made baptism honourable by his own descent to baptism.'[39] The imagery of the womb is paramount:

---

[35] Ibid., p. 365.

[36] Ibid., pp. 367–71, Paras 833–5.

[37] Gerard Garite, *Documents pour l'étude du livre d'Agathange*, Vatican City, 1946, pp. 98–100, giving the Greek and the Latin recension. Cf. Winkler, *Das Armenische Initiationsrituale*, pp. 103–32.

[38] Robert W. Thomson, *The Teaching of Saint Gregory*, 2nd edn, St. Nersess Armenian Seminary, New Rochelle, NY, 2001, pp. 120ff.

[39] Ibid., p. 123.

> He made verdant the womb of generation of the waters, purifying by the waters and renewing the old deteriorated earthy matter, which sin had weakened and enfeebled and deprived of the grace of the Spirit. Then the invisible Spirit opened again the womb by visible water, preparing the newly born fledglings for the regeneration of the font to clothe with robes of light all who would be born once more.[40]

The end result is regeneration:

> For in the same way as the skilled smith takes iron and forges it, throwing it into the furnace of fire and making it glow at red heat, just so have the just been plunged into the furnace of righteousness and dyed in the hues and colours of the Holy Spirit. They have put on Christ Himself in person, and like a light have kindled the love of the Godhead in themselves. They have received power from on high, like strong workers they have hastened to fill all tongues with the seed of the service of God.[41]

The *Teaching* also mentions the horn of Exodus 31:11, and links anointing with priesthood, kingship and prophecy.[42] The horn is explained as the example of the anointing of Christ. The document seems to know a tradition akin to that of East Syria, in that it understands that the unction of priests, kings and prophets was passed on from Moses to John, though it does not actually claim that the same horn of oil was used.[43]

Gabrielle Winkler has concluded that the two accounts of baptism indicate a Syrian origin for the Armenian baptismal tradition. She draws parallels with the accounts found in the *Acts of Judas Thomas* and *Didascalia* with only a single pre-baptismal anointing. In addition, using philological methodology, she argues that they use the same technical baptismal terminology. This latter methodology is somewhat reminiscent of nineteenth-century philological methodology, where a word has a particular meaning which it always retains in whatever context and whatever translation or transliteration. This lexiconographical method was once used in biblical studies, but has been severely criticized because, although words are not quite like Humpty Dumpty's view in *Alice in Wonderland*, meaning whatever one wants them to mean, there is far more flexibility in linguistic usages than Winkler seems to allow. Thus, the fact that a word is related to a Syriac word (inevitable, given the strong Iranian/Parthian component of the Armenian language) does not mean that its origin was indisputably Syrian, and even less, that the words always have identical technical meanings. The two accounts we have are fifth-century recollections and traditions of Gregory's late third and early fourth-century activities. In one account only the oil of anointing is mentioned; in the other, myron and oil, suggesting more than one usage. As in the *Acts of Judas Thomas*, *Didascalia*, and Narsai, we have no post-baptismal anointing. But Chrysostom apparently also knew of the same pattern in Greek-speaking Antioch, so

---

[40] Ibid., p. 122.

[41] Ibid., pp. 219–20.

[42] Ibid., pp. 128–9.

[43] Ibid.

that that pattern was certainly not peculiar to Edessa and the Syriac-speaking tradition. Given that Gregory was from Caesarea, and that the earliest anaphora of the Armenian Church is an early version of St Basil (which probably means the anaphora of Caesarea), it could equally be the case that the ritual pattern of baptism of early Armenia was derived from Caesarea, and that the two accounts tell us as much about the baptismal practice of Caesarea as they do about the early Syrian tradition.

Whatever the origin of those early accounts, the later developed rite of baptism shows structural similarities to the other Eastern rites. Armenians in Jerusalem or Cilicia would have known the ritual pattern as outlined by Cyril and Theodore of Mopsuestia, with a post-baptismal anointing. According to a twelfth-century source, the baptismal rite was the work of John Mandakuni, who died *c.* 480. He was one of a number of people reputed to have trained at Constantinople and Edessa to translate Greek and Syriac writings into Armenian and, at least in the opinion of H. Ansgar Kelly, was working with the Constantinople/Antioch Greek tradition.[44] Mario Lages has argued that the remnant of the Catechetical rites was derived from Jerusalem.[45] Conybeare's *Rituale Armenorum* gives the text in the ninth or tenth-century uncial codex no. 457, viii, 6 of the Library of San Lazaro in Venice. Charles Renoux has drawn attention to another manuscript of similar date, Erévan Maténadaran 1001. Renoux notes that both draw on the Greek *Barbarini* 336. In its evolution, the Armenian rite seems to have moved towards a 'Byzantinization'.[46] The rite has a distinct stress on the pneumatic imagery of John 3, and an absence of verbal exorcisms. It includes prayers after the eighth day for making a catechumen, and for mother and child after forty days. The rite of baptism begins with prayers and psalms, a renunciation of Satan and a trinitarian confession. The opening prayer, prayed over the catechumen, echoes phrases from the eucharistic prayer of St Basil (named St Gregory) such as the 'paradise of delight', and the 'condescension of the incarnation'. The Creed is recited together with Psalm 118. There is a blessing of the oil, and blessing of the water, and this includes pouring the blessed oil into the water. The prayer of blessing the oil associates the oil with the Holy Spirit and priests, kings and prophets, as seen above in the *Teaching of St Gregory*. Scholars speculate that there was once a pre-baptismal anointing at this point, but that it was later transferred until after the rite; this theory finds some support in the fifth-century accounts of Agathangelos and the *Life*. A prayer bids the Holy Spirit to come upon the oil. Biblical readings follow, and a litany. The emphasis on the baptism in water concerns themes of enlightenment, redemption, adoption and co-heirs rather than the image of death and resurrection. Like the Syrian rites, and the emphasis in the *Teaching,* the font is

---

[44] Henry Ansgar Kelly, *The Devil at Baptism. Ritual, Theology, and Drama*, Cornell University Press, Ithaca, NY and London, 1985, p. 188.

[45] Mario Lages, 'The Hierosolymitian Origin of the Catechetical Rites in the Armenian Liturgy', *Didaskalia* 1 (1971), 233–50.

[46] Charles Renoux, *Initiation chrétienne. 1. Rituels arméniens du baptême*, Les Éditions du Cerf, Paris 1997, pp. 5ff.

seen as womb rather than tomb. Baptism is by triple immersion and is followed by the Lord's Prayer, another prayer, and the anointing. Each part of the body has its particular formula, for example, 'The nostrils: May this seal be to thee a watch set before thy mouth and a door to keep thy lips.' There is also a vesting prayer, which mentions the 'garment of salvation'. The candidate is then taken to the *bema* (sanctuary) and the rubric directs that communion is given. A rubric also mentions the crown, or white hood, which is to be worn for eight days.

Conybeare shows other manuscript readings such as, for example, a manuscript of *c.* 1300 in which abjuring of Satan is nearer the Byzantine version. Conybeare also gives the text of a thirteenth-century homily attributed to Eznkatzi, though he thought parts of it could date from the sixth or seventh centuries.[47] The homily explains:

> ... it is called a birth afresh ... And of this birth God is father and the Church mother, and the font is the womb, which brings forth her child by water and spirit. For as water washes and cleanses the uncleanness of the flesh, so the holy Spirit cleanses and purifies the spirit and renders it a temple of God. [48]

Although the homily goes on to refer to Romans 6:3, it immediately returns to the waters of the font, which it likens to those of creation, bringing forth living things. It also refers to the pouring of oil into the water:

> And he drops the myron crosswise into the water, for the myron is Christ and the cross-wise shape is the cross of Christ. And as Christ died by the cross, so also the Christian along with Christ in the font is mystically made a sharer of the cross. And as he hath died unto the world and its sin, so he is made alive only by the beneficence of Christ. [49]

This seems to be a more detailed explanation of the *Life*'s reference to myron and 'perfecting a cross'.

The modern rite for infants as used in the Armenian Orthodox Church in the USA begins with:

1   At the door of the Church: The Lord's Prayer and penitential Psalms: 51 (and 25–7, but omitted from text), Psalm 131;
2   The blessing of the baptismal braid (*Narot*); hymn to the Holy Spirit, bidding of the cross, prayer of the cross, the Lord's Prayer;
3   The abjuring of Satan with bidding, prayer and renunciation;
4   The Creed and Gospel (Matthew 28:16–20);
5   Entrance into the Church with Psalm 118:19–29, hymn and bidding; prayer;
6   The baptism, with hymn, prayer over the oil, readings (Psalm 29:3, 2–4; Ezekiel 36:25–8; Galatians 3:23–9; John 3:1–8), diaconal litany, prayer over the water,

---

[47] F.C. Conybeare, 'The Character of the Heresy of the Early British Church', *Transactions of the Society of Cymmrodorion*, 1897–98, pp. 106–107.

[48] Ibid., p. 107.

[49] Ibid.

signing of the water, the pouring of oil crosswise into the font, hymn of the Holy Spirit, prayer, threefold immersion, Galatians 3:27, Psalm 34, Romans 6:3–11, Matthew 3:13–17, the Lord's Prayer;

7   Holy Chrismation, with hymn of the Holy Spirit, prayer, formulae for parts of the body anointed, Lord's Prayer;

8   Adoration of the altar, with hymn, prayer, Psalm 43, including putting on the baptismal garment;

9   Communion with prayers;

10 Blessing and dismissal.[50]

The main focus in this rite is forgiveness of sins, the washing of second birth, and putting on the incorruptible robe.

The Coptic and Ethiopic Rites

The earlier rites in Egypt that we have noted, namely the prayers found in the euchology of Sarapion and the *Canons of Hippolytus* do not seem to have persisted, though the rite which emerged has warranted the term 'maverick' in that it seems to reflect an amalgam of usages.[51] Thus, for example, the use of an interrogatory form of credal confession, together with the active baptismal formula, reflects the same usage as the Western Church, but many of the formulae have parallels in the Byzantine rite.[52] The present rite may be summarized as follows:[53]

1   The ritual of the catechumenate
    • Names of the catechumen
    • Unction with the oil of catechesis
    • Renunciation of Satan
    • Exorcism with exsufflation
    • Adherence to Christ
    • Threefold credal profession
    • Anointing with the '*agellielaion*', oil of exorcism
    • Laying-on of hands and prayer.

---

[50] *The Order of Baptism according to the Rite of the Armenian Apostolic Orthodox Church*, Evanston, IL, 1964.

[51] For this term see Paul Bradshaw, 'Baptismal Practice in the Alexandrian Tradition: Eastern or Western?', in Maxwell Johnson (ed.), *Living Water, Sealing Spirit*, Pueblo Liturgical Press, Collegeville, MN (1995), pp. 82–100, p. 95.

[52] See O.H.E. Khs-Burmester, 'The Baptismal Rite of the Coptic Church. A Critical Study', *Bulletin de la Société d'Archéologie Copte* 11 (1945), 27–86, and *The Egyptian or Coptic Church. A Detailed Description of Her Liturgical Services and the Rites and Ceremonies Observed in the Administration of her Sacraments*, Publications de la Société d'Archéologie Copte, Cairo, 1965.

[53] Whitaker/Johnson, *DBL*, pp. 132ff; R.M. Woolley, *Coptic Offices*, SPCK, London, 1930.

2   The ritual of the baptistery
   - Private prayer of the priest
   - Blessing of the font, including pouring in of unmixed oil, prayer of exorcism, insufflation, a sealing of the waters with the cross, a eucharistic preface with *sanctus, epiklesis*, pouring of chrism
   - Threefold immersion
   - Post-baptismal chrismation
   - Clothing with white garments and crowning
   - Communion of neophytes.

There are also services for absolution of women after childbirth, and a service of the basin which is performed before baptism, and is optional.

The rite shows truncation or telescoping of the ritual, but, as in some of the Syrian rites, it has been influenced by the eucharistic liturgy. The opening prayers of catechesis includes prayers for the catechumens and prayers over the oil of exorcism, though Bradshaw suggests that the earlier Egyptian tradition referred to the anointing of oil or the chrism of catechesis, and had the function of healing and re-creation rather than exorcism.[54] Candidates are stripped, and looking towards the west, stretch out the right hand to renounce Satan. After the adherence and Creed and a prayer, there is a prayer of exorcism and being prepared for the reception of the Spirit. The *agallielaion* is then used, with the formula, 'You are anointed, child of N., with the oil of gladness, availing against all workings of the Adversary, to your grafting into the sweet olive tree of the holy catholic Church of God.' Prayers for protection follow.

The actual baptism, which begins with entry into the baptistery, is a lengthy rite, complete with readings from Titus 2:11–3:7, John 1:5–13, Acts 8:26–39, and John 3:1–21, interspersed with prayers and followed by intercessions, all reminiscent of the eucharistic liturgy. This rite concludes with the private prayer for worthiness said by the priest, which is the same prayer found in the Byzantine rite. Holy oil is poured into the font, with a prayer that God will 'change, transform, hallow them [the waters], and give them power', and that through the oil and water evil spirits and other sinister agencies will be brought to nought. This is followed by salutations, and then the *sursum corda* as in eucharistic prayers, followed by a *eucharistia* outlining God's saving use of water from its creation through various incidents in the Old Testament. It includes a *sanctus*, though one devoid of any angelological context. The post-*sanctus* asks God that 'by the descent of your Holy Spirit upon it, bestow upon it the blessing of the Jordan'. The next section echoes the Byzantine prayer, with negative *epikleses*, and includes the same biblical quotation, Ephesians 4:22. The water is signed three times with the request that the water and oil be blessed, glorifed and purified in the name of the Trinity. After two further prayers the priest pours the chrism into the water in the form of a cross. This use of two oils may be a combining of once separate

---

[54] Bradshaw, 'Baptismal Practice', p. 92.

usages. After some psalm verses, the candidate is baptized with a threefold immersion, with the active formula used. A prayer is provided for the release of the water, and after the baptism another prayer asks that the Spirit be bestowed in the chrism. This rite ties the Spirit to the post-baptismal anointing in a far more explicit way than in other Eastern rites hitherto discussed. Formulae for the anointings of the various parts of the body are provided, analogous to the Armenian rite. After the signing comes the prayer for the laying-on of hands, which asks for blessing and is accompanied by breathing on the candidate and a petition that he/she receive the Holy Spirit. Then follows the clothing, and a prayer over the 'crowns' with formula, and a girdle. Afterwards the people say:

> Crown unfading the Lord has set upon them who received the Holy Baptism of Jesus Christ. Blessed are you in truth O my Lord Jesus, with your good Father and the Holy Spirit; for you received Baptism, you redeemed us.

The giving of communion follows.

The rite seems to have preserved a complex ritual pattern, though the theology which it attempts to articulate is not as sharp as in, for example, the Maronite rite.[55] The making of the catechumen, with the renunciation, and even the consecration of the water, all show a concern to cast out both evil spirits and evil practices, and to invoke blessing for protection. The use of two oils in the font may suggest different usages which have been amalgamated. The Holy Spirit is clearly associated with the oil, but the reception of the Spirit is articulated in the formulae as linked specifically with the post-baptismal ceremonies. Crowning receives rather more explicit attention than the white garment.

Whereas the Ethiopian eucharistic rite shows considerable creativity and independence from the Coptic rite, its baptismal rite is very similar to that of the parent Coptic Church. The text with Latin translation was published in 1927, though the Latin is that of Tasfa-Seyon made in 1549.[56] There are one or two changes in the sequence of prayers, and chrismation apparently disappeared in the seventeenth century, which Robert Cabié suggested may have been as a result of strained relations with Egypt which prevented the acquisition of chrism.[57]

Concluding Remarks

Although both Armenia and Egypt had their own baptismal rituals, in the course of time the Byzantine rite has heavily influenced both. The theological focus in these

---

[55] For the theological tradition, see Waheed Hassab Alla, *Le Baptême des Enfants dans la Tradition de l'Église copte d'Alexandrie*, Éditions Universitaires Fribourg Suisse, Fribourg, 1985.

[56] Selvain Grebaut, 'Ordre du Baptême et de la confirmation dans l'Église Éthiopienne', *Revue de l'Orient Chrétien* 6 (1927–28), 105–89.

[57] In A.G. Martimort (ed.), *The Church at Prayer*, Vol. 3, *The Sacraments*, Geoffrey Chapman, London, 1988, p. 83.

Eastern rites is less clear than is the case in the Syrian rites. However, all focus more on cleansing and rebirth or regeneration rather than on the paschal theme of death/resurrection. As with the Syrian rites, so with these, the rite is one entire rite which includes anointing (and in the Armenian and Coptic rites, communion). The post-baptismal anointings 'seal' the rite, but whatever this may mean, the anointings should not be understood as a 'sacramental equivalent' to that which became known as 'Confirmation' in the West; that is to force Eastern rites into later Western categories.

CHAPTER 6

The Western Rites: From John the Deacon to Anglo-Saxon England

Just as the Eastern rites are divided into families, so too are the pre-Reformation Western rites. By far the most important is the Roman rite, important because Charlemagne encouraged its use throughout his kingdom. The result was the hybrid Romano-Germanic rite, which came to supplant most other usages, namely the Spanish or Visigothic (also called Mozarabic) and the Gallican/Frankish rites. Augustine of Canterbury introduced the Roman rite to England, where it displaced the Celtic rite. The Milanese rite alone survived as a living rite alongside the Roman rite.[1] The hybrid forms, however, though mostly Roman, did include some material from the other supplanted usages. In this chapter we turn to consider the different families and the new hybrid forms, and in particular their Anglo-Saxon recensions.

Rome

Writing in 1965, in light of the then-recent challenge by J.M. Hanssens to the authenticity of the so-called *Apostolic Tradition* attributed to Hippolytus, J.D.C. Fisher remarked that, apart from the letter of Innocent, 'we have no earlier knowledge of the Roman rite of initiation which is both full and of undisputed authenticity than that which we derive from John the Deacon and the *Gelasian*'.[2] He added that the rite at a later stage of development may be seen in *Ordo Romanus XI* and in the *Hadrianum*, the version of the *Gregorian Sacramentary* sent by Hadrian I to Charlemagne in the eighth century. Though in hindsight few have been convinced by Hanssens' reassignment of the so-called *Apostolic Tradition* to Egypt, the more recent studies we have previously mentioned, which cast doubt on its provenance and date, show that Fisher's words are once more *à propos*.

At around 500 CE, John the Deacon (perhaps the later Pope John I, 523–526) wrote a letter to a layman, Senarius, who asked certain questions relating to baptism. John does not tell us everything we should like to know, since he seems to assume a certain knowledge on the part of Senarius. Nevertheless he sets out the overall baptismal ritual in Rome at that time.[3] He first explains the meaning of catechumenate and scrutiny:

---

[1] Though the Spanish rite survived in a chapel of Toledo Cathedral.

[2] J.D.C. Fisher, *Christian Initiation. Baptism in the Medieval West*, SPCK, London, 1965, p. 2, referring to J.M. Hanssens, *La Liturgie d'Hippolyte*, Pontifical Oriental Institute, Rome, 1959.

[3] Text in Whitaker/Johnson, *DBL*, pp. 208ff.

the whole human race has fallen in death because of the waywardness of the first man. Before anyone is reborn in Christ, he or she is held close in the devil's power. By renouncing the devil and making a true confession a person can come to the laver of regeneration. However, in order to be able to do that, he or she must become a catechumen and be instructed, and so journey from being a slave to a son. The catechumen receives the laying-on of hands, exsufflation and exorcism, and blessed salt. The candidates come to stability and permanence, which is achieved by 'frequent laying-on of the hand, and by the blessing of his Creator called over his head three times in honour of the Trinity'.[4]

On receiving exsufflation and renouncing 'the toils and pomps of the devil', the candidate may receive the Creed, and is now called a 'competent' or 'elect'. The *competens* participate in three liturgical gatherings called scrutinies, when they are anointed with the oil of sanctification on their ears and nostrils. At the third gathering, which seems to be immediately before the baptism, they are also anointed with the oil of consecration on their breast. They go down naked into the water and are baptized with a threefold immersion. John then explains that the candidate

> … is next arrayed in white vesture, and his head anointed with the unction of the sacred chrism: that the baptized person may understand that in his person a kingdom and a priestly mystery have met. For priests and princes used to be anointed with the oil of chrism, priests that they might offer sacrifices to God, princes that they might rule their people. For a fuller expression of the idea of priesthood, the head of the neophyte is dressed in linen array, for priests of that time used to deck the head with a certain mystic covering. All the neophytes are arrayed in white vesture to symbolize the resurgent Church, just as our Lord and Saviour himself in the sight of certain disciples and prophets was thus transfigured on the mount, so that it was said: *His face shone as the sun: his raiment was made white as snow.*[5]

Here John links the post-baptismal anointing with the ideas of priesthood and kingship, and even sees the white head covering as being an expression of a priestly people. He goes on to describe the white vesture as the costume of second birth, and the raiment of glory, and a wedding garment. He notes that all these things are also done in the case of infants, though these, being presented by their parents or others, are saved through the profession of other people. John attests the practice found in the Verona/ Leonine masses, of milk and honey being given with communion. He also witnesses to chrismation and blessing by the pontiff.[6]

The Old Gelasian Sacramentary, *Codex Vaticanus Reginensis Latinus* 316, dates from *c.* 750 from the nunnery of Chelles near Paris, and seems to reflect a prototype of the rite *c.* 628–715.[7] It is not a pure Roman liturgy, and already shows signs of inclusion of Gallican material. Nevertheless, its provisions for baptism are regarded

---

[4] Ibid., p. 209.

[5] Ibid., p. 211.

[6] For a discussion see J.D.C. Fisher, *Confirmation Then and Now*, SPCK/Alcuin Club, London, 1978, pp. 128–9.

[7] Text, Whitaker/Johnson, *DBL*, pp. 212ff.

as reflecting seventh-century Roman usage. It gives mainly liturgical texts, with a few rubrics. What is interesting is that, although the structure has the rituals staged over a period of time, and presupposes adults, the rite in fact is focused on *infantes*. Though this can be another term for the elect or *competens*, the rubrics –such as an acolyte holding an *infantes* in his arms as he recites the Creed – show that actual infants are intended here. Mass texts are provided for three Sunday scrutinies, or catechetical examinations, on the third, fourth and fifth Sundays of Lent, and additional exorcisms take place on weekdays, bringing the number to seven. Indeed, in this rite the candidates were already called 'elect' at the scrutinies, and the scrutinies themselves were no longer catechesis but only the rites of exorcism.

The last of these took place on the Monday of the third week in Lent. There were blessings of salt, and separate prayers of exorcism for males and females, which may point back to a time when candidates were stripped for these rites, and female exorcists or deaconesses took charge of the women. There was a solemn, but symbolic, giving of the Gospels to the elect at the 'opening of the ears'. The Creed and the Lord's Prayer were handed over to the candidates, with brief explanations. Provisions for blessing the chrism and the oil of exorcism were provided for Maundy Thursday.

On the morning of Holy Saturday the infants made their 'return of the Creed', which included an exorcism of Satan, the *effeta* of nostrils and ears with spittle, and anointing the breast and between the shoulder blades with the oil of exorcism, with a threefold renunciation, and then the recitation (by the officiant) of the Creed and prayers. The actual baptism took place during the Easter Vigil, after the vigil readings and a litany. The blessing of the font consists of four sections:

1 *Benedictio fontes*, with a collect which prays God to be present and send down the Spirit of adoption.
2 *Item Consecratio fontes*. This title is followed by a longer prayer, 'God, who by your invisible powers', and prays, 'let your Holy Spirit by the secret admixture of his light give fruitfulness to this water prepared for human regeneration, so that, sanctification being conceived therein, there may come forth from the unspotted womb of your divine font a heavenly offspring, reborn unto a new creature'.[8] This prayer also requests that the water be free from every assault of the enemy and be purified by the departure of all wickedness, similar to that in the Byzantine rite.
3 After a rubric 'Here you sign [the water]', a prayer follows which is addressed to the water, 'Wherefore, I bless you, O Creature of water ... I bless you also through Jesus Christ ... .'
4 After another rubric directing a change of voice, there is a further prayer asking 'May the power of your Holy Spirit descend into all the water of this font and make the whole substance of this water fruitful with regenerating power.' It asks that all stains of sin be removed, and for cleansing and rebirth.

---

[8] Ibid., pp. 233–4.

These four sections have been carefully studied by Dominic Serra.[9] Although a number of authors have argued that the opening collect is Gallican, Serra accepts the arguments advanced by Coebergh that the prayer is Roman. It has parallels with the blessing of oil for the sick, and the preparatory prayers for the ordination of a bishop in the *Hadrianum*, and uses the Roman *cursus*. He concludes that it is a preparatory prayer, typical of Roman usage before a major blessing.

The second prayer consists of an address to God, a petition to God to bless the water, and a petition for cleansing the water. Most scholars are agreed that this is Roman. Parallels are to be found in the sermons of Peter Chrysosogus of Ravenna, and in Leo, and perhaps both used the language of the Roman prayer. Of the third prayer, noting that direct address to an element is not regarded as typically Roman, Serra commented:

> We can be sure that [this] is not a Roman creation because of its address to the water rather than to God, and because of its use of the first person singular. It is quite likely that it was originally a Gallican exorcistic text which somehow entered the Roman liturgy at a very early date prior to the migration of the great liturgical documents from Rome to Francia.[10]

The fourth prayer too is regarded as probably Gallican in origin. Serra thus made the suggestion that if we take out (3) and (4), which are Gallican, we are left with a Roman preparatory prayer, and a Roman blessing in three sections, which was concluded by the rubric 'Here you sign [the water]'. This direction came to be, at a later date, a cue for the additional Gallican third prayer. What is interesting is that even with the Gallican additions, these prayers do not make much of the Romans 6 typology, and the second, Roman, prayer specifically picks up womb language alongside purification and regeneration.

The blessing of the water is followed by triple immersion, but the formula is a threefold credal form:

> Do you believe in God the Father Almighty ? **R**. I believe.
> And do you believe in Jesus Christ his only Son our Lord, who was born and suffered?
> **R**. I believe.
> And do you believe in the Holy Spirit; the holy Church; the remission of sins; the resurrection of the flesh? **R**. I believe.[11]

The Matthean Trinitarian formula seems to have replaced this by the time of Pope Zachariah I *c.* 744.[12]

After baptism the presbyter signs the head of the infant with chrism with the formula:

---

[9] Dominic E. Serra, *The Blessing of Baptismal Water at the Paschal Vigil (Ge 444–448): Its Origins, Evolution, and Reform*, published Doctoral Dissertation, Pontifical Institute of Liturgy, St. Anselmo, Rome, 1989.

[10] Ibid., p. 170.

[11] Whitaker/Johnson, *DBL*, p. 235.

[12] J.D.C. Fisher, *Christian Initiation. Baptism in the Medieval West*, SPCK, London, 1965, p. 17.

The Almighty God, the Father of our Lord Jesus Christ, who has made you to be regenerated *of water and the Holy Spirit,* and has given you remission of all your sins, himself anoints you with the chrism of salvation in Christ Jesus unto eternal life.[13]

A rubric directs that then the sevenfold Spirit is given them by the bishop. He seals them (*ad consignandum*), and lays hands on them with the following:

Almighty God, Father of our Lord Jesus Christ, who has made your servants to be regenerated *of water and the Holy Spirit,* and has given them remission of all their sins, Lord, send upon them your Holy Spirit the Paraclete, and give them the *spirit of wisdom and understanding, the spirit of counsel and might, the spirit of knowledge and godliness, and fill them with the spirit of fear* of God, in the name of our Lord Jesus Christ with whom you live and reign ever God with the Holy Spirit, throughout all ages of ages. Amen.[14]

This prayer, which seems to be a reiteration of the presbyteral prayer, extended by a request for sending the Spirit with Isaiah 11:2ff., is then followed by the bishop chrismating the forehead with the brief formula 'The sign of Christ unto eternal life'.

We shall return to this episcopal prayer, hand-laying and anointing later. For the moment it should be observed that it is a peculiarly Roman ceremony in terms of the ritual having both a presbyteral and an episcopal post-baptismal chrismation. The rubric says 'bishop' and not pontiff, and Fisher suggests that even at Rome, the Pope's suffragans were expected to preside over baptisms in the Stational Churches. The hand-laying prayer certainly seems to identify the reception of the Spirit with this moment of the rite.

Since at a later date this episcopal section would become detached in time, and would spin off to become a separate episcopal rite called 'Confirmation', it has attracted a great deal of attention. Aidan Kavanagh has argued that it was originally an episcopal *missa*; that is, it has a structure comparable to rites used to dismiss various categories of people from the liturgical assembly. Such groups as catechumens would come before the bishop for a blessing, which was a hand-laying rite.[15] Paul Turner, in response, suggested it was more of a welcome than a dismissal, representing 'the first public gesture of ratification for the bishop and the faithful who did not witness the pouring of water', since baptisms in Rome were not all in the same place, and were certainly not public events.[16] It may be that, structurally, Kavanagh is correct, but contextually Turner might be nearer the mark. It is odd that in the so-called *Apostolic Tradition,* the provision in initiation for an episcopal hand-laying and chrismation is one of the few things which is Roman. Perhaps it arose in response to the exigencies

---

[13] Whitaker/Johnson, *DLB,* p. 235.

[14] Ibid.

[15] Aidan Kavanagh, *Confirmation: Origins and Reform,* Pueblo, Collegeville, MN, 1988.

[16] Paul Turner, 'The Origins of Confirmation: An Analysis of Aidan Kavanagh's Hypothesis', in M. Johnson (ed.), *Living Water, Sealing Spirit,* Pueblo, Collegeville, MN, 1995, pp. 238–58.

of the emergence of a monarchical bishop at Rome, asserting the monarchical bishop's authority over all initiations in the various ethnic churches in Rome, by completing or supplementing the older rite of baptism and chrismation still administered by previously semi-autonomous presbyter-bishops. This 'non-identical repetition' would partly account for the repetition of the first part of the presbyter's chrismation prayer. As to the ritual pattern of hand-laying, Alistair Stewart-Sykes has argued that it originated in Africa as a result of the patronage system and manumission of slaves.[17] Whatever its origin and nature, it was peculiarly Roman, and was later either adopted or imposed elsewhere in the West.

An *Ordo* is a set of liturgical instructions, and *Ordo Romanus XI* gives us some insight into how baptism was practised in Rome in the seventh century.[18] It can be summarized as follows:

TIME	LITURGICAL ACTION
Third week in Lent	*Electi* summoned to the first scrutiny on Thursday of the third week.
Thursday of third week	An acolyte records the names of infants and their sponsors and calls each infant into church by name, males on the right, females to the left. Candidates are signed, hands are laid on them, salt is placed in the mouth. At five points the *patrini* and *matrinae* (godparents) sign the infants' foreheads with their thumb, in the triune name. The infants then wait outside until the scrutinal mass is finished. The first scrutiny ends with a summons to the second.
Sunday of third week	The second scrutiny is the same as the first.
Scrutiny of fourth week	The scrutiny is similar to the first, but includes the *effeta* and handing-over of the Gospels, Creed and Lord's Prayer. Infants left with others for safe-keeping, but parents and sponsors re-enter the church. Fourth scrutiny is announced.
Scrutiny of fifth week	Fourth scrutiny is the same as the first.
Scrutiny of sixth week	Fifth scrutiny is the same as the first.
Scrutiny of seventh week	Sixth scrutiny is the same as the first.

---

[17] Alistair Stewart-Sykes, 'Manumission and Baptism in Tertullian's Africa: A Search for the Origin of Confirmation', *Studia Liturgica* 31 (2001), 129–49.

[18] Text in Whitaker/Johnson, *DBL*, pp. 244ff.

Scrutiny of Holy Saturday	Seven scrutinies explained as symbolizing sevenfold gift of the Spirit. The infants are catechized, with exorcism, *effeta* with spittle, and a presbyter 'returns' the creed. The infants are taken out until the Vigil.

After the blessing of the candle and the vigil lessons, the pontiff and clergy go in procession from the church to the 'fonts', singing a litany. The font is blessed with prayers, *Almighty Everlasting God*, and *God, who by your invisible power*, 'and the rest'. Chrism is poured 'over the water into the fonts in the manner of a cross. With his hand he stirs the chrism and water'. (Water can be taken afterwards for sprinkling in houses or on fields, vineyards and orchards.) The pontiff baptizes one or two infants, and the rest are baptized by a deacon. The infants are given to a presbyter for anointing. Towels are ready for the infants. The infants are brought to the pontiff and he gives each a *stola,* a *casula*, a chrismal cloth and ten coins. Once robed, they are arranged in order as their names are written, in a circle, and the pontiff 'makes a prayer over them, confirming them with an invocation of the sevenfold grace of the Holy Spirit'.

After the prayer he signs them with chrism. The infants receive communion.

These three sources give us some idea of how baptism was practiced in Rome during the sixth and seventh centuries. The *Hadrianum*, or *Gregorian Sacramentary*, of the eighth century does not differ greatly from the textual provisions found in the *Gelasian*.

Milan and North Italy

After the witness of Ambrose, evidence for the rite in Milan is found in the *Tractates on Baptism* attributed to Pseudo-Maximus of Turin, dated to the sixth century, the *Manuale Ambrosianum* of the tenth century, and the *Ordo of Beroldus* of the twelfth century. The *Tractates* witness to the anointing of candidates' ears and nose with the oil of blessing, the renunciation of Satan and baptism in the font 'sanctified with heavenly power'. They also attest the three baptismal credal interrogations. The third Tractate discusses the post-baptismal anointing with chrism, which confers kingly and priestly authority, and the washing of the feet. There is no mention of a counterpart to Ambrose's 'spiritual seal'.

At one time it was claimed that Odilbert of Milan (*c*. 803–814) also gave an account of rites, which he sent to Charlemagne.[19] However, Susan Keefe has shown that at best, if authored by Odilbert, it gives the Roman and not the peculiarly Milanese rite (it has an episcopal hand-laying, but no *pedilavium*) but that most probably a Carolingian compiler fabricated Odilbert's name.[20]

However, amongst the many baptismal commentaries produced in the Carolingian period in response to Charlemagne's questionnaire, H. Boone Porter drew attention to that written by Maxentius, Archbishop of Aquileia (811–*c*. 826), which witnesses to a local use rather than the Roman use.[21] Porter noted the exposition of the Creed, borrowed from an *Ordo* of Aquileia attributed to Lupsus; it omits an answer to Charlemagne's question 'Why the nose is touched?' because his rite knew an anointing of the nose and ears with oil rather than spittle as in the Roman usage. Maxentius also attributed to the single post-baptismal anointing the 'fullest infusion of the Holy Spirit'. Porter pointed out that he speaks of the Creed after the baptism, anointing and robing, in the place where the *pedilavium* is to be found in the Milanese usage. Porter suggested that, since in Ambrose the *pedilavium* was described as a profession of faith, Maxentius was using irony at this point, describing the Creed rather than the *pedilavium* to disguise the fact that his rite differed from the Roman usage.

The tenth-century *Ambrosian Manual* provides two baptismal orders.[22] The first provides for the handing-in of names on the second Sunday of Lent, with scrutinies on Saturdays, and the delivery of the Creed on the day before Palm Sunday. On the second Sunday of Lent provision is made for the blessing of ashes and renunciation of the devil. The renunciation is repeated on two other Saturdays, and was twofold, as in the time of Ambrose. The blessing of the font has the first Gelasian collect and another prayer asking that God will grant remission of sins in 'this healthful laver and give sanctification to the waters'. A lengthy prayer follows, asking for pardon of sins, and the celebrant breathes on the water and exorcizes it. Then, in a prayer beginning 'O celestial flood, be sanctified by the Word of God', he addresses the water using Old Testament allusions and types, and asks in rather sexist and anti-sexual words for the restoration of the innocence of Adam 'which his wife let go, which cruel incontinence spoiled'. It asks for renewal in the 'mystic waters'. After a threefold credal interrogatory with litany (rather confusing, since the unit is repeated three times), the candidates are baptized, and the presbyter signs them with chrism, using the same formula as found in the Roman *Gelasian* rite. The bishop washes the feet of the infants. A prayer is provided after the return to the font.

[19] Fisher, *Christian Initiation*, pp. 39ff.

[20] Susan Ann Keefe, 'The Claim of Authorship in Carolingian Baptismal Expositions: The Case of Odilbert of Milan', in *Fälschungen im Mittelalter: Internationaler Kongress der Monuementa Germaniae Historica, München 16–19 September 1986*, Hahnsche Buchhandlung, Hannover, 1988, pp. 385–401.

[21] H. Boone Porter, 'Maxentius of Aquileia and the North Italian Baptismal Rites', *Ephemerides Liturgicae* 69 (1955), 3–8.

[22] Whitaker/Johnson, *DBL*, pp. 183ff.

The second order begins with the making of a catechumen, and has an exorcism of salt (as in the *Gelasian*), an exorcism of the oil, renunciation, *effeta* and anointing. It also includes a signing with the sign of the cross with formula, and giving of salt. There is also an 'Exorcism of St Ambrose', and then provision for baptism of a sick person.

The *Ordo of Beroldus* gives lengthy details regarding the scrutinies, of which there were three.[23] The candidates were enrolled on the Saturday of Lazarus (fourth Saturday of Lent), and the document describes the giving of the Creed. On Holy Saturday the archbishop blessed and exorcized the font. There was a threefold credal interrogation, and a threefold baptism with the Matthean formula. The archbishop anointed the heads of the baptized children (the rite assumes that the candidates are children) with the formula 'God the Almighty Father of our Lord Jesus Christ, who has generated you with water and the Holy Ghost', which presumably continued as in the *Ambrosian Manuale* and Roman *Gelasian*. The archbishop then washed their feet, and the mass followed. Fisher concluded that, at least until the twelfth century, to which the *Ordo of Beroldus* belongs

> ... the Milanese rite of Paschal initiation consisted in catechumenate, baptism, unction with chrism for the imparting of the Holy Spirit, *pedilavium*, and the communion of the baptized. In Milan itself the whole rite was presided over by a bishop, often, we may suppose, by the archbishop himself.[24]

However, there is nothing in the formulae to link the chrism with the Holy Spirit. It is significant, though, that despite the fact that Milan was so close to Rome and used some of the Roman (*Gelasian*) prayers, there is no hint of the laying-on of hands and formula of the sevenfold gift of the Holy Spirit.

Gaul and the Frankish Lands

There are three major liturgical sources for Gaul and the Frankish lands: the *Missale Gothicum*, *c.* seventh century, the *Missale Gallicanum Vetus*, *c.* 700, and the *Bobbio Missal* of the eighth century. In addition we have a number of ninth-century commentaries, written partly in response to the series of questions posed by Charlemagne. As a result of Charlemagne's desire to promote liturgical uniformity throughout his kingdom according to the use of Rome, we have the *Hadrianum Sacramentary*. The cumulative evidence suggests a diversity of practice, which partly explains Charlemagne's concern to achieve uniformity.

J.D.C. Fisher summarized the main liturgical texts as follows:

> The Gallican rite, as described in the books which are here being considered, consisted in (i) catechumenate, about which little is said, (ii) baptism, (iii) anointing

---

[23] Ibid., pp. 198ff.
[24] Fisher, *Christian Initiation: Baptism in the Medieval West*, p. 45.

of the candidates, (iv) *pedilavium*, (v) vesting in white robes,(vi) communion at the mass of the Paschal vigil. These rites have an obvious resemblance with the Milanese rite after it had lost the 'spiritual seal' of Ambrose.[25]

In the *Missale Gothicum,* the provisions for making a Christian ask first for a blessing on the child, with reference to Matthew 19:14, and that they be 'signed with the sign of your cross', and so counted worthy to receive baptism.[26] Collects, which in fact are formulae, were provided for the signing, and the second refers to eyes, ears, nose and mouth. An introduction to the blessing of the fonts (also called a collect) speaks of new voyagers embarking and plying their trade. A very short prayer asks that the angel of blessing may descend on the waters, so that those over whom the water is poured may receive remission of sins and, being born of water and Holy Spirit, may serve God faithfully. A *contestatio* (proper preface for the eucharistic prayer, but here the first section of the blessing of the water), prays:

> Look down, O Lord, upon these waters which are made ready to blot out men's sins; may the angel of your goodness be present in these sacred fonts, to wash away the stains of the former life and to sanctify a little dwelling for you: so that the souls of them that are reborn may flourish unto eternal life and may truly be renewed by the newness of baptism. O Lord our God, bless this creature of water, may your power descend upon it, pour down from on high your Holy Spirit the Comforter, the Angel of truth, sanctify O Lord the waves of this flood as thou didst sanctify the stream of Jordan, so that all who go down into this font in the Name of the Father and the Son and the Holy Spirit shall be counted worthy to receive pardon of their sins and the infusion of the Holy Spirit …[27]

The celebrant exorcized the water and commanded wickedness to give place to the Holy Spirit, so that the font may be a laver of the baptism of regeneration for the remission of sins. He then breathed on the water and poured in chrism in the form of a cross. Baptism was in the Matthean formula with the words 'unto the remission of sins, that you may have eternal life'. The chrismation speaks of the chrism being 'the garment of immortality' which Jesus received, which suggest a christological meaning bound up with a new humanity and akin to the Syrian idea of the robe of glory. Then came the washing of feet, and putting on a white robe, and the collect (an explanation) refers to those who have been regenerated with water and the Holy Spirit. There is thus only a single post-baptismal chrismation, and the formula articulates no association of the Spirit with the chrism.

In the 'Mass for the Vigil of the Pascha', the *Immolatio* (*contestatio,* and here a proper preface for the eucharistic prayer) describes this as the night in which God offers pardon to sinner, makes new men from old, restores worn-out old men as full-grown infants, and brings new creations from the font. There is no provision for an extra episcopal hand-laying and chrismation.

---

25 Ibid., p. 48.

26 Whitaker/Johnson, *DBL*, pp. 258ff.

27 Ibid., p. 260.

The *Bobbio Missal*'s provisions for baptism reproduce some material found in the *Gelasian*, but still other material has parallels with the *Ambrosian Manual*.[28] Thus, the section, 'At the Creed for the Opening of the Ears of the Elect', contains the exhortation and explanations of the Gospel found in the *Gelasian* (33–41). But there follows an explanation of the Creed which has no parallel in the Roman book. The 'Order for Making a Christian' is similar to that found in the *Missale Gothicum*, with collects and signing with the cross and breathing on the mouth. The latter is enacted with the formula '*N*, receive the Holy Spirit, may you guard him in your heart.' [29]

The exorcism of the water which begins the 'Order of Baptism' is based on the *Gelasian*, as is the first part of the blessing of the font. What appears to be a second prayer of blessing asks that the Holy Spirit be sent down on the water so that those baptized may be purified and regenerated and received into the number of the saints. Chrism is poured in the sign of the cross. There is then an exorcism for a man before baptism, the *effeta*, and anointing with the formula, 'I anoint you with sanctified oil, as Samuel anointed David to be king and prophet', and a formula addressing the oil, asking it to do its work.[30] A threefold renunciation of Satan comes next, followed by a threefold interrogatory creed, and baptism is in the threefold Matthean formula, to which is added 'who have one substance, that you may have a part with the saints in everlasting life'.[31] Chrism is poured on the brow, followed by the giving of a white garment and washing the feet.

Another document connected with this tradition is the *Expositio Antiquae Liturgiae Gallicanae*, under the name of St Germanus of Paris.[32] This document explains some of the ceremonial and ritual of baptism, but particularly the blessing of chrism. Oil is said to be 'indicating the grace of the Holy Spirit'. The document explains that the Creed is delivered to the *competentes,* and that when the priest comes to deliver the Creed

> ... soft feather cushions and white towels are spread out over the screen around the choir, vessels of chrism and oil are poured into the chalices for blessing, and the book of the Holy Gospel, covered in red: for the people as they approach the faith may be likened to an infant.[33]

These rites, according to Gabrielle Winkler, testify to the fact that in the northern part of Gaul and possibly from the north-western region of the Alps, 'there were communities outside of Rome which practiced only one post-baptismal anointing. This anointing was done apparently by either the bishop, if he was present, or by a presbyter'.[34]

---

[28] Ibid., pp. 265ff.

[29] Ibid., p. 270.

[30] Ibid., p. 272.

[31] Ibid., p. 273.

[32] E.C. Ratcliff (ed.), *Expositio Antiquae Liturgiae Gallicanae*, Henry Bradshaw Society, London, 1971; Text: Whitaker/Johnson, *DBL*, pp. 263ff.

[33] Whitaker/Johnson, *DBL*, p. 264.

[34] Gabriele Winkler, 'Confirmation or Chrismation? A Study in Comparative Liturgy', in *LWSS*, p. 208, though there is no need to conclude that this was in turn derived from Syria.

We have already noted that one of the policies of Charlemagne was to have more liturgical uniformity throughout his kingdom, and that this should be achieved by the use of the Roman rite. It was part of a wider policy of control. Of that policy Susan Keefe writes:

> The rite of baptism played a crucial role in the Carolingian world with its great divide between the baptized and the unbaptized: the faithful and the infidels. Baptism established one's identity in society and membership in the church ... Charlemagne took advantage of baptism as an exchange of lords. The name acquired by baptism, 'fidelis', was the name for a vassal. In one of the more infamous acts of Christian history, he forced-baptized people he conquered in order that they would keep the fealty owed him by their act of submission.[35]

But this policy was also part of a renaissance of Christian education. In 811 Charlemagne addressed to his bishops a questionnaire asking after the manner in which they administered baptism. Subsequently, and as a response to the questionnaire, a whole genre of baptismal instructions were produced. Susan Keefe identifies three models. First, a whole number of these texts were based upon the *Ordo of Alcuin*, which may well have been written by Alcuin himself, *c.* 789. Keefe paraphrases it thus:[36]

1 (*caticuminus et renuntiatio*) First a pagan coming to baptism becomes a catechumen so that he renounces the evil spirit and all his damning pomps.

2 (*exsufflatio*) He is also breathed upon so that, with the devil having fled, an entrance is prepared for Christ our God.

3 (*exorcismus*) The evil spirit is exorcised, that is, conjured, so that he goes out and departs, giving place to the true God.

4 (*sal*) The catechumen receives salt so that his filthy and dissolute sins are cleansed with salt, the divine gift of wisdom.

5 (*traditio symboli*) Then the faith of the Apostle's Creed is delivered to him so that the home, empty and abandoned by its former inhabitant, is decorated with the faith, and a dwelling place is prepared for God.

6 (*scrutinia*) Next, scrutinies are done so that he is examined often whether, after the renunciation of Satan, he has fixed the sacred words of the given faith deeply in his heart.

7 (*nares*) His nostrils also are touched so that as long as he draws breath he may endure in the received faith.

8 (*pectus*) His breast is also anointed with the same oil so that with the sign of the holy cross an entrance for the devil is closed.

---

[35] Susan A. Keefe, *Water and the Word. Baptism and Education of the Clergy in the Carolingian Empire*, 2 vols, University of Notre Dame Press, Notre Dame, IN, 2002, vol. 1, p. 3. For the importance of fealty and kinship in baptism see Joseph H. Lynch, *Godparents and Kinship in Early Medieval Europe*, Princeton University Press, Princeton, NJ, 1986.

[36] Ibid., pp. 81–2.

9   (*scapulae*) His shoulder blades are also signed so that he is armed on all sides. Also in the anointing of the breast and shoulder blades firmness of faith and perseverance in good works is signified.

10   (*trina mersio*) And thus in the name of the Holy Trinity with a triple immersion he is baptized. And rightly man, who was made in the image of the Holy Trinity, is renewed to the same image through the invocation of the Holy Trinity; and who died through the third grade of sin, that is, by deed, raised three times from the font through grace rises to life.

11   (*alba vestimenta*) Then he is dressed in white vestments because of the joy of his rebirth, his chastity of life, and his angelic beauty.

12   (*caput, mysticum velamen*) Then his head is anointed with sacred chrism and covered with a mystic veil so that he realizes by this diadem that he bears the dignity of the kingdom and the priesthood, as the Apostles said: 'You are a royal and priestly people, offering yourselves to the living God, a holy sacrifice pleasing to Him.'

13   (*corpus et sanguis domini*) Thus he is confirmed with the Lord's Body and Blood so that he is a member of that One who suffered for him and rose.

14   (*impositio manus a summo sacerdote*) Finally, he receives the sevenfold gift of the Holy Spirit through the imposition of the bishop's hand, so that he is strengthened through the Holy Spirit to preach to others, who through grace in baptism was bestowed with eternal life.

Susan Keefe notes that, although this is based on John the Deacon, and has many elements which are shared with the Roman usage, it departs from it in a number of ways. The renunciation seems to come at the beginning; there is an exsufflation with an exorcism before the salt; the Apostles' Creed rather than the Nicene is given; the scrutinies come after the delivery of the creed to test its retention; there is no touching the ears but only the nose; there may be a double anointing of the breast and back; white garments are put on before the head is anointed, and episcopal hand-laying comes after the eucharist.[37] The result is hybrid, and it formed the basis for a whole number of the Carolingian baptismal instructions.

A second model is that based directly on the questionnaire Charlemagne sent to his archbishops. The questionnaire itself was not designed to promote unity, but to promote education of the clergy. It had used something similar to the *Ordo of Alcuin*. Instructions such as that written by Archbishop Magnus of Sens responded to the order of the questions in the questionnaire.[38]

A third model was Hrabanus Maurus' baptismal instruction in his *De institione clericorum*. Chapters XXV–XXX describe an *Ordo* of baptism in which all the ceremonies seem now to be administered at one time. These chapters formed the

---

[37] Ibid., p. 83.
[38] Ibid., p. 87ff.

basis of several of the instructions, some simply extracting the chapters, and some elaborating on them.[39] The chapters also give an outline of ceremonies which are included in the Mainz *Romano-Germanic Pontifical*. Keefe points out that, while most approximate to the Roman usage, there are many variations which perhaps reflected local conditions. However, some 'barely stifle, or openly teach, non-Roman forms of baptism'.[40]

Charlemagne's request from Pope Hadrian for a book giving the Roman rite resulted in the *Hadrianum* – a Gregorian sacramentary from Rome, with a Supplement compiled probably by Benedict of Aniene. The resulting book exercised considerable influence throughout the Carolingian empire. In this sacramentary we find no mention of the scrutinies, which have been compressed into a unitary rite on Easter Eve preceding the actual baptism. Amongst minor additions, we find the first appearance in the Roman rite of requesting and giving the child's name immediately prior to the credal interrogations. There is also development in the Ordines, or instructions for celebrating liturgy.[41] In *Ordo* XV we find a baptismal rite for an Epiphany Vigil. *Ordo* XXVIII contains a complete baptismal rite. Here the pre-baptismal anointing has a formula: 'I anoint you with the oil of sanctification in Jesus Christ our Lord as a propitiation to eternal life.' This seems to be a move away from an exorcistic meaning to a more salvific meaning for the anointing.

The directive Ordines came to be combined with material from sacramentaries. One such product of this combination was the *Romano-Germanic Pontifical* of Mainz, *c.* 950/62,[42] which in turn influenced many subsequent books in the later medieval period. As already noted, the provisions for baptism are akin to those outlined by Hrabanus Maurus.[43] The once-staged rites of the *Gelasian Sacramentary*, spread over a period of time, are now telescoped into one occasion. Infants are brought to the church and the males stand on the right, females on the left. The renunciations and giving of the Creed follow, and then exorcism and giving of salt, with separate prayers for males and females. Then come exorcisms of Satan, with further renunciations, signing with the sign of the cross, and anointing with the oil of exorcism. The older use of oil of exorcism is retained alongside the formula found in *Ordo* XXVIII.

The candidates then go to the font for the blessing and exorcism of the water. The priest signs the sign of the cross in the water three times during the blessing, and makes various other ceremonial gestures, including dipping the (Paschal) candle into the font as a gesture of fecundity. Candidates are baptized with the Matthean formula,

---

[39] Ibid., pp. 94ff.

[40] Ibid., p. 99.

[41] See Cyrille Vogel, *Medieval Liturgy. An Introduction to the Sources*, Pastoral Press, Washington, DC, 1986.

[42] Cyrille Vogel (ed.), *Le Pontifical Romano-Germanique Du Dixième Siècle*, 3 vols, Biblioteca Apostolica Vaticana, Vatican City, 1963–72.

[43] Ibid., vol. 2, pp. 155ff.

chrismated and clothed. The bishop then lays hands on the baptized and says the prayer for the sevenfold gifts of the Spirit, and anoints them saying, 'I confirm (*confirmo te*) you in the Name of the Father, and of the Son and of the Holy Spirit.' The rite presupposes infants, and because it is a Pontifical, it assumes the episcopal completion of the rite. But where baptisms took place without a bishop, the older Gallican anointing by the presbyter as completion of the rite was no longer allowed. The Roman practice of insisting on episcopal completion enabled the episcopal part to become separated and postponed until a bishop was present. The older Gallican single anointing gave way to the Roman usage.

Spain

Our main evidence for the Mozarabic, or Visigothic, rite of Spain comes from Martin of Braga, Ildephonse of Toledo, and Isidore of Seville in the seventh century, and the *Liber Ordinum*.[44] Martin came to Braga from Tours at the request of the Suevic king. In addition to his writings, he arranged councils in Braga in 561 and 572. From his writings we learn of the catechumenate, the handing-over of the Creed, the use of sackcloth, the renunciation, and the chrism which is associated with the Spirit.[45] Martin also entered into controversy with a neighbour, Boniface, over the number of immersions. Some Christians in Spain used a single immersion to distinguish themselves from the Arians who were using the inherited triple immersion.[46]

Isidore of Seville wrote in the seventh century, and in his *Ecclesiasticis Officiis* described the rites associated with baptism. He notes that there are catechumens who become *competentes* and then are baptized. The catechumens are exorcized, receive salt and are anointed, which Isidore linked to Matthew 17:18. The giving of the salt he explained as being

> ... instituted by our forefathers, so that by tasting it they receive a seasoning of wisdom, and may not stray in folly from the flavour of Christ; that they may not be foolish and look backward, as did Lot's wife, lest giving a bad example they may themselves remain to infect others.[47]

Isidore noted that catechumens proceed to being competents, who in addition to listening, are also catechized, and receive the Creed. The font is 'the source of all graces', and he stressed that one must be dipped into the sacrament, and that each

---

[44] See T.C. Akeley, *Christian Initiation in Spain c.300–1100*, Darton, Longman and Todd, London, 1967; Whitaker/Johnson, *DBL*, pp. 164ff.

[45] Akeley, *Christian Initiation*, pp. 46–7.

[46] Ibid., p. 47. See Rowan Williams, 'Baptism and the Arian Controversy', in Michael R. Barnes and Daniel H. Williams (eds), *Arianism After Arius*, T & T Clark, Edinburgh, 1993, pp. 149–80; Maurice Wiles, 'Triple and Single Immersion: Baptism in the Arian Controversy', *Studia Patristica* 30, Peeters, Leuven (1997), 337–49.

[47] Whitaker/Johnson, *DBL*, p. 159.

person of the Trinity must be named. Isidore also made much of the seven steps of the font and their meaning. He linked anointing to kingship and priesthood, with 1 Peter 2:9 as a scriptural source. The laying-on of hands is linked with the giving of the Spirit through the hands of the bishop, and here Isidore quotes Acts 19:2–8 and 8:14–17.

Ildephonse explained the scrutiny and the exorcisms, and noted that 'In some places, so it is reported, they receive salt, signifying as it were the seasoning of wisdom.'[48] He is of the opinion that this has no foundation in Scripture, and so departs from Isidore in this matter. It may be a case of differing local customs, or perhaps that Isidore's rites reflect Roman influence. In Ildephonse's description, the *effeta* included, for the young, being led over a carpet of goatskin in token of repentance. The Creed was given to the competents on the day of their anointing, and 'returned' on Maundy Thursday. Like Isidore, Ildephonse says that the font has seven steps, and he uses similar words – down three for renunciation, up three for the Father, Son and Spirit, with the seventh also the fourth, the Son of Man, as in Daniel 3:15. Ildephonse noted that both triple and single immersion and sprinkling were practised, triple signifying the three days in the tomb, and single standing for the one godhead.

Susan Keefe has pointed out that at least one text amongst the many Carolingian baptismal instructions witnesses to the Spanish usage.[49] It is an anonymous text, and sets out four stages of coming to the faith – being first a catechumen, then a competent, a *fidelis*, and finally a Christian. This description seems to have been taken from the *Commentary on the Apocalypse*, c. 776, by the Spanish monk Beatus of Liebana. The first event he associates with catechumens is the recitation of the Creed, and he indicates that a catechumen is anointed before becoming a competent. As Keefe noted, the day of delivery of the Creed, Palm Sunday, essentially marked the beginning of the catechumenate in Spain, and that is why the author associated the Creed with the beginning of the catechumenate.[50] More Spanish features include allowance for either a single or a triple immersion, and the single post-baptismal anointing, of which the writer says, 'Through the priest's imposition of hands the Holy Spirit invoked upon him flows down … .'[51] The chrismation is followed immediately by the imposition of hands by the priest. Yet the text also allows for the ceremony of the giving of salt, which, according to Ildephonse, was observed in some places in Spain, but not everywhere. Keefe thus concludes that this text reflects a time (the beginning of the ninth century) when the liturgy was open to Romanization.[52]

The *Liber Ordinum*, an eleventh-century manuscript, provides 'An Order of Baptism for Occasional Use', with an exorcism, signing and naming, a further exorcism, and anointing with blessed oil on the mouth and ears with the *effeta*.[53] The priest then lays

---

[48] Ibid., p. 162.

[49] Keefe, *Water and the Word*, pp. 100ff.

[50] Ibid., p. 102.

[51] Ibid., p. 103.

[52] Ibid., p. 105.

[53] Whitaker/Johnson, *DBL*, pp. 164ff. Cf. Akeley, *Christian Initiation*, pp. 201ff., which is composed

hands upon the candidate and recites a *cento* blessing compiled from Luke 3, 1 John 1, and Psalm 45. After the blessing, the Creed is handed over. The font is then exorcised and blessed with a prayer, the wording of which is very similar to much in the *Ambrosian Manual*. God is asked to 'breathe kindly upon these waters mixed with the oil of sanctification' and 'bless them with your power, and from your throne pour upon them the grace of holiness'. A threefold renunciation follows and, after the celebrant asks the candidate's name, a brief threefold credal confession. Baptism is with the Matthean formula with 'that you may have eternal life'. The infant is clothed and anointed by the priest, and then the priest lays hands on the child and says:

> O God, who in this sacrament wherein men are reborn you send your Holy Spirit upon water, in such fashion that the Creator commands his creature and by its office cleanses those who are washed thereby, whom you would perfect (*confirmaret*) with your bountiful gift; you who by water would take away the stain of sin and by your own self would complete the grace of the sacrament, and therefore has commanded that the unction of chrism shall follow the ministration of baptism: we therefore pay and ask you, O Lord, following your commandments according as we are able, to pour your Holy Spirit upon these your servants. Amen.
>
> *The Spirit of wisdom and understanding.* Amen.
> *The Spirit of counsel and might.* Amen.
> *The Spirit of knowledge and godliness.* Amen.
>
> Fill them, both men and women, with the *spirit of your fear*, who inspires men to follow your saving commandment and breathes upon them a heavenly gift. And so grant that being strengthened in the Name of the Trinity, they may by this chrism be accounted worthy to become Christ's, and by the power of Christ to become Christians.

A veil is set over the heads of the infants, and they are communicated. There is also a blessing over the white robes for the third day after baptism, and a separate provision for the delivery of the Creed on Palm Sunday.

In Spain, then, we find a ritual pattern similar to that found in Milan and in some parts of Gaul, namely, a truncated catechumenate, and a single presbyteral anointing and hand-laying following baptism.

The Celtic and Anglo-Saxon Rites

The liturgical evidence for the Romano-British Church is sparse and elusive, but the Church seems to have been closely allied with the Church in Gaul. At some point in the fifth century, because of the successful incursions of the pagan Anglo-Saxons, the British Church became isolated from the continental churches, but its members turned to their fellow Christians in Ireland. According to Bede, when St Augustine arrived

---

from a variety of manuscripts and texts, to give a progression from Lent 1 until the blessing of the white robes.

as missionary to the Anglo-Saxons and encountered the British bishops, he asked them to 'fulfil the ministry of Baptism through which we are born again to God, according to the custom of the holy Roman Apostolic Church'.[54]

There has been considerable speculation over what this 'fulfil'or 'completion' might be, particularly about the force of *'conpleatis'*, complete. Conybeare was of the opinion that the British either did not use the three names of the Trinity, or used a single immersion.[55] Margaret Pepperdene argued that it more likely refers to an omission of any post-baptismal anointing.[56] She suggested that if the British followed early Gallican practice, there would have been a single presbyteral post-baptismal anointing and laying-on of hands, and quite possibly a single immersion, as with later practices in Milan and Spain. However, these practices would hardly have been regarded as invalid. She suggests that, as with later Irish practice, the post-baptismal anointing was omitted because of the shortage of available oil at a time when both British and Irish churches were isolated from the continental Church, and when trade between the islands and the source of supply on the continent was disrupted by political and economic upheavals within the old Roman Empire.[57] However, it could equally mean that Augustine expected the Roman usage of episcopal chrismation and hand-laying rather than the presbyteral practice of the Gallican and British rite.

Equally little is known of the Irish practice. Sybil McKillop pointed to a number of references in the *Confessio* and *Epistola ad Coroticum* of Patrick (which might well reflect British usage too), to show that Patrick knew of baptism in the Lord, anointing of the forehead with chrism, a completion (*in Christo confirmavi*) and robing in white.[58] Patrick also grounds baptism in Matthew 28:19, and makes use of the Pauline imagery of Romans 6:3. However, McKillop's supposed reconstruction to include exorcism, renunciation, and consecration of the water, while probable, goes beyond the evidence in Patrick's writings.[59]

The only extant Irish baptismal rite is the one found in the *Stowe Missal*, which dates from the eighth century. The text of the baptismal rites are strongly Roman as in the *Gelasian*.[60] There are, however, no indications of time, and so no preference for Easter baptism, and the making of a catechumen takes place immediately before the baptism. The few rubrics seem to imply adults, although two rubrics, one in Irish and one in Latin, indicate that the rite was also used for young children. Two things are particularly noteworthy. There is a single anointing after baptism, with formulae

---

[54] Bede, *Historia Ecclesiastica* 2.2, <http://www.ccel.org/ccel/bede/history.v.ii.ii.html>.

[55] F.C. Conybeare, 'The Character of the Heresy of the Early British Church', pp. 84–117.

[56] Margaret Pepperdene, 'Baptism in the early British and Irish Churches', *Irish Theological Quarterly* 22 (1955), 110–23.

[57] Ibid., p. 117.

[58] Sybil McKillop, 'A Romano-British Baptismal Liturgy?,' in Susan M. Pearce (ed.), *The Early Church in Western Britain and Ireland,* BAR British Series 102 (1982), pp. 35–48.

[59] See ibid., p. 40.

[60] Whitaker/Johnson, *DLB*, pp. 274ff.

very similar to that found in the *Bobbio*, and the *pedilavium* comes after the clothing with a white robe. In other words, the ritual pattern is that of Gaul, not Rome.

Since the mission to Anglo-Saxon Briton came directly from Rome, it is logical to infer that the liturgical books reflect Roman usage. Little documentary evidence remains from the seventh or eighth centuries; our sources for Anglo-Saxon baptismal rites are tenth and eleventh century, and show the influence of the *Hadrianum*.[61] The *Leofric Missal* is named after Bishop Leofric (1050–72), though the baptismal rite is a portion of the manuscript which dates from the tenth century. The *Missal of Robert of Jumieges*, Bishop of London (1044–50) and Archbishop of Canterbury (1050–52) is eleventh century and, as in the *Stowe Missal* rite, the making of a catechumen is followed immediately by the blessing of the font and baptism. The *Winchcombe Sacramentary* was copied in the last part of the tenth century, and taken to Fleury in France in the eleventh century.[62] It too assumes a single occasion for the ritual, and in this rite the candidate receives a lighted candle. The renunciation has been moved from the *effeta* to a position directly preceding the Creed. Two other sources are unpublished manuscripts in Corpus Christi College, Cambridge. The first is a copy of the *Romano-Germanic Pontifical*, and contains nothing new.

The second, known as the *Red Book of Darley*, is more interesting.[63] In this manuscript, the *effeta* and the renunciation have been moved to immediately precede the Creed, and the rite provides a lengthy litany for the procession to the font. Of far greater interest is that many of the rubrics are in Anglo-Saxon; there is nothing really comparable in any other country to this use of the vernacular until much later in the Middle Ages.[64] So, for example,

> Do nu rode tacn [m]id þinum ðuman on ðæs cildes forhe[afod.] *and* cweð
> (Now make a sign of the cross with your thumb on the child's forehead and say).[65]

> cweð þon*ne* letanias ær þu fanthalgige
> (Then he says litanies before the holy font)[66]

The celebrant is carefully guided through the rite with directions as to actions over males or females, reciting the Creed and Lord's Prayer, and making the sign of the cross on the child's 'strong' hand. There are intricate instructions for ritual acts during

---

[61] Sarah Larratt Keefer, 'Manuals', in Richard W. Pfaff (ed.), *The Liturgical Books of Anglo-Saxon England*, Old English Newsletter Subsidia 23, Medieval Institute Publications, Western Michigan University, Kalamazoo, MI, 1995, pp. 99–109. M. Bradford Bedingfield, *The Dramatic Liturgy of Anglo-Saxon England*, The Boydell Press, Woodbridge, 2002, pp. 171–90.

[62] Anselme Davril (ed.), *The Winchcombe Sacramentary*, Henry Bradshaw Society, London, 1995.

[63] Christopher Hohler, 'The Red Book of Darley', *Nordiskt Kollokvium II. 1. Latinsk Liturgiforskning*, Stockholm University, 1972, pp. 39–47.

[64] Ibid., p. 42. R.I. Page, 'Old English Liturgical Rubrics in Corpus Christi College, Cambridge, MS 422', *Anglia. Zeitschrift für Englische Philologie* 96 (1978), 149–58.

[65] Page, 'Old English Liturgical Rubrics', p. 151, No. 2. The rubrics are faded, but Page managed to retrieve them using ultra-violet light.

[66] Ibid., No. 20, p. 152.

the blessing of the font, including dividing the water with the sign of the cross three times, blowing on the water three times, dripping a sign of the cross with candle wax, and mixing oil in the water. Godparents are named as such and have a considerable role in the rite. Thus for the renunciation:

> 'Ahsi her þ[æ]s cild[e]s [naman] þonne secge se godfæder þ[æ]s cildes naman þonne cweðe.'
> *Abrenuntias satane*
> (Here he asks the child's name, then the godfather says the child's name, then he says:
> Do you renounce Satan?)
>
> þa godfæderas
> *Abrenuntio*
> (The godfather[s]: I renounce)
>
> þon*ne* cweþe se preost
> *Et omnibus operibus eius*
> (Then the priest says: And all his works?)
>
> Don*ne* cw þe se godfæd*er*.
> *Abrenuntio*
> (Then the godfather says, I renounce)[67]

While it is assumed that infants were originally sponsored by their parents, the participation of biological parents was gradually abandoned in favour of having spiritual parents for a spiritual birth. In sixth and seventh-century Byzantium, Italy and Frankish Gaul, biological parents and the sponsors of their children came to be regarded as related to one another in spiritual kinship through the child. In *c.* 840 the Frankish scholar Walafrid Strabo explained the matter thus:

> A father or mother must not receive their own offspring [in baptism], so that there may be a distinction between spiritual and carnal generation. If by chance that [sponsorship] happens, they who have taken the spiritual bond of coparenthood in their common child will not henceforth have the sharing of carnal intercourse.[68]

As we have noted with Charlemagne and fealty, baptismal sponsorship or godparents involved not only friendship but implied also strong social bonds of patronage and the loyalty of kinship. The Frankish and Roman practices were introduced to the Anglo-Saxons, but Joseph Lynch has argued that in Anglo-Saxon England the prohibition of marriage between spiritual kin was not introduced until the time of Wulfstan of York (996–1023).[69]

Godparents could be adopted at any of three stages of the initiation, during the catechumenate, baptism, or confirmation – or all of them. Indeed, in Old English

---

[67] Ibid., p. 153.

[68] Walafrid Strabo, *Libellus de exordiis et incrementis quarundam in observationibis ecclesiae*, c. 27, in Joseph H. Lynch, *Christianizing Kinship. Ritual Sponsorship in Anglo-Saxon England*, Cornell University Press, Ithaca, NY and London, 1998, p. 17.

[69] See Lynch, *Christianizing Kinship*.

cristnen meant to be made a catechumen, but as the rites themselves coalesced into one, the term *cristnen* came to mean naming in baptism. Every baptism created a second father or mother for every infant, a *godfæder* or a *godmodor*.[70] In the *Red Book of Darley*, a rubric directs that the priest puts the infant in the water, but it is the godfather who takes it out of the water – a dramatic symbol of spiritual ownership of the newborn from the womb of the font.

It is possible to glean something of how baptism was understood in the Anglo-Saxon Church from some of the homilies – those of the Venerable Bede (673–735), and in the Anglo-Saxon language, the *Vercelli Homilies* (early tenth century) and those of Aelfric (c. 955–1020) and Wulfstan (d.1023).

In his 'Homily on the Gospels for Advent', on Mark 1:4–8, Bede stresses that baptism brings forgiveness of sins. Speaking of John the Baptist he says:

> Now he was baptizing with a baptism of repentance for the confession and correction of sins, and he was preaching a future baptism of repentance in Christ for the forgiveness of sins. Only in this baptism [of Christ] is the forgiveness of sins granted to us.[71]

This purification of baptism is needed, and is prefigured in the washing of the disciples' feet, and without it we cannot arrive at fellowship with Christ.[72] Elsewhere, in Luke 2:21, Bede links the need for forgiveness with Adam. Speaking of circumcision, he says:

> That is, because Adam by his transgression went against the pact of life given to human beings in paradise, and in him all sinned, [a person] will vanish from the society of saints if he is not aided by a saving remedy. Both purifications, namely that of circumcision under the law and that of baptism under the gospel, were provided as graces for taking away the first transgression.[73]

Through the grace of baptism human beings can be 'changed from sons of the devil into sons of God'.[74] Baptism extinguishes the flaming sword which guards paradise, but this extinguishing takes place as a result of Christ's own baptism.[75] Of this Bede explained:

> He came to be baptized in water, though he was the maker of water, so that to us, who were conceived in iniquity and brought to life in moral faults, he might suggest the mystery of the second nativity, celebrated through water and the Spirit, that we are to try to reach. He deigned to be washed in the waters of the Jordan although he was clean of all stains, so that he might sanctify the flowing of water for the washing away of the stains of all our wicked deeds.[76]

---

[70] For full discussion, including the difference between godparents and co-parents, see ibid.

[71] Bede the Venerable, *Homilies on the Gospels*, Book 1. Advent to Lent, trans. Lawrence T. Martin and David Hurst, Cistercian Publications, Kalamazoo, MI, 1991, p. 1.

[72] Ibid., Book 2. Lent to the Dedication of the Church, Homily II.5, p. 46.

[73] Ibid., Homily I.11, p. 105.

[74] Ibid., Homily I.12 (Epiphany), p. 119.

[75] Ibid., p. 116–17, and p. 120.

[76] Ibid., Homily I.12., p. 114.

Elsewhere Bede reiterated that 'the reason he was baptized with water was so that he might make the flowing of all waters fruitful for the cleansing of our wicked deeds'.[77] Commenting on Jesus healing the deaf and dumb man, Bede explains:

> As to his saying 'Effeta' (that is, 'be opened'), he did this in order to heal the ears which a longstanding deafness had closed up, but which his touch now opened that they might hear. Hence I believe a custom prevailed in the Church that his priests, first among all the elementary stages of consecration [that they perform] for those whom they are preparing to receive the sacrament of baptism, touch their nostrils and ears with saliva from their mouth, while they say, 'Effeta'. By the saliva from their mouth they symbolize the taste of heavenly wisdom to which they are being introduced. By touching the nostrils [they indicate] that, once they have cast aside all harmful delights, they should always embrace only the odor of Christ, about which the Apostle says, *We are the good odor of Christ to God in every place*, and they should remember that, following the example of blessed Job, they are not to speak falsehood with their lips, nor with their tongue meditate on lying, as long as breath is in them and the Spirit of God is in their nostrils. Moreover, by the touching of the ears [they indicate] that, once they have left off listening to wicked tongues, they are to listen to the words of Christ and do them, like the prudent man, who built his house upon a rock.

> Each one of us, dearly beloved brothers, who has received the baptism of Christ according to the sacred rites, has been consecrated in this way. All who are going to receive this healing and saving bath according to the sacred rites, either at the approaching time of Easter, or at some other time, will be consecrated in this way.[78]

Baptism is of course in the triune name, and Bede stressed that the whole Trinity was present at Christ's baptism.[79] The result is spiritual regeneration:

> We see the one being baptized descend into the font, we see him being immersed, we see him come up out of the water; but what is being done in that washing of regeneration cannot be seen. Only the piety of the faithful knows that a sinner descends into the font, and a purified person comes up; that a child of death descends, and a child of the resurrection comes up; that a child of original sin descends, and a child of God comes up. Only the Church, a mother who gives birth, knows these things; otherwise, to the eyes of the foolish, the person seems to come forth from the font just as he went in, and the entire action seems to be a game … What is born of the Spirit is spirit, because the person who is regenerated invisibly of water and the Spirit is changed into a new human being, and from being fleshly he becomes spiritual.[80]

Bede saw baptism as the preparation for the Spirit. On the feast of Pentecost he wrote that each year the mysteries of baptism are celebrated, 'and as a result a venerable temple is made ready for the coming of the Holy Spirit upon those who believe and

---

[77] Ibid., Homily I.7, p. 71.

[78] Ibid., Homily II.6, p. 54.

[79] Ibid., Homily I.12, p. 118.

[80] Ibid., Homily II.18, p. 181.

are cleansed at the salvation-bearing baptismal font'.[81] Christ alone is the one who baptizes with the Holy Spirit, 'since he bestowed the Spirit on us and produces virtues in us'.[82] Noah's ark is a type of the Church, and the flood is our baptism, and the olive branch which the dove brought is a type of the anointing of the Spirit.[83] Through the anointing of the sacred chrism we are signed with the grace of the Holy Spirit.[84]

Vercelli Homily 16 is for the Epiphany, and in treating the baptism of Jesus it also imparts some teaching on baptism. Jesus was baptized because he wished to set an example through Himself for the eternal salvation of mankind.[85] He was baptized to make us 'as children to God Himself'.[86] Jesus submitted to the baptism of John because 'the Lord had intended that the eternal salvation should come to mankind through baptism'. The homilist notes:

> 'Jordan' is called that river which the Savior was baptized in. And it is a very great river, and it has a very strong current, and runs into the sea-flood. And it happened at that time, when the Savior descended into that water, the sea-flood and the entire current turned backwards and the river stood still.[87]

The effect of the baptism of Jesus is summarized thus:

> And He with this signified that there will always be for us through the service of that holy baptism, through a vision spiritually and mystically, open heavens; and He gave all sins forgiveness, if we henceforth are willing to hold and to love that sacrament [i.e., mystery] spiritually, with true belief and with good deeds.[88]

Aelfric alluded to baptism in a number of his homilies. Commenting on the circumcision of Jesus, he noted that this 'token' was as great amongst believers then as baptism is now.[89] In baptism the Church still works miracles, but whereas the Apostles worked bodily miracles, the church works spiritual miracles: 'When the priest christens the child (þonne se preost cristnað þæt cild), then casts he out the devil from that child; for every heathen man is the devil's, but through the holy baptism he is God's, if he observe it.'[90] In a sermon on Pentecost, Aelfric said that by holy baptism our persecutors (the devil) are sunk just like Pharaoh and the Egyptians in the Red Sea.[91] And in a sermon for Christmas, Aelfric noted,

---

81 Ibid., Homily II.17, pp. 170–71.

82 Ibid., Homily I.1, p. 7.

83 Ibid., Homily I.14, p. 140.

84 Ibid., Homily I.12, p. 123.

85 Lewis E. Nicholson (ed.), *The Vercelli Book Homilies*, University Press of America, Lanham, MD and London, 1991, p. 105.

86 Ibid.

87 Ibid., p. 106.

88 Ibid., p. 108.

89 *The Homilies of the Anglo-Saxon Church*, B. Thorpe (ed.), 2 vols, The Aelfric Society, London 1844–6, p. 95.

90 Ibid., p. 305, Sermon on the Lord's Ascension. Here 'christen' seems interchangeable with 'baptism' (*fulluht*).

91 Ibid., p. 313.

> Each man is filled with sins and is born through Adam's transgression, but he is afterwards born to Christ in the holy community, that is in God's church, through baptism. That water washes the body and the Holy Ghost washes the soul from all sins, and the baptized man is then God's son.[92]

Finally, Wulfstan, Archbishop of York, outlined the importance and meaning of some of the ceremonies of the rite in a sermon on baptism. Through good instruction the priest should cause a person to perceive his Lord rightly and reject resolutely the devil's companionship and forsake and shun his evil teaching.[93] The priest must teach the *Pater Noster* and the Creed. Of the catechumenate ritual Wulfstan explains:

> When the priest christens, he breathes on the man, when it is fitting, *in modum crucis*, and then at once, through God's might, the devil becomes exceedingly disheartened, and with the exorcism of the priest the devil is driven out from the human creature who earlier through Adam was undone, and a dwelling-place in the man is immediately provided to the Holy Ghost.[94]

The salt signifies the divine wisdom – here Wulfstan simply explains what the Latin text itself says. He notes, 'just as the body feels the salt's sharpness, so should the soul perceive wisdom's prudence'.[95] Wulfstan's rite was one in which the priest sings the Creed, which 'prepares his heart as a dwelling for God'. The unction is a putting-on of God's shield.[96]

Of the blessing of the font, Wulfstan explains:

> And through the consecrating of the font there the presence of the Son of God Almighty is brought about. And through the breath that the priest breathes on that water when he consecrates the font, the devil is thence driven out. And when the priest places the consecrated taper in the water, then the water is filled entirely with the Holy Spirit. And, quickest to tell, all that the priest does through the holy sacrament visible, the Holy Spirit perfects it all mystically.[97]

The post-baptismal anointing 'signifies the Christian crown which he receives in heaven'.[98]

Towards the end of the sermon Wulfstan turns to explain the meaning of the words *Abrenentio* and *Credo*, and addresses Christian parents:

> Therefore parents among the Christian people have a great need to beget their youngsters for God and to wean them from the devil. Consequently everything which they permit of sin to their children, all that will be contrary to that which

---

[92] Aelfric, Abbot of Eynsham, *Aelfric's Catholic Homilies: The Second Series*, Malcolm Godden (ed.), Oxford University Press, London, 1979, i, p. 6.

[93] *Sermo de Baptismate*, VIIIc in Wulfstan, Archbishop of York, *The Homilies of Wulfstan*, Dorothy Bethurum (ed.), Clarendon Press, Oxford, 1957, pp. 175–84. My gratitude to my colleague Professor Lana Schwebel for translating this homily into modern English.

[94] Ibid., p. 176. 'Cristen' here seems to retain its older meaning.

[95] Ibid., p. 178.

[96] Ibid.

[97] Ibid., p. 179.

[98] Ibid.

they promised to God when they obtained baptism for them. They must suffer stiff punishment according to God's judgement unless they atone for that which they could have done.[99]

He urged that all should learn the Lord's Prayer and Creed at least in English 'unless he is able to do so in Latin'.[100]

In these homilies we find that it is the ritual which is outlined and explained, so that clergy and people understand the meaning of the rite. Though Old Testament types can be utilized, there are no extended reflections in these homilies on original sin and guilt, or grace. The theology is still akin to the classical catechetical homilies – a pragmatic liturgical theology.

Concluding Remarks

Just as the Byzantine rite has influenced the Armenian and Coptic rites, and yet both the latter have retained their distinctive rituals, the same holds true with regard to the Roman usage and the Gallican and Spanish rituals in this period. The Roman ceremonies and liturgical prayers find their way into the Gallican and Spanish liturgical literature. However, the latter retained some distinctive features – particularly with regard to the persistence of the *pedilavium* in the Gallican rite, and the single post-baptismal anointing. In this era infants became the prime candidates for baptism. Needing sponsors, godparents develop as a social network in addition to a spiritual network. The focus of the theology of the rites covered remission of sins, rebirth and the gift of the Spirit. As in the east, the theme of death/resurrection, though not absent, is never prominent. The explanation of baptism was accomplished by explaining and exegeting the stages of the ritual itself. This, as we shall see, began to be abandoned with the rise of Western scholastic methodology.

---

[99] Ibid., p. 182.
[100] Ibid., p. 183.

CHAPTER 7

The Western Rites: The Later Medieval Rites, Technical Theologies and the Tridentine Reform

Local Variations

In the Western tradition from the twelfth century to the sixteenth, we find the disappearance of the 'national' rites such as the Gallican and Spanish rites (other than in Toledo), and the almost universal use of the hybrid forms of the Roman-Germanic ritual. However, there was certainly no one single 'ur-text', though on the whole the prayer formulae and ritual sequence were fairly uniform. Each diocese was able to evolve and maintain its local usages, variants and variables. The advent of printing brought some stability to each diocesan usage, but certainly did not result in a universal uniform text and ritual. This may best be illustrated by Tables 7.1 and 7.2. The first compares the outline of the rites in the twelfth-century Rheinau ritual, the fifteenth-century Constance ritual, and fifteenth-century Magdeburg Agenda, the latter being one of the liturgical sources which would be used by Luther.[1] These texts (chosen for convenience of access), are separated in time and place, but amply illustrate what would be the case in a multiplicity of rituals.[2] What the comparison illustrates is basically common texts, but with differing rubrics, and sometimes a different sequence; for example, the formulae which open the rite, and the prayers surrounding the Gospel reading. It is also notable that Mark 10 is the Gospel reading in Magdeburg and some other German rituals. Some rites opened with a *votum* from Psalm 124, 'Our Help is in the Name of the Lord, who made heaven and earth.'

The second table compares the two principal rites in use in England (though there were also uses of Hereford and Lincoln), which again shows a very uniform text, with minor rubrical and short formulae differences.[3]

---

[1] Gebhard Hürlimann, *Das Rheinauer Rituale*, Universitätsverlag Freiburg Schweiz, 1959; P. Alban Dold, *Die Konstanzer Ritualientexte in ihrer Entwicklung von 1482–1721*, Ascendorff, Münster in Westfalia, 1923; The Magdeburg Agenda, text in J.D.C. Fisher, *Christian Initiation. The Reformation Period,* SPCK, London, 1970.

[2] See a larger number tabulated in Kent Burreson, 'The Saving Flood: The Medieval Origins, Historical Development, and Theological import of the Sixteenth Century Lutheran Baptismal Rites', Doctoral Dissertation, University of Notre Dame, 2002.

[3] A. Jefferies Collins, *Manuale ad usum Percelebris Ecclesie Sarisburiensis,* Henry Bradshaw Society, Chichester, 1960; W.G. Henderson, *Manuale et Processionale ad usum Insignis Ecclesiae Eboracensis*, Surtess Society, London, 1875.

It will be seen from Table 7.2 that there are differences at the beginning regarding asking the name, and the formulae, and the Gospel and 'Be not deceived' are reversed. However, the differences are minimal, and reflect local usage of one rite rather than two separate rites. Of particular interest are the vernacular instructions in the *Sarum Manual*, to which we will return later.

Sacramental Definitions and Teachings

Alongside these rites this period witnesses the rise of scholastic theology, with the development of formal definitions of the sacraments. The word 'sacrament' was used in Latin-speaking Christianity at least from the time of Tertullian, and was given considerable discussion and definition by Augustine. But, as Marcia Colish observed, from the twelfth century onwards, 'there was a felt need, for the first time in the history of the western Christian tradition, for an organized, systematic, general theology of the sacraments'.[4] The definition of a sacrament as a sign of a sacred thing was deemed no longer adequate. Thus we find in the schools of theology treatises on sacraments which quite naturally include baptism. However, where the emphasis in earlier periods was on description and reflection on the ritual process of baptism (even if at times fanciful), there was now a move towards a generic definition of sacraments and a theology of the sacrament of baptism, tied less to the ritual sequence and what the text said, and concerned more with those elements of the rite which could fit the prior definitions of what sacraments are and what they confer. Here we will consider the teachings of Hugh of St Victor, Peter Lombard, Thomas Aquinas, Bonaventure, Duns Scotus and Gabriel Biel.[5]

Hugh of St Victor

Hugh of St Victor (1096–1141), the Paris theologian, wrote an extended work on sacraments. Sacraments, he noted, were instituted 'with our first parents', since marriage itself is described as a great mystery (sacrament). According to Hugh, a sacrament is 'a corporeal or material element set before the senses without, representing by similitude and signifying by institution and containing by sanctification some invisible and spiritual grace'.[6] For something to be a sacrament it must have a similitude – something which makes it capable of representing the same thing; it must have an institution through which it is ordered to signify this thing; and it must have sanctification, through which it contains that thing and makes it efficacious. He immediately illustrated this by way of the water of baptism:

---

[4] Marica L. Colish, *Peter Lombard,* 2 vols, E.J. Brill, Leiden, 1994, Vol. 2, p. 516.

[5] These are chosen because of their influence, but others such as Roland of Bologna were also key figures. See ibid.

[6] Roy J. Deferrari, *Hugh of Saint Victor on the Sacraments of the Christian Faith,* Mediaeval Academy of America, Cambridge, MA, 1951, p. 155.

Table 7.1   Local Medieval Variations (1)

Rheinau Ritual 12th C.	*Constance Ritual 1482*	*Magdeburg Agenda 1492*
Before the church entrance.	[Before the church entrance.]	
Exsufflation: *Go out unclean spirit* Sign of the cross: *In the name of ...*	Enquiry of name (in vernacular) of each child *Do you renounce Satan ...* *Go out from him, unclean spirit ...* Sign of the cross: *Receive the sign of Christ crucified ...*	Exsufflation *Go out unclean spirit* Enquiry of name Sign of the cross: *Receive the sign of God the Father almighty ...*
Making into a Catechumen *Almighty everlasting* Blessing of salt *I exorcize you, creature of salt.* Enquiry of name *Receive the salt of wisdom.*	*Almighty everlasting ...* (Exorcized salt required) *N, receive the salt of wisdom*	*Almighty everlasting ...* Blessing of salt *I exorcize you, creature of salt.* Enquiry of name *Receive the salt of wisdom*
God of our fathers	*God of our fathers*	*God of our fathers*
Sign of the cross, for males: *God of Abraham ...* *Therefore accursed devil* Signs the females: *God of heaven, God of earth* *Therefore accursed devil* Over males: *Hearken accursed Satan* *Therefore accursed devil* Signing of females: *God of Abraham ...* *Therefore accursed devil* Signing males: *I exorcize you, unclean spirit* *Therefore accursed* Signing females: *I exorcize you, unclean spirit* *Therefore accursed devil* Signing males:	Sign of the cross, for males: *God of Abraham ...* *Therefore accursed devil* *Hearken accursed Satan* *Therefore accursed devil* *I exorcize you unclean spirit* *...* *Therefore accursed devil*	Sign of the cross, for males: *God of Abraham* *Therefore accursed devil* Signing of females: *God of heaven, God of earth* *Therefore accursed devil* Over males: *Hearken accursed Satan* *Therefore accursed devil* Signing of females: *God of Abraham* *Therefore accursed devil* Signing of males: *I exorcize you, unclean spirit* *Therefore accursed* Signing of females: *I exorcize you, unclean spirit* *Therefore accursed devil*
I beseech your eternal and most just goodness ... Matthew 19:13–15 Laying-on of hands and singing the Creed and Lord's Prayer	*I beseech your eternal and most just goodness ...* Matthew 19:13–15 The presbyter teaches the Lord's Prayer, angelic salutation and Creed to the parents.	*O Lord, holy* Mark 10 Placement of *stola* Delivery of Lord's Prayer and Creed

continued

Table 7.1   *concluded*

Rheinau Ritual 12th C.	Constance Ritual 1482	Magdeburg Agenda 1492
	Laying of hands on each head and saying: *Lord's Prayer, Ave Maria, and Creed.*	
	Be not deceived Satan	
Be not deceived Satan …	*Effeta* (ears, nose)	*Be not deceived Satan*
Effeta (Lt. ear, nose, rt. ear)	Admittance into the church as *competentes*	*Effeta* (Lt. ear, nose, rt. ear)
		Entrance into church
	Exorcism of the water	
Litany of Saints		*The Lord preserve your…*
Blessing of font		
(Tracing of cross on water, dividing water into four sections, placing candle in the water, breathing on the water three times, lifting candle from the water, pouring chrism into the water)	Pouring of chrism in font with formula for blessing	
	Renunciation (in Latin and	
Renunciation	vernacular)	Renunciation
	Credal interrogations	
Credal interrogations	Anointing with Holy Oil	Credal interrogations
Anointing with oil of	*Do you wish baptism?*	Anointing with oil of
exorcism	*I wish*	exorcism
		Do you wish baptism?
	Threefold baptism with	*I wish*
Threefold baptism with	Matthean formula	Threefold baptism with
Matthean formula	Presbyteral chrismation	Matthean formula
Presbyteral chrismation	*Almighty God …*	Presbyteral chrismation
Almighty God …	Places cap on the head	*Almighty God …*
White Cap on the head	*Receive your cap*	Robing
N, Receive …	*Go in peace. Your faith has*	*Receive*
(They go out)	*saved you.*	Giving of candle
Communion		
Almighty everlasting God …		
(Confirmation of Infants)		

Table 7.2   Local Medieval Variations (2)

Sarum Manual 1543	*York Manual 1509*
The *Ordo* for making a Catechumen	The *Ordo* for making a Catechumen
	Enquiry of name
	Breathes in the face three times:
	N, receive the Holy Spirit ... go out unclean spirit.
Signing with the cross on forehead:	Signing with the cross on forehead:
The sign of our Saviour ...	*N, the sign of the Holy Cross ...*
On the breast:	On the breast:
The sign of our Saviour ...	*N, the sign of our Saviour..*
Holding his right hand on the head:	Holding his right hand on the head:
Almighty and everlasting God ...	*Almighty and everlasting God ...*
(asks name)	
We beseech you, Lord ...	*We beseech you, Lord ...*
O God who created the human race ...	*O God who created the human race ...*
Exorcism of salt:	Exorcism of salt:
I exorcize you, creature of salt ...	*I exorcize you, creature of salt ...*
Enquiry of the name	
N, receive the salt of wisdom ...	*N, receive the salt of wisdom ...*
O God of our fathers ...	*O God of our fathers ...*
Over males:	Over males:
God of Abraham, God of Isaac ...	*God of Abraham, God of Isaac ...*
Therefore accursed devil ...	*Therefore accursed devil ...*
O God, the immortal defence of all that ...	*O God, the immortal defence of all that ...*
Hearken, accursed Satan ...	*Hearken, accursed Satan ...*
I exorcize you, unclean spirit ...	*I exorcize you, unclean spirit ...*
Therefore, accursed one ...	*Therefore, accursed one ...*
Over females:	Over females:
God of heaven, God of earth ...	*God of heaven, God of earth ...*
Therefore, accursed devil ...	*Therefore, accursed devil ...*
God of Abraham, God of Isaac ...	*God of Abraham, God of Isaac ...*
Therefore accursed devil ...	*Therefore accursed devil ...*
I exorcize you, unclean spirit ...	*I exorcize you, unclean spirit ...*
Therefore, accursed one ...	*Therefore, accursed one ...*
Signing with the cross:	
I beseech your eternal and most just goodness ...	*I beseech your eternal and most just goodness ...*

continued

Table 7.2   *concluded*

Sarum Manual 1543	York Manual 1509
Be not deceived, Satan	Matthew 19:13–15
Matthew 19:13–15	*Be not deceived Satan*
Effeta (rt. ear, nose, lt. ear)	*Effeta* (rt. ear, nose, lt. ear)
Godfathers, godmothers and all say:	Godfathers, godmothers and all say:
Our Father, Hail Mary, I believe.	*Our Father, Hail Mary, I believe.*
Priest repeats:	Priest repeats:
Our Father ... Hail Mary ... I believe ...	*Our Father, Hail Mary, I believe.*
Sign of the cross on right hand:	Sign of the cross on right hand:
N, I give you the sign of ...	*N, receive the sign of ...*
Blessing of infant:	*N, I sign you with the sign ...*
The blessing of God ...	
Introduction to the Church:	Introduction to the Church:
N, enter into the temple ...	*N, enter into the temple ...*
The Blessing of the Font.	The Blessing of the Font
Vernacular exhortation to godparents	
Litany	Litany
Almighty God ...	*Almighty God ...*
It is very meet ...	*It is very meet ...*
Blessing includes signing, parting the	Similar ceremonial, though breathing is
water in the form of a cross, casting	in the sign of a triangle
water in four directions, breathing on	
the water, dropping wax in the water,	
dividing the water with the candle,	
putting the candle in the water, lifting it	
out, adding chrism	
Renunciation	Renunciation
Anointing	Anointing
Threefold Credal interrogation	Threefold Credal interrogation
What do you seek? With responses.	*What do you seek? With responses*
Threefold dipping, with head to north,	Threefold immersion
east, then south, then west	
Anointing:	Anointing:
Almighty God, the Father ...	*Almighty God, the Father ...*
N, receive a white garment ...	*N, receive a white garment ...*
N, receive a lamp ...	*N, receive a lamp ...*
(Confirmation if bishop present, and	(Confirmation if bishop present, and
communion)	communion)
Mark 9:17–29; John 1:1–14	Mark 9:17–29; John 1:1–14

For in it is the visible element of water which is a sacrament, and these three things are found in one: representation from similitude, signification from institution, virtue from sanctification. Similitude itself is from creation, institution itself from dispensation, and sanctification itself from benediction. The first was imposed through the Creator, the second was added through the Saviour, and the third was administered through the Dispenser. Accordingly visible water is the sacrament, and invisible grace the thing or virtue of the sacrament. Now all water has from its natural quality a certain similitude with the grace of the Holy Ghost, since, just as the one washes away the stains of the body, so the other cleanses the iniquities of souls. And, indeed, from this inborn quality all water had the power to represent spiritual grace, before it also signified the latter by superadded institution. Now the Saviour came and instituted visible water through the ablution of bodies to signify the invisible cleaning of souls through spiritual grace. And hence water now does not represent from natural similitude alone but also signifies spiritual grace from superadded institution. But since these two things, as we have said, do not yet suffice for the perfect sacrament, the word of sanctification is added to the element and a sacrament is made; thus that visible water is a sacrament representing from similitude, signifying from institution, containing spiritual grace from sanctification.[7]

Here we can see Hugh's intellectual extrapolation, building on Augustine, but freely using terminology of which much is very far removed from the actual liturgical rite. According to Hugh, sacraments were founded for three reasons – for humiliation, instruction and exercise of the mind.[8] But there are three types of sacraments: those in which salvation is received, such as baptism; those which give sanctification, such as the reception of ashes, and the consecration of things by those in Holy Orders.[9] There are thus, for Hugh, myriads of rites and ceremonies which count as sacraments.

When he turns specifically to baptism, he says that it is the sacrament upon which salvation rests. He notes that in the Old Testament this salvation was by way of circumcision, that in the time of Jesus there was both circumcision and baptism, and then finally baptism alone. Baptism is 'the water sanctified by the word of God for washing away sins'.[10] Following Augustine, Hugh holds that there can be no sacrament until the word is added to the element. The word is identified as Matthew 28:19 (which would put a question mark against the validity of the Gelasian form which baptized with the threefold credal interrogations).[11] Faith is necessary, but it 'is within and lies hidden until it begins to be named and to come into manifestation'.[12] Baptism was instituted because circumcision could free from perdition, but could not lead to the glory of the kingdom. Baptism, being sanctified by the passion of Christ, confers more than circumcision – the baptism of John the Baptist was a sacrament, but only the baptism of Christ contains the virtue of the sacrament.

---

[7] Ibid.
[8] Ibid., p. 156.
[9] Ibid., p. 164.
[10] Ibid., p. 283.
[11] Ibid.
[12] Ibid., p. 286.

When Hugh finally turns to the baptismal rites, he offers some explanation of the ceremonies not unlike the Frankish commentaries. Catechizing is important, because Matthew 28 instructs the Church to first teach and then baptize. Exorcism follows teaching. Hugh explained:

> For three things must be accomplished towards the reception of the new, by which the one to be baptized is, as it were, received and nourished and promoted up to the integrity of the new life. Now these are the catechisms, the exorcisms, the prayers. Thus first the one to be baptized is catechized that he may be moved to faith by the decision of his own will. Then he is exorcized that the evil power of the devil may be cast from him. Prayer is also added that grace may go before and follow after to furnish strength for free decision and to make the entire illusion of the evil spirit afar off.[13]

He further explains:

> The font is consecrated in the name of the Father and of the Son and of the Holy Ghost, that the sanctity of the sacrament may be known to exist not from him who ministers but from Him who sanctifies.[14]

Godparents answer for the child 'so that he who was bound by another's iniquity is loosed by another's faith and confession'.[15] The threefold immersion is the threefold cleansing of thought, speech and operation. The post-baptismal anointing indicates that the baptized share in the Spirit of Christ and are co-heirs of the kingdom:

> Then there is given to the Christian a white garment, that he who darkened the splendor of the first nativity by the garments of age may with the habit of regeneration hold forth the cloak of glory. Also, after the holy anointing his head is covered with a holy veil, that he may understand that he possesses the diadem of the kingdom and sacerdotal dignity. Finally a lighted candle is put into his hand, that he may be taught to fulfil that part of the gospel where it is said: 'So let your light shine before men, that they may see your good works, and glorify your Father who is in heaven,' (Matt. 5:16). Thus if he keeps the lamp inextinguishable, he will enter nuptials with the celestial spouse in the midst of the wise virgins.[16]

Hugh makes a final comment on godparents – they are so called because 'they offer children to be reborn to a new life and become in a manner authors of the new regeneration'.[17]

Peter Lombard

Peter Lombard (1100–60), Archbishop of Paris, was a lasting force in later medieval theology through his *Sententiae in IV Libris Distinctae* which formed the basis of medieval theological learning. In the fourth book he turned to consider the nature of

---

13 Ibid., p. 298.
14 Ibid.
15 Ibid., p. 299.
16 Ibid.
17 Ibid.

sacraments. He based his treatment on that of Hugh, but with some important differences. He begins with Augustine's definition of a sacrament as a sign of a sacred thing, but added that it is also 'a sacred thing signifying and the sacred thing signified'.[18] Again, following Augustine, he notes that some signs are natural, such as smoke signifying fire, whereas others are given. Not all signs are sacraments, but all sacraments are signs.[19] But they are much more than signs; their power is not in their resemblance, but in their institution: 'For a sacrament is properly said to be that which is so great a sign of the grace of God and the form of invisible grace, that it bears its image and exists as its cause.'[20] Here Lombard omits Hugh's reference to 'corporeal or material element', which enables him to include penance as a sacrament, and to join with contemporaries such as Master Simon and Roland of Bologna in listing only seven sacraments.[21] Lombard thus implies a greater difference between sacraments of the Old and New Testaments, though he notes that circumcision conferred the same remedy against sin which is now accomplished in baptism. The sacrament of baptism is more common and more perfect because it has accumulated a full grace.[22] Baptism is one of the seven New Testament sacraments, which may be divided into three groups:

> Now we come to the sacraments of the new Law: which are baptism, confirmation, blessing of bread, that is, eucharist, penance, extreme unction, ordination, marriage. Of which some offer a remedy against sin and confer assisting grace (*gratiam adiutricem*), such as baptism; others that are a remedy only, such as marriage; others uphold us in grace and virtue, such as the eucharist and ordination.[23]

Thus baptism is already defined as conferring assisting grace. He sides with those who distinguished the baptism of Christ from both circumcision and the baptism of John. The latter can be called a sacrament out of courtesy; Christ accepted the baptism of John out of humility rather than for its efficacy.[24] Lombard distinguishes between the *sacramentum*, or external rite alone, and the *res sacramentum*, or matter and effect of the sacrament. Infants received both the *sacramentum* and the *res*, while adults who are baptized without faith receive only the *sacramentum*.[25] All baptized infants are freed from original sin, but only the elect will be saved. For adults who come to

---

[18] 'Sacrum signans et sacrum signatum', Bk 4.1.2. Magistri Petri Lombardi, *Sententiae in IV Libris Distinctae*, 2 vols, Collegii S. Bonaventurae ad Claras Aquas, Grottaferrata, 1981. Bk 4 is in vol. 2. <http://franciscan-archive.org/lombardus/index.html#writings>.

[19] Ibid., Bk 4.1.4.

[20] '*Sacramentum enim proprie dicitur, quod ita signum est gratiae Dei et invisibilis gratiae forma, ut ipsius imaginem gerat et causa exsistat*', Ibid.

[21] See Marcia Colish, *Peter Lombard*. Master Simon was from Flanders or the lower Rhine area.

[22] Lombard, Bk 4.1.9, '*Ideo autem mutata est circumcisio per baptismum, quia sacramentum baptismi et communius est et perfectius, quia pleniori gratia accumulatum*'.

[23] Ibid., Bk 4.2.1.

[24] Ibid., Bk 4.2.2–4.

[25] Ibid., Bk 4.4.1–4.

baptism, more than faith is required. They must come to the font with the intention of leaving behind a sinful manner of life, and uncharitable dispositions. They must conform to Christ in order to put on Christ.

Lombard then returns to the subject of infant baptism. He says infants are granted operating and cooperating grace (*gratiam operantem et cooperantem cunctis parvulis in baptismo dari*) as well as remission of original sin.[26] This grace enables both infants and adults to gain access to sanctification and to develop virtue and merit, though in infants this remains latent until they are old enough to accept it and cooperate with it. The operating and cooperating grace assists the baptized to resist the inclination to sin.

Lombard raised the question of single versus triple immersion, and allowed both, according to local custom. He notes that in earlier centuries the Church baptized at certain seasons, but concludes that those conditions no longer apply; it should be administered whenever needed. As a liturgical event, water was the sacramental medium – chosen because it is generally available and resembles the *res* of the sacrament – and the correct invocation is the triune formula of Matthew 28:19 (again putting a question mark against the *Gelasian* formula). Faith is required – even if different for infants – as is the minister's intention to baptize. Together these make a valid baptism. In summary, for Peter Lombard, because baptism imparts operating and cooperating grace, it is a rebirth and a renewal of the mind, and it arms the Christian with grace with which he or she can grow to virtue and sanctification.

Bonaventure

Bonaventure (1221–74) became Cardinal Bishop of Albano and Minister General of the Friars Minor. He treated sacraments in *Commentaries on Lombard's Sentences* and in the *Breviloquium*. In the former work, discussing the hypothetical question of whether sacraments should have been instituted, he argues that they are a medicine for spiritual ills.[27] Their institution was fitting for God and expedient for us, and, drawing on Hugh, he says they are for our erudition, humiliation and exercitation.[28] Sacraments assist grace, and baptism adjoined by grace looses us from punishment.[29]

More illuminating is Bonaventure's discussion in Part VI of the *Breviloquium*, 'On sacramental Remembrance'. Drawing on Isidore of Seville, he states that sacraments are 'sensible signs divinely instituted as remedies through which "beneath the cloak of material species God's power operates in a hidden manner"'.[30] He reiterates that they are a spiritual medicine, to help cure the disease of original sin. But,

---

[26] Ibid., Bk 4.4.7.

[27] Bonaventure, Commentary on Lombard Bk 4, Part 1, Q.4, English translation from <www.franciscan-archive.org/bonaventure/opera>, pp. 5–6.

[28] Ibid., *Conclusio*, p. 6.

[29] Ibid., p. 8.

[30] Jose de Vinck, *The Works of Bonaventure*, Vol. 2, St. Anthony Guild Press, Paterson, NJ, 1963, vol. 2, p. 223.

> ... because in themselves the sensible signs cannot produce any effect in the order
> of grace, although they are by nature distant representations of grace, it was
> necessary that the Author of grace institute [appoint] them for the sake of
> signifying and bless them for the sake of sanctifying; so that through natural
> similitude they would represent, through conjoined institution they would signify
> and through superadded benediction they would sanctify and prepare for grace,
> by which our soul is healed and cured.[31]

Sacraments are vessels of grace, and cause grace, though grace is not substantially
present in them, for grace dwells only in the soul and can only be infused by God.[32]
Their origin is with Christ the Lord. Their efficient cause is God's institution; their
material cause, representation through sensible signs; their formal cause, sanctification
through grace, and their final cause, the healing of humanity through a proper
medicine.[33]

Bonaventure notes that there was once a diversity of sacraments, both historical
variations and numerical variety, such as tithes and circumcision, but that now under
the New Covenant there are, as Lombard had said, seven. Not all were instituted in
the same way: 'He instituted Baptism first by being baptized Himself, then by
determining the form of Baptism, and by making it universal.'[34] Thus Bonaventure
here combines the baptism of Jesus with the Matthean command.

He maintains that the door to the sacraments is baptism, and that it is a remedy
against original sin. It is for those entering the battle, whereas Confirmation is for
those fighting.[35] For a baptism to be valid, Bonaventure follows Hugh and Peter
Lombard:

> For anyone to be validly and fully baptized, the form established by the Lord must
> be said aloud: 'I baptize thee in the name of the Father, and of the Son, and of the
> Holy Spirit. Amen.' No word should be omitted, none added, nor should the order
> given here be changed, nor should the word 'name' in the beginning be altered.
> There must also be immersion or ablution of the whole body, or at least of its most
> noble part, by means of the element water, in such a way that the immersion [or
> ablution] and the vocal expression are performed simultaneously by one and the
> same minister.[36]

It is for the sake of greater effectiveness that a preparatory instruction and exorcism
precede baptism. In the case of adults, faith is required, but in the case of children,
the faith of another suffices.[37] Bonaventure believed that the power of the Trinity is
present in baptism, and that even when baptism was conferred in the name of Christ,
this comprised the Trinity by implication. Threefold immersion represents the death,

---

[31] Ibid., p. 224.
[32] Ibid., p. 225.
[33] Ibid.
[34] Ibid., p. 236.
[35] Ibid., pp. 230–32.
[36] Ibid., p. 245.
[37] Ibid.

burial and resurrection of Christ.[38] This sacrament brings about regeneration and is fittingly performed in water; it provides a grace which regenerates.[39] Bonaventure concludes:

> And because the purpose of Baptism is to deliver both children and adults from the power of the prince of darkness, both should be exorcized, that the hostile spirits may be expelled, and both instructed, that the adults may be delivered from the darkness of error and formed to the faith, and that the godparents representing the children may learn what to teach them; lest the sacrament of Baptism be prevented by human default from achieving its intended end.[40]

Thomas Aquinas

Thomas Aquinas (1225–74) was the towering figure of medieval scholastic theology, and had a brilliant mind. He gave full treatments to sacraments and baptism in his *Summa Theologiae*, building on Hugh and Peter Lombard. Having stated that sacraments fall under the general category of 'sign', Aquinas asserted:

> It [the term 'sacrament'] can be applied to something for several different reasons: either because the thing concerned contains some hidden sanctity within it, so that, as applied to it, the term 'sacrament' is equivalent to 'sacred secret'; alternatively the term 'sacrament' may be applied to something because it is related to this sanctity either as its cause or its sign, or in virtue of some other kind of connection with it. Now for our present purposes when we speak of the sacraments we have in mind one specific connection with the sacred, namely that of a sign. And it is on these grounds that we assign sacraments to the general category of signs.[41]

Agreeing with Augustine that a word needs to be conjoined to the element, Aquinas gave three aspects which supported this proposition. First, they can be considered from the sanctifying cause which is the incarnate Word; secondly, from the aspect of humans who are sanctified by them, and third from the aspect of the actual signification itself. Thus, 'water, considered as a sign, can equally well represent washing in virtue of its wetness and refreshing in virtue of its coldness. But once the words *I baptize you* are uttered it becomes manifest that we are using water in baptism to signify a spiritual cleansing'.[42] Mispronunciation of the formula by accident does not alter the validity of the sacrament, but deliberate distortion does.[43] Aquinas held that to omit one of the divine names invalidates the sacrament: 'It is indeed unlawful to add any words to the words of sacred Scripture so as to change their meaning.'[44]

---

[38] Ibid., p. 246.

[39] Ibid., p. 247.

[40] Ibid., p. 248.

[41] *St. Thomas Aquinas, Summa Theologiae, ST* 3a.60.1, vol. 56, David Bourke (ed.), Blackfriars and Eyre and Spottiswoode, London, 1974, p. 5.

[42] *ST* 3a.60.6, in ibid., p. 23.

[43] *ST* 3a.60.7, in ibid., p. 27.

[44] *ST* 3a.60.8, in ibid., p. 33.

The chief effect of sacraments is grace, and sacraments cause grace in some way. For Aquinas, the main discussion on this matter is whether the cause is principal or instrumental. The former produces its effect by virtue of its form, while the latter does so solely by virtue of the impetus imparted by the principal agent. Hence sacraments are instrumental causes, with God being the principal agent. A sacrament therefore is an instrument of grace, and sacraments also impart a 'proper character', or seal. Here Aquinas seems to dissent from Bonaventure, for whom sacraments are an occasion for a divine action and grace. Baptism enables the baptized to receive other sacraments. Although Aquinas noted that Hugh allowed for a large number of sacraments, he accepts that there are but seven. Not all sacraments are necessary for salvation, but baptism is so required.

When Aquinas turns specifically to consider baptism, he dissents from Hugh of St Victor's view that the water of baptism itself sanctifies. Rather, he holds that sanctification is in the external washing with the prescribed form of words, which is the sacramental sign of interior justification.[45] He notes that baptism was instituted by Christ himself in his own baptism. Prior to Christ's passion, it had its effectiveness from the passion in so far as it prefigured the passion; after the passion and resurrection, it is made necessary for all in the command of Matthew 28.[46] By divine institution water is the proper matter for baptism (*propria materia*).[47] Aquinas noted:

> 4. The power of Christ flowed into all waters not because of physical continuity, but because of likeness of species. As Augustine says, *The blessing which flowed from the Saviour's baptism, like a spiritual river, filled the course of every stream and the channel of every spring.*
> 5. The blessing of the water is not necessary for baptism but is a part of its solemnity by which the devotion of the people is aroused, and the cunning of the devil kept in check lest the effect of baptism be impeded.[48]

The proper form is the triune formula of Matthew 28:19, because 'Christ commanded that the sacrament of baptism be given with the invocation of the Holy Trinity. As a result, anything lacking in the full invocation of the Trinity destroys the integrity of baptism.'[49]

Aquinas felt that immersion, though not essential, best symbolizes the burial of Christ. Either single or triple immersion are permissible modes of baptism, the former symbolizing the unity of the death of Christ and the Godhead, whereas the latter signifies the three days of burial and the Trinity. In the baptismal rite, certain things are necessary and others, such as the use of oil and chrism, pertain to the solemnity

---

[45] *ST* 3a.66.1, in vol. 57, James J. Cunningham (ed.), 1975, p. 7.

[46] *ST* 3a.66.2, in ibid., p. 13.

[47] *ST* 3a.66.3, in ibid., p. 13.

[48] *ST* 3a.66.4, in ibid., p. 17, though the reference is to *Pseudo-Augustine, Serm. Suppos.* 135. PL 39, 2012.

[49] ST 3a.66.6, in ibid., p. 29.

of the sacrament. Exorcisms are not necessary, and do not confer the sacrament, but they do save a person from the demon's power to impede the sacrament.

The effect of baptism, through the virtue of Christ's passion, is the removal of sin. Through baptism a person receives grace and virtues. According to Aquinas, infants need to be baptized because, 'since by birth they incurred damnation through Adam, so by rebirth they might attain salvation through Christ'.[50] The sponsors at baptism profess not that the child will believe, but they profess the faith of the Church in the name of the child. Catechesis should follow.

Aquinas gave a very thorough explanation of the sacrament, and was less concerned than Hugh, Lombard and Bonaventure with the details of the baptismal rite. Ceremonies which pertain to the solemnity, as well as catechesis and exorcisms, can be defended, but he offers little elaboration on the liturgical ceremonies, since the heart of the rite, which is about validity, is water with the triune formula.

This discussion of Hugh, Lombard, Bonaventure and Aquinas gives some idea of the direction in which theological reflection about baptism and its effects was moving during this period. We can illustrate this further by briefer reference to Duns Scotus and Gabriel Biel.

Duns Scotus

Scotus (1266–1308), who taught theology at Oxford and then Paris, defined sacraments thus:

> A sacrament is a sensible sign, ordered to the salvation of the wayfaring human being, efficaciously signifying – by divine institution – the grace of God, or a gratuitous effect of God.[51]

He accepted that there were seven sacraments. However, Scotus believed that Aquinas' view of sacramental causality was philosophically problematic, and sided with Bonaventure. He agreed with Aquinas that instrumental causes do not have intrinsic causal powers, but require a principal agent.[52] Yet Scotus questioned the idea that a material object could have a supernatural causal power. In his view sacraments do not cause God's grace; rather, God has decided that whenever a sacrament is received, he will give the appropriate supernatural gift. This divine decision has been formalized in a covenant (*Pactio Divina*) with the Church. God's pact guarantees sacramental reliability. The Old Testament 'sacraments' owe their efficacy to Christ's foreseen merits, whereas the New Testament sacraments owe their efficacy to the actual merits of Christ.

---

[50] ST 3a.68.9, in ibid., p. 109.

[51] *Ordinatio* 4.i.2, n. 9, cited in Richard Cross, *Duns Scotus*, Oxford University Press, New York, 1999, p. 136. I am reliant on Cross for this section, though see also Raphael M. Huber, 'The Doctrine of Ven. John Duns Scotus. Concerning the Causality of the Sacraments', *Franciscan Studies* 4 (1926), 9–38.

[52] *Ordinatio* 4.1.1, nn. 26–7, Cross, p. 137.

Scotus is clear that the effect of sacraments is the gift of grace. He distinguishes baptism and penance from the other sacraments in that these two confer first grace, or grace that saves. By baptism God causes the remission of original sin and actual sin, spiritual birth, adoption as sons of God and church membership.[53] Some sacraments, including baptism and confirmation, also confer some indelible mark or character, by which the recipient conforms to Christ and is under some obligation to Christ. Whereas for Aquinas this character was a quality, for Scotus it is a relational property which inheres in the will.

Gabriel Biel

According to Heiko Oberman, Biel (d. 1495) who taught theology at Tübingen, followed in the school of Duns Scotus and Jean Gerson.[54] After discussing first and second causes, Biel argued that no creature or created matter can cause its own salvation, and so he sided with Scotus. He made a distinction between primary and secondary causes. Thus of baptism he asserted:

> So the sacraments had the same nature – e.g. the water of baptism (among others) had the same nature which it now has – but they were not causes or signs or sacraments of a spiritual effect before Christ's institution of them, which was accomplished after His incarnation; rather, they are called *causes sine qua non.*
>
> And so it seems that the problem lies more in the terms than in the things, as far as concerns the difference between a cause properly speaking and a cause *sine qua non.*[55]

Biel cites in support Pierre d'Ailly, that the power of cause in secondary causes is from God alone. So he asserted that, although the sacraments cause grace as causes *sine qua non*, they none the less do not create grace: 'This picture celebrates the active power in God, since it holds that God alone, through the proper act of his free will, principally and properly causes every positive effect, it itself and in everything belonging to it.'[56]

In Biel's view, baptism removes the *culpa* and *poena* of original sin, and infuses grace (*prima gratia*). This is the first justification (*iustitia prima*), which is lost when mortal sin is committed. The baptized also acquire *fides acquisita*, which is necessary for *fides infusa*, the supernatural habit of faith infused into the soul at the moment of reception of first grace.[57]

---

[53] Cross, p. 138.

[54] Heiko Oberman, *The Harvest of Medieval Theology*, Harvard University Press, Cambridge, MA, 1963, p. 4.

[55] Whether the sacraments of the New Covenant are effective causes of grace, English translation, <http://www.nd.edu/~afreddos/translat/biel.htm>, p. 4.

[56] Ibid., p. 10.

[57] Oberman, *The Harvest of Medieval Theology*, pp. 134–5.

These brief reviews of Scotus and Biel illustrate how disputes over the sacraments were pursued at a philosophical level, concerned with the causality of grace, effects of grace, and 'character', as well as categorizing types of grace, justification and faith. This of course was regarded as the proper study of theology in the medieval academy, though it resulted in a different vocabulary to that found in the liturgies themselves, and perhaps a somewhat esoteric faith slightly removed from the experiential pastoral practice. Sacraments and baptism could be thought of without too close a reference to the liturgical text.

However, the writings of the academy were for the academy; what of preaching and more popular teaching? In a collection of sermons from the twelfth and thirteenth centuries, one for the first Sunday in Lent views baptism as the first washing, and confession as a second washing. Everyone must be washed twice, 'once at the baptismal bath, for ere the child is baptized it is the devil's; the second time thou shalt be washed at true confession, when thou renouncest thy sins'. This almost suggests that a sense of sin and confession is the completion of baptism.[58]

Another short homiletic piece explained, 'Each Christian man, so soon as he steppeth out of the font, where he is baptized of his sins, maketh to himself three foes … these three foes are – the devil and his host, the second is this earth, the third … his own flesh.'[59] In a homily on the Creed, the homilist stressed that baptism was necessary for the washing-away of sin. But even cleansed from sin, the Christian still had an obligation to learn the Creed:

> At the beginning of the Christian religion each man learnt his belief ere he received baptism. But then there were many children that died without baptism and perished, therefore it was ordained by God's command that children should be baptized in holy church, and their godfathers and godmothers should answer for them at the church-door, and enter into pledges at the font-stone, that they should be believing men, and know their belief when they were able to learn it. And this the godfathers and godmothers cannot do, except they themselves know their belief, that is, *Pater noster* and *Creed*.[60]

A sermon from a fourteenth and fifteenth-century collection noted that God had ordained seven sacraments 'the which shall easily bring us to the bliss if we be of good governance'. The first is in our youth, and is baptism, 'that cleanses men of the first sin, that we had of our elders, and gives great grace to us that have been purged'.[61] John Mirk's sermon for Epiphany (early fifteenth century) emphasized that the Trinity was present at the baptism of Jesus, and that when people see the water in the font in their church, they should know that the Trinity is present.[62] Roger Edgeworth,

---

[58] Richard Morris (ed.), *Old English Homilies and Homiletic Treatises*, Greenwood Press, New York, 1968, p. 36.

[59] Ibid., pp. 240–42.

[60] Ibid., pp. 72–4.

[61] Woodburn O. Ross, *Middle English Sermons*, Oxford University Press, London, 1940, p. 30.

[62] *Mirk's Festial: A Collection of Homilies*, Early English Text Society, Kegan Paul, Trench and Trübner, London, 1905.

preaching in the sixteenth century, having quoted from Augustine that the word added to the element makes a sacrament, explained in Sermon XIII:

> God clensith theyr hartes by fayth, the water and worde concurringe with the same fayth. Then this clensing of the soule must not be attribute to the water, excepte we put the worde, and then joyne theim both together, and they shall be of suche strength, that they may purge and make cleane the least chylde that ever was borne, whiche (as I have sayde in tymes past) beleveth in the fayth of the churche, lyke as he or she that is of discretion to beleveth by his own fayth. This blessed Sacramente of baptisme, by whiche we be regenerate and gotten agayne to God, was signified by the water that drouned the earth, and earthly craneall people, and saued the eyght liues that then were saued. And that the water of the sayde flud saued none that were oute of the shippe, signifieth that all heretikes that be out of the common receaued fayth of the churche, althoughe they be cristened, and glorieth to be called christen men, yet by the same water they shall be drouneed into hell, by which the ship, the catholike churche was lifte and borne vp into heauen and saued, as the materiall shippe of Noe was lifte vp into the ayre aboue grounde, and saued by water.[63]

At a more pragmatic level, John Mirk's fourth sermon of his *Quatuor Sermones* (early fifteenth century?) gave instructions to midwives to baptize in the threefold formula if a child was likely to die, and outlined degrees of affinity as a result of being a godparent.[64] His *Instructions for Parish Priests* warns that an infant must not be allowed to die unbaptized. If a child is in danger the midwife or parent should baptize it, though they must use the correct form:

> I folowe (baptize) the, or elles I crystene þe, in the nome of the fader & þe sone and the holy gost. Amen. Or elles thus, Ego baptize te. N. In nomine patris & filij & spiritus sancti. Amen.[65]

Any vessels and water used in emergency baptism must not be used for anything again. Godparents are to teach the Lord's Prayer, Hail Mary and Creed. This is echoed in the Sarum baptismal rite, where a vernacular charge to the godparents is given:

> *God faders and godmodyrs of thys chylde whe charge you that ye charge the foder and te moder to kepe it from fyer and water and other perels to the age of vii. yere. and that ye lerne or se yt be lerned the* Pater noster. Aue maria. *and* Credo. *after the lawe of all holy churche and in all goodly haste to be confermed of my lorde of the dyocise or of hys depute and that the moder brynge ayen the crysom at hyr puryfycation and washe your hande or ye departe the chyrche.*

Not everyone accepted the cumulative traditions about sacraments and baptism. One notable exception was John Wyclif, the fourteenth-century Oxford scholar. In his

---

[63] *Sermons very fruitfully, godly and learned, preched and sette forth by Maister Roger Edgeworth, doctoure of diuinitie*, London, 1557, fol. 226r. Edgeworth was a Henrician preacher, and refrained from preaching during the Protestant years of Edward VI's reign.

[64] R. Pynson (ed.), London, 1502.

[65] John Myrc (John Mirk), *Instructions for Parish Priests*, Edward Peacock (ed.), Kegan Paul, Trench, Trübner, London, 1902, p. 5.

Trialogus he listed the by then customary seven sacraments. However, he developed the predestinarian theology of Aquinas to a point where logically the sacraments were greatly reduced in importance. They could not deliver grace, but were signs of grace for the elect only. He acknowledged the scriptural foundations of baptism, but did not regard it as absolutely necessary for salvation. It could avail only for the elect, who would still be elect without it, and it did no good to the non-elect.[66]

Jan Huss and the Unity of Brethren in Bohemia and Moravia were influenced by Wyclif's views. Many of the early Brethren abandoned infant baptism, and postponed the rite until maturity. From 1478 they once more adopted infant baptism, though the practices were not uniform. Baptism was administered by pouring, and not by immersion. The rite of confirmation was developed to place an emphasis on a mature confession of faith rather than imparting the Holy Spirit.[67]

Ritual Adaptability and Uniformity

Although every diocese might have its own ritual, certain rituals became more widely used than others, particularly as larger dioceses had their liturgical books printed. For example, in England the Sarum rite was the dominant rite in use, lending a certain unformity. In Germany a prevalent ritual was the *Agenda Communis*. Deriving from the diocese of Ermland on the Baltic Sea in northern Prussia, and probably originating in the eleventh century, this *Agenda* and its rite of baptism was widely used in Germany. The baptismal rite as published in the sixteenth century acknowledged the fact that baptism now meant infant baptism, and headed the first rites as 'Order for Catechizing Infants'.[68] It simplified certain formulae, such as the signing of the child, which omits the reference to the Trinity. Two catechumenal prayers were provided, one of which was in the *Gelasian*, an exorcism said over males. It assumed that the salt had already been blessed and exorcised. The exorcisms are abbreviated, though they are certainly prominent. The account of blessing the children from Mark 10 is the Gospel lection, and there is a vernacular address to godparents to teach the child the Lord's Prayer, Hail Mary and Creed. The rite provided no blessing of the font, on the assumption that this had been done at Easter or Pentecost. It provided no credal questions, but simply a rubric asking of candidates' faith. The remainder of the rite tended to follow the fairly uniform Western pattern.

H.O. Old noted that, with the spirit of the Renaissance and the new Christian Humanism, there was a desire for a more universal approach over against local variety:

---

[66] See Richard Rex, *The Lollards*, Palgrave, New York, 2002.

[67] Rudolf Rican, *The History of the Unity of Brethren*, The Moravian Church in America, Bethlehem, PA, 1992.

[68] A. Kohlberg, *Die älteste Agende in der Diozese Ermland und den Deutschordensstaate Preussen nach dem ersten Druckausgaben von 1512 und 1529*, R. Rudlowski, Braunsberg, 1903.

> In regard to the rite of baptism, the new desire for liturgical uniformity first emerged in the work of the Venetian Dominican Alberto Castellani, who in 1523 published an order for the administration of baptism which aimed at establishing a more universal rite.[69]

The work published by Castellani, *Liber Sacerdotalis*, appeared in part as a response to the need for services of adult baptism after the Spanish reconquest of the Iberian peninsula. Yet, as Jaime Lara has shown, this rite proved useful for the missionary friars in Mexico and Peru, and was incorporated into the *Manual* prepared for Japan in the early seventeenth century.[70] Castellani claimed that he had consulted manuscripts in the Vatican Library which attested to the 'ancient and venerable customs and rites of the Western Church'. The rite is prefaced with a short indication that if the candidate is an adult, catechesis and exorcisms are necessary. It reproduces much of the *Gelasian* material in the manner of the Sarum rite.

Castellani's rite proved inadequate for some of the missionaries in Mexico, and in 1540 Vasco de Quiroga published the *Manual de Adultos*, though it was suppressed in the 1560s.[71] According to secondary sources which quoted from this *Manual*, it provided for translation of some parts of the rite into the vernacular dialects. It included a concern for welcome:

> If a native comes to you requesting baptism, receive him [or her] in a friendly manner and with great warmth say: *What do you wish, my friend?* If he says 'I want to be a Christian', answer: *You are most welcome, friend. You ask for an excellent thing because to be a Christian is to be an adorer of God and his servant, and even more so, to be a friend and child of God. Have courage then that I may teach you what you have to learn. To be a Christian you ought to believe in God and I shall instruct you in these things so that you may know them.*[72]

Lara noted that this rite apparently delayed the anointing with the oil of catechumens until the actual day of baptism. On that day the priest asked the candidates in their own language what they had learned, and then anointed them.

> Then in their language ask: *Do you believe in God the Father* ... etc. Immerse them in the water three times, as is the laudable custom of the Church, in the name of the Father ... etc. It would also be enough to immerse them only once [with the Trinitarian form]. Finally, anoint them on the crown of the head with the chrism and say the prayer as in the book. Put the white vesture on them. If the number is very large you can give the candle and white garment to two or three only.[73]

---

[69] H.O. Old, *The Shaping of the Reformed Baptismal Rite in the Sixteenth Century*, Eerdmans, Grand Rapids, MI, 1992, p. 6.

[70] Jaime Lara, '"Precious Green Jade Water": A Sixteenth-Century Adult Catechumenate in the New World', *Worship* 71 (1997), 415–28. My thanks to Professor Lara for loaning me his text of the Liber Sacerdotalis. *Liber Sacerdotalis nuperrime ex libris sanctae Romanae ecclesiae et quarundam ecclesiarum: et ex antiquis codicibus apostolicae bibliothecae*, Venice, 1523.

[71] Ibid. I am indebted to my colleague Professor Lara for the information on baptism in the New World in the sixteenth century.

[72] Ibid., p. 419.

[73] Ibid., p. 422.

Since in the early Church Christians greeted one another with a holy kiss, male candidates were to receive an embrace, while female candidates were to kiss the priest's stole but be embraced only by other Christian women.[74] The rite concluded with tambourines, cymbals, stringed instruments and native flutes, and the singing of the Te Deum or some other motet.

This *Manual*, however, was suppressed, and replaced by the *Manuale Sacramentorum secundum ecclesiae Mexicanae* (1560). Some attempt was made to accommodate the local culture, and the friars tried to translate liturgical words into native concepts. Lara gives an example from the *Psalmodia Christiana*, a collection of hymns published in 1538, which also included short doctrinal statements. Using the imagery of jewellery associated with the royal and priestly class of Aztec society, one such statement says:

> When the sun shone, when day broke, when the Word of God descended upon you, when you received the Sacrament – when you accepted the deep green jade water of baptism – when God, God the King, adopted you all as His sons, you became spiritual children of the holy Church; your souls acquired godliness [and] in them was placed Christianity, which become your adornment, a gift for you, your lot.[75]

God and the Church give the baptized 'incomparable feathered bracelets and a variety of precious spiritual flowered vestments', which are the sign of the cross, the Creed, Lord's Prayer, Hail Mary and the *Salve Regina*. The psalms which follow contain the Creed, an explanation of the Lord's Prayer and *Ave*.

The New World was not the only challenge facing the Western Church. The scope of the Renaissance and Christian Humanism also included the Reformation and the breakup of the Western Catholic Church. To counter the teaching of the Reformers, the Pope summoned the Council of Trent, which met on and off from December 1545 to December 1563. During Session VII (1547), the Council defined the Catholic teaching on sacraments and baptism. The work of revising the liturgy was handed to the Pope, and the rite of baptism, which was included in the Roman Ritual, was not issued until 1614.

Already in Session V in 1546, the Council had treated the subject of Original Sin, and affirmed its belief that this is removed in baptism.[76] It asserted that infants needed to be baptized, and that, by the grace of the Lord Jesus Christ, the guilt of original sin is remitted. Session VI considered Justification, and affirmed that 'the final cause indeed is the glory of God and of Jesus Christ, and life everlasting; while the efficient cause is a merciful God who washes and sanctifies gratuitously, signing, and anointing with the holy Spirit of promise'.[77] The instrumental cause is the sacrament of baptism

---

[74] Ibid., pp. 422–3.

[75] Ibid., p. 427, from *Psalmodia Christiana*, Trans Arthur Anderson, University of Utah Press, Salt Lake City 1993, p. 31.

[76] *The canons and decrees of the sacred and oecumenical Council of Trent*, ed. and trans. J.Waterworth, Dolman, London, 1848, p. 22.

[77] Ibid., p. 34.

'which is the sacrament of faith, without which no man was ever justified'.[78] The formal cause is the justice of God.

Session VII affirmed seven sacraments, of which some are necessary to salvation, and some, including baptism, imprint in the soul 'a certain spiritual and indelible Sign'.[79] The canons specific to baptism differentiated between the baptism of John and that of Jesus, insisted on the use of water, required the Matthean formula and intention to baptize for valid baptism, and said it was necessary to salvation. Other canons condemned those who regarded infant baptism as invalid, and those who suggested that baptism freed a person from obligations of moral conduct (antinomianism).

During Session IV in 1546 it was suggested that the council should draw up a catechism. The resulting work did not appear until 1566. It was patterned on earlier simpler catechisms, as well as being a Catholic response to Reformation catechisms. The section on sacraments explained that sacraments are signs instituted by God and as such 'have in themselves the power of producing the sacred effects of which they are the signs'.[80] They are signs of a sacred thing, and the words 'sacred thing' are to be understood as 'the grace of God, which sanctifies the soul and adorns it with the habit of all divine virtues'.[81]

Thus in baptism the solemn ablution of the body not only signifies, but has power to effect a sacred thing which is wrought internally by the operation of the Holy Spirit. Every sacrament consists of the matter (*materia*) which is the element, and the form (*forma*) which is commonly called the word.[82] In addition, certain ceremonies also accompany the sacraments. The Catechism affirms that 'the Sacraments of the Catholic Church are seven in number'.[83] The effect of sacraments is to give sanctifying grace, and in certain sacraments a character is sealed. So, in baptism, 'when we are washed in the sacred font His grace is infused into our souls', and it qualifies us to receive other sacraments.[84] Because baptism impresses a character, it can never be repeated.

When the Catechism turns specifically to baptism, it notes that, although not everything about baptism can be said during a celebration of the rite, nevertheless the pastor should expound one or two points 'when the faithful can contemplate with a pious and attentive mind the meaning of those things which they hear and at the same time see it illustrated by the sacred ceremonies of Baptism'.[85] It is '*the Sacrament of regeneration by water in the word*. By nature we are born from Adam children of wrath, but by Baptism we are regenerated in Christ, children of mercy'.[86] Water is the

---

[78] Ibid., p. 35. It is not clear whether this refers to faith or baptism.

[79] Ibid., p. 55.

[80] *Catechism of the Council of Trent for Parish Priests. Issued by Order of Pope Pius V*, English translation, John A. McHugh and Charles J. Callan, Joseph F. Wagner, Inc., New York, 1923, p. 146.

[81] Ibid., p. 146.

[82] Ibid., p. 150.

[83] Ibid., p. 152.

[84] Ibid., pp. 158–9.

[85] Ibid., pp. 161–2.

[86] Ibid., p. 163.

matter, although, 'guided by Apostolic tradition', the Church has observed the practice of adding holy chrism to more fully signify the effect of baptism.[87]

The form is the Matthean formula. Most essential is the naming of the Trinity; hence the Eastern passive form is valid. However, baptism in the name of Christ should be interpreted as meaning 'The Name', that is, Father, Son and Holy Spirit.[88] Baptism may be administered by immersion, infusion or aspersion, and whether it is single or threefold is a matter of indifference.

The Catechism defends infant baptism, and explains the effects of baptism as remission of sin, remission of all punishment due to sin, and the means by which the soul is replenished with divine grace: 'This grace is accompanied by a most splendid train of all virtues, which are divinely infused into the soul along with grace.'[89] Furthermore, by baptism 'we are sealed with a character that can never be effaced from the soul'; it 'opens to us the portals of heaven which sin had closed against us'.[90]

That much of this was too complex for many lay people is perhaps demonstrated by Robert Bellarmine's (1542–1621) *Christian Doctrine*, which is a much simpler catechism. Here sacraments are defined as the means of obtaining grace. In answer to the question of number, the by-now standard seven is listed. To the question 'What effect doth Baptism work?,' Bellarmine simply says, 'It maketh a man become the Child of God, and Heir of Paradise: it blotteth out all Sins, and filleth the Soul with Grace, and spiritual gifts.'[91]

The Catechism of the Council of Trent also treated the ceremonies or rituals of baptism. It divided them into three categories. The first set of rituals, enacted before coming to the font, consisted of standing at the church door, catechetical instruction (consisting of many interrogations; in the case of infants, the sponsor answered on the child's behalf), exorcism, salt, sign of the cross, and saliva. The second, after coming to the font, comprised renunciation of Satan, profession of faith and the desire to be baptized, and baptism. The third consists of ceremonies after baptism, namely the chrism, the white garment and the lighted candle.[92] The summary of the ritual which the Catechism gave did indeed cover the ceremonial common to the many Western diocesan rituals, and avoided having to deal with the minute variations of formulae and precise sequence.

The Tridentine rite of baptism did not appear until 1614. In theory, any diocesan or monastic rite which could show an antiquity of more than two hundred years, could continue to enjoy its distinctive rites. In practice, over a period of time, many dioceses abandoned their own usage and adopted the common Tridentine form. The rite,

---

[87] Ibid., p. 166.

[88] Ibid., pp. 167–8.

[89] Ibid., p. 188.

[90] Ibid., pp. 188,191.

[91] Robert Bellarmine, *Christian Doctrine*, English edn 1676, p. 26.

[92] Ibid., pp. 192–7.

though not specifically for infants, certainly envisaged infants as the main candidates. It began with brief interrogations and a brief admonition to keep the Gospel summary of the law. This was followed by the exsufflation and signing of the cross, followed by a prayer for the candidate. The priest then laid hands on the child, and prayed the Gelasian prayer (slightly altered), 'Almighty everlasting God'. The salt was blessed and then given with the Gelasian prayer, 'God of our fathers', and exorcisms, followed by a signing and the Gelasian prayer, 'O Lord, holy Father'. The priest then placed the stole on the child's left shoulder, and led her into the church with a formula for the entry. The Creed and Lord's Prayer were recited. Then came a further exorcism, the effeta, renunciation and anointing with the oil of catechumens. Credal questions and a question about the desire for baptism are followed by the baptism in the threefold name. The rite concluded with the anointing with chrism, the white garment and the lighted candle, and dismissal. A long and a short form for blessing of the font was contained elsewhere in the ritual, together with forms for adult baptism; the latter was inspired in part by the *Liber Sacerdotale* of Castellani, and the short blessing was taken from the *Manuale Mexicaniensis*. On the whole, though, the prayers articulated the theology which had been that of Rome in the *Gelasian Sacramentary*. This form, with occasional minor revision to accord with canon law, remained the use of the Roman Catholic Church until the latter part of the twentieth century.

Concluding Remarks

In the later Middle Ages the Western baptismal rite was textually mainly that found in the *Gelasian Sacramentary*, though with local additions and variations. Furthermore, the rite was telescoped – the various stages of initiation were now celebrated at one time, and for the most part, to infants only. With the rise of scholastic theology, thinking on sacraments resulted in definitions taking over, and a theology developing alongside the ritual and in some ways independent of the ritual. This would have an impact later at the Reformation. The Reformers would formulate a theology, and then attempted to adjust the baptismal rite to fit the theology. With the discovery of the New World and the need once more for rites of baptism for adults, an attempt was made at some cultural accommodation. This experiment was short-lived. The Counter-Reformation required a certain uniformity of doctrine and liturgical practice to safeguard against the inroads of Protestantism. This was the main contribution of Trent: to define Catholic doctrine, and to rein in and discourage much of the earlier local variations.

CHAPTER 8

In the Floods of Great Waters

Both historically and theologically all baptismal rituals look back to the baptism of Jesus in the Jordan. In so far as that event, recorded in kerygmatic genre, crystallizes the whole salvific work of God in Christ both for, and in place of, humanity, it is foundational, and all liturgical rituals need to be grounded in that one baptism. An Amcan Travel staffers' visit to Israel, March 2001, logged:

> We stopped at a baptismal area on the Jordan River near where it flows out of the Sea of Galilee. Lots of people were singing Amazing Grace in their white robes and being baptized.[1]

For sentimental, historical and no doubt many personal reasons, some people like to take their ritual and theology back to where it all began, in the River Jordan. Theologically, however, there is never a need to return to the River Jordan, and all baptismal rites have developed beyond the Jordan. This study has described the lavish rituals of the Syrian Orthodox and the Church of the East, and surveyed the diversity of rites in the West. These older, foundational rites seem to be a ritual unpacking of the baptism of Jesus with dipping (Christological), naming (trinitarian), and gestures to symbolize the descent of the Spirit (pneumatological) and adoption into an eschatological community (ecclesiological). Other rituals have been added to express sin and repentance, coming to faith, being a new creation, or a resurrected being. For all the differences between the various Eastern rites, and the Western Tridentine and former usages such as the Mozarabic, all rites look back to the Jordan, and ritualize baptism in the conviction that what happened there once, still happens now in every baptism.

One of the first ritual supplements to baptism was anointing. Although attempts have been made to find an original pattern and linear development, the diversity found in the ancient texts seems to reflect a diversity found in common secular bathing etiquette. There we find evidence of anointing before or after, or before and after bathing, and also of oil being poured into the baths themselves. All these are reflected in the diversity we find in the early centuries in the emerging baptismal rituals. The peculiar hand-laying and anointing by the bishop in the Roman use would spin off to become a separate and new rite of Confirmation. This was at first a Roman, and then Western peculiarity – and later a theological problem, and it is anachronistic to try to find 'Confirmation' in Eastern rites.

Most of the themes relating to baptism found in the New Testament are reflected in some way or other in the developing baptismal rites. Some became more important

---

[1] <Http://www.goamcan.com/travelogues/IsraelTrip.html>.

than others. In many of the rites the theme of rebirth/regeneration and font as womb predominate, and although the death/resurrection theme of Romans 6 is frequently present, it usually takes second place; womb, not tomb, is the major focus. The theme of repentance took on a deeper meaning in the West through the theological influence of St Augustine, though the dramatic renunciation found in the classical rites shows that rejection of sin and evil was always an important theme. In the Eastern rites, though, the emphasis was on restoration of the old Adam in Christ rather than concern with Original Sin. This is expressed most forcefully in the blessing of the font in the Maronite rite where the font is not so much the Jordan as womb of God giving birth to a 'heavenly Adam'.

Though there have been changes in the Eastern rites throughout the centuries and even in recent times, the texts have been more or less stable for many centuries. The variations and similarities between the various Eastern rites witness to a once greater diversity. Even within some Churches – the Maronite and Syrian Orthodox – there are manuscripts witnessing to a once greater variety of usages.

In the West the diversity of usages – Roman, Milanese, Gallican, Mozarabic, Celtic – began to shrink, partly by osmosis and mutual borrowing of material, and partly by the gradual adoption of the Carolingian hybrid Roman usage. However, the commentaries from this period still reflect some of the earlier diversity. With the rise of scholastic theology, we find the beginning of a separation between the theology and rite. Definitions of sacrament and baptism resulted in generic definitions, often unrelated to the liturgical text and practice. Finally in the West, with the Council of Trent, we find a suspicion of regional variation, and the move towards a uniform rite. Certainly some diocesan rituals and usages continued, but the standard rite of Trent curtailed many local usages, and discouraged any cultural adaptation. The Tridentine rite held sway in the Roman Catholic Church until the reforms of the Second Vatican Council in the 1960s.

These foundational rites of the ancient Churches remain as an important paradigm for the postmodern world, where once again there is an interest in ritual and symbolism. Although some of the more esoteric medieval interpretations of the ritual, and perhaps much of the terminology of the Western scholastic theologians will be unappealing, beneath these ancient ritualizings, there are important expressions of Christian salvation, perhaps summed up in a *ghanta* in the Syrian Orthodox rite:

> You did give us the font of true purification which cleanses us from all sins. Through this water, which is consecrated by Your invocation, we receive the holiness granted to us by the Baptism of Your Christ. We beseech You, O Lord, to fill this water with the power which you did bestow by the passion of Your Only-Begotten Son. Sanctify and purify us from all iniquities and make us ready to receive Your Holy Spirit.

Bibliography

'Beckhams host glitzy christening.' *BBC News*, UK edition. 23 December 2004. <http://news.bbc.co.uk/l/hi/uk/4120477.stm>.

'Israel Trip Report.' *Amcan Travel,* March, 2001, pp. 149–80 <http://www.goamcan.com/travelogues/IsraelTrip.html>.

Aelfric, Abbot of Eynsham. *Aelfric's Catholic Homilies: The Second Series.* Edited by Malcolm Godden. London and New York: Oxford University Press, 1979.

Agende für die Evangelische kirche in den königlich Preußischen Landen, Berlin, 1829.

Akeley, T.C. *Christian Initiation in Spain c.300–1100.* London: Darton, Longman and Todd, 1967.

Aland, Kurt. *Did the Early Church Baptize Infants?* Translated by G.R. Beasley-Murray. Philadelphia, PA: Westminster Press, 1963.

Alla, Waheed Hassab. *Le Baptême des Enfants dans la Tradition de l'Église copte d'Alexandrie.* Fribourg: Éditions Universitaires Fribourg Suisse, 1985.

Ames, William. *The Marrow of Theology.* Edited and translated by John Dykstra Eusden. Grand Rapids, MI: Baker Books, 1997.

Amish Country News. Edited by Brad Igou. 2005. <http://www.amishnews.com/amisharticles/religioustraditions.htm>.

Aquinas, Saint Thomas. *Summa Theologiae.* Vol. 56, edited by David Brooks, 1974; Vol. 57, edited by James J. Cunningham, 1975. London: Blackfriars and Eyre and Spottiswood.

Arensen, Sherl. 'The Rite Stuff.' *Today's Christian* 38 (2), March/April 2000, p. 63. <http://www.christianitytoday.com/tc/2000/002.7.63.html>.

Armour, Rollin Stely. *Anabaptist Baptism.* Eugene, OR: Wipf and Stock, 1998.

Armstrong, O.K. and Marjorie Armstrong. *The Baptists in America.* New York: Doubleday, 1979.

Arndt, Johann. *Paradislustgard.* Stockholm: F. and G. Bekjers Forlag, 1975.

———. *True Christianity.* Translated by Peter Erb. New York: Paulist Press, 1979.

Arranz, M. ' Les Sacrements de l'ancien Euchologe constantinopolitain.' *Orientalia Christiana Periodica* 52 (1986), 145–78.

Attridge, Harold W. 'The Original Language of the *Acts of Thomas*.' In *Of Scribes and Scrolls. Studies on the Hebrew Bible, Intertestamental Judaism, and Christian Origins presented to John Strugnell on the Occasion of his Sixtieth Birthday.* Edited by Harold W. Attridge, John J. Collins and Thomas H. Tobin. Lanham, MD: University of America Press, 1990, 241–50.

Augustine, Saint. *De Peccatorum Meritis et Remissione et de Baptismo Parvulorum.* <http://www.newadvent.org/fathers>.

———. *Sermons on the Liturgical Seasons.* Translated by Mary Sarah Muldowney. New York: The Fathers of the Church, 1959.

Aytoun, K.A. 'The Mysteries of Baptism by Moses bar Kepha Compared with the Odes of Solomon.' In *The Syrian Churches Series 6,* edited by J. Vellian. Kottayam, Kerala, India: CMS Press, 1973, 1–15.

Baker, J.Wayne. *Heinrich Bullinger and the Covenant: The Other Reformed Tradition.* Athens, OH: Ohio State University Press, 1980.

Balke, Willem. *Calvin and the Anabaptists.* Translated by William J. Heynen. Grand Rapids, MI: Eerdmans, 1981.

Baptism, Confirmation and the Eucharist in the Church of the East. Syriac Commission Study Seminar, Holy Apostolic Catholic Assyrian Church of the East Commission on Inter-Church Relations and Education Development. February–March 2000 <http://www.cired.org/east/0402_initiation_rites.pdf>.

Baptism, Eucharist and Ministry. Faith and Order Paper No. 111. Geneva: World Council of Churches, 1982.

Baptism, Rites of Passage, and Culture. Edited by S. Anita Stauffer. Geneva: Lutheran World Federation, 1999.

Barber, E. *A Small Treatise of Baptisme or Dipping.* London, 1642.

Bardy, Gustave and Maurice Lefévre. 'Hippolyte: Commentaire sur Daniel.' *Sources Chrétiennes* 14 (1947).

Barrett, Ivan J. *Joseph Smith and the Restoration.* Provo, UT: Brigham Young University Press, 1973.

Barth, Karl, *Church Dogmatics*, I Part 1–IV Part 4 Fragment. Edinburgh: T & T Clark, 1936–69.

————. *The Teaching of the Church Regarding Baptism.* Translated by Ernest Payne. London: SCM Press, 1948.

Barth, Markus. 'Baptism.' In *The Interpreter's Dictionary of the Bible, Supplementary Volumes.* Edited by Keith Crim. Nashville, TN: Abingdon, 1972.

————. *Die Taufe – Ein Sakrament?* Zollikon-Zurich: Evangelischer Verlag, 1951.

Basil, Saint. 'Concerning Baptism.' In *Ascetical Works.* Translated by Sister M. Monica Wagner. New York: Fathers of the Church, 1950, 339–430.

Battles, Ford Lewis. *Institutes of the Christian Religion*, 1536 edition. Grand Rapids, MI: Eerdmans, 1975.

Baun, Jane. 'The Fate of Babies Dying Before Baptism in Byzantium.' In *The Church and Childhood, Studies in Church History 31.* Edited by Diana Wood. Oxford: Blackwell, 1994, 113–125.

Baxter, Richard. *The Practical Works of Richard Baxter.* 23 volumes. Edited by William Orme. London: J. Duncan, 1830.

Beardslee III, John W. *Reformed Dogmatics: J. Wollebius, G. Voetius [and] F. Turretun.* Edited and translated by John W. Beardslee III. New York: Oxford University Press, 1965.

Beasley-Murray, G.R. *Baptism in the New Testament.* London: Macmillan, 1963.

Bede, the Venerable. 'Chapter 2.' Bede, *Historia Ecclesiastica* 2.2. <http://www.ccel. org/ccel/bede/history.v.ii.ii.html>.

————. *Homilies on the Gospels*. Translated by Lawrence T. Martin and David Hurst. Kalamazoo, MI: Cistercian Publications, 1991.

Bedingfield, M. Bradford. *The Dramatic Liturgy of Anglo-Saxon England*. Woodbridge: The Boydell Press, 2002, 171–90.

Bellarmine, Robert. *Christian Doctrine*, English edition, 1676.

(Bender, Harold S.) 'An Amish Church Discipline of 1781.' *The Mennonite Quarterly* 4 (1930), 140–48.

Bernard, J.H. *The Odes of Solomon*. Cambridge: Cambridge University Press, 1912.

Bettenson, Henry. *Documents of the Christian Church*. Oxford: Oxford University Press, 1979.

Betz, Hans Dieter. 'Transferring a Ritual: Paul's Interpretation of Baptism in Romans 6.' In *Paul in His Hellenistic Context*. Edited by Troels Engberg-Pederson. Edinburgh: T & T Clark, 1994.

Biel, Gabriel. 'Whether the Sacraments of the New Covenant are effective causes of grace.' Edited and translated by Alfred J. Freddoso <http://www.nd.edu/~afreddos/translat/biel.htm>.

Bierma, Lyle D. *German Calvinism in the Confessional Age. The Covenant Theology of Caspar Olevianus*. Grand Rapids, MI: Baker Books, 1996.

Bomberger, J.H.A. 'The Old Palatinate Liturgy of 1563.' *Mercersburg Review* 2 (1850), 277–83.

Bonaventure, Saint. *Commentaries on Lombard's Sentences*. English translation in <http://www.franciscan-archive.org/bonaventure/opera>.

Bonner, G. *St. Augustine of Hippo. Life and Controversies*. Philadelphia, PA: Westminster Press, 1963.

The Book of Concord. Edited by T.G. Tappert. Philadelphia, PA: Westminster, 1962.

The Book of Marganitha on the Truth of Christianity. Translated by His Holiness Nar Eshai Shimun XXIII. Ernakuluam, Kerala, India: Mar Themotheus Memorial Printing House, 1965.

Borgen, Ole E. *John Wesley on the Sacraments*. Grand Rapids, MI: Francis Asbury Press, 1972, 1985.

Bornert, René. *Le Reforme Protestante du Culte. Strasbourg au XVI siècle (1523–1598)*. Leiden: E.J. Brill, 1981.

Botte, Bernard. 'L'Eucologe de Serapion est-il authentique?' *Oriens Christianus* 48 (1964), 50–57.

————. *From Silence to Participation*. Washington, DC: Pastoral Press, 1988.

Bouhot, Jean-Paul. *La confirmation, sacrament de la communion ecclésiale*. Lyons: du Chalet, 1968.

Bradshaw, Paul F. 'Baptismal Practice in the Alexandrian Tradition: Eastern or Western.' In *Essays in Early Christianity*. Edited by Paul Bradshaw. Bramcote: Alcuin/GROW Liturgical Study, Grove Books, 1988, 5–17. Reprinted in *Living Water, Sealing Spirit*. Edited by Maxwell Johnson. Collegeville, MN: Pueblo Liturgical Press, 1995, 82–100.

———— (ed.). *Companion to Common Worship*, Vol. 1. London: SPCK, 2001.

————. 'Redating the *Apostolic Tradition*: Some Preliminary Steps.' In *Rule of Prayer, Rule of Faith*. Edited by Nathan Mitchell and John Baldovin. Collegeville, MN: Pueblo Liturgical Press, 1996, 3–17.

————. *The Search for the Origins of Christian Worship*. New York: Oxford University Press, 2002.

————, Maxwell E. Johnson and L. Edward Phillips. *The Apostolic Tradition*. Minneapolis, MN: Augsburg Fortress Press, 2002.

Braniste, Ene. 'Le déroulement de l'Office de l'Initiation dans les Églises de Rite Byzantin et son Interprétation.' *Ostkirchliche Studien* 20 (1971), 115–29.

Bremmer, Jan N. 'The *Acts of Thomas*: Place, Date and Women.' In *The Apocryphal Acts of Thomas*. Edited by Jan N. Bremmer. Louvain: Peeters, 2001, 74–90.

Brent, Allen. *Hippolytus and the Roman Church in the Third Century: Communities in Tension before the Emergence of a Monarch-Bishop*. Leiden: E.J. Brill, 1995.

Brock, Sebastian. 'The Baptismal Anointings According to the Anonymous Expositio Officiorum', *Journal of Syriac Studies* 1 (1998), 1–9.

————. 'Baptismal Themes in the Writings of Jacob of Serugh.' *Symposium Syriacum 1976*, Rome: Pontificial Oriental Institute, 1978, 325–47.

————. 'The Consecration of the Water in the Oldest Manuscripts of the Syrian Orthodox Baptismal Liturgy.' *Orientalia Christiana Periodica* 37 (1971), 317–31.

————. *The Luminous Eye*. Rome: Placid Lectures, CIIS, 1985.

————. 'A New Syriac Baptismal *Ordo* attributed to Timothy of Alexandria.' *Le Muséon* 83 (1970), 367–431.

————. 'A Remarkable Syriac Baptismal Ordo.' *Parole de l'Orient* 2 (1971), 365–78.

————. 'Severos' letter to John the Soldier.' In *Erkenntnisse und Meinungen II*. Edited by G.Wiessner. Wiesbaden: Otto Harrassowitz, 1978, 53–75.

————. 'Some Early Syriac Baptismal Commentaries.' *Orientalia Christiana Periodica* 46 (1980), 20–61.

————. 'Studies in the Early History of the Syrian Baptismal Liturgy.' *Journal of Theological Studies* 23 (1972), 16–64.

————. 'The Transition to a Post-baptisal Anointing in the Antiochene Rite.' In *The Sacrifice of Praise. Studies on the themes of thanksgiving and redemption in the central prayers of the Eucharistic and baptismal liturgies*. Edited by Bryan D. Spinks. Rome: Edizioni Liturgiche, 1981, 214–25.

Brooks, E. *Letters*. London: Text and Translation Society, 1903.

Brown, R.E. *The Gospel According to John*, 2 volumes. Garden City, NJ: Doubleday, 1966/70.

Buchanan, Colin. *Infant Baptism and the Gospel. The Church of England's Dilemma*. London: Darton, Longman and Todd, 1993.

Buerger, David John. *The Mysteries of Godliness: A History of Mormon Temple Worship*. San Francisco, CA: Smith Research Associates, 1994.

Bullinger, Heinrich. *Decades*, Volume 5. Cambridge: Parker Society edition, Cambridge University Press, Cambridge, 1850.

Bultmann, Rudolph. *The Gospel of John.* Philadelphia, PA: E.T. Westminster Press, 1971.

Bunyan, John. *The Miscellaneous Works of John Bunyan*, Volume 4. Edited by Roger Sharrock. Oxford: Clarendon Press, 1976–94.

Burges, Cornelius. *Baptismall regeneration of Elect Infants, Professed by the Church of England, according to the Scriptures, the Primitive Church, the present reformed Churches, and many particular Divines apart.* London, 1629.

Burrage, Champlin. *The Early English Dissenters,* 2 volumes. Cambridge: Cambridge University Press, 1912.

Burreson, Kent. 'The Saving Flood: The Medieval Origins, Historical Development, and Theological import of the Sixteenth Century Lutheran Baptismal Rites.' Ph.D Dissertation, University of Notre Dame, 2002.

Cabasilas, Nicholas. *The Life in Christ.* Translated by Carmino J. de Catanzaro. Crestwood, NY: St.Vladimir's Seminary Press, 1974.

Calvin, Jean. *Institutes of the Christian Religion.* 1536 edition, translated by Ford Lewis Battles. Grand Rapids, MI: Eerdmans, 1975; 1559 edition, translated by Henry Beveridge, 2 volumes. London: James Clarke & Co. Ltd, 1962.

———. *Tracts and Treatises on the Doctrine and Worship of the Church. Volume 2.* Translated by H. Beveridge, edited by T.F. Torrance. Revised edition, Edinburgh and London: Oliver and Boyd, 1958.

Campbell, Alexander. *Christian Baptism: with its Antecedents and Consequents.* Bethany, VA: Alexander Campbell, 1851.

———. *The Christian System.* Cincinnati, OH: Standard Publishing Company, 1901.

The Canons and Decrees of the Sacred and Oecumenical Council of Trent. Edited and translated by J. Waterworth. London: Dolman, 1848.

Capelle, B. 'L'Anahore de Serapion: Essai d'exégèse.' *Le Muséon* 59 (1964), 425–43.

Cardale, John. *Readings in the Liturgy and Divine Offices of the Church,* 2 volumes. London: Thomas Bosworth, 1874–75.

Catholic Church. *Catechism of the Catholic Church.* Città del Vaticano: Liberia Editrice Vaticana, 2000.

———. *Catechism of the Council of Trent for Parish Priests. Issued by Order of Pope Pius V.* Translated by John A. McHugh and Charles J. Callan. New York: Joseph F. Wagner, 1923.

———. *Le Pontifical Romano-Germanique Du Dixième Siècle.* Edited by Cyrille Vogel in collaboration with Reinhard Elze. Vatican City: Biblioteca Apostolica Vaticana, 1963–72.

———. *The Rites of the Catholic Church as Revised by the Second Vatican Council,* 2 volumes. New York: Pueblo Press, 1976, 1980.

————. *The Winchcombe Sacramentary.* Edited by Anselme Davril. London: Henry Bradshaw Society, 1995.

————. Diocese of St. Maron. *Mysteries of Initiation. Baptism, Confirmation, Communion According to the Maronite Antiochene Church.* Washington, DC: Diocesan Office of Liturgy, 1987.

Chalfoun, P. Khalil. 'Baptême et Eucharistie chez 'Ammar Al-Basri.' *Parole de l'Orient* 27 (2002), 321–34.

Charlesworth, J.H. 'The Odes of Solomon – not Gnostic.' In *The Catholic Biblical Quarterly* 31 (1969), 357–69.

————. *The Old Testament Pseudepigrapha,* Volume 1. Garden City, NJ: Doubleday, 1983.

————. *The Pseudepigrapha and Modern Research.* Chico, CA: Scholars Press, 1981.

Chemnitz, Martin. *Ministry, Word, and Sacraments. An Enchiridion.* Edited, translated and briefly annotated by Luther Poellot. St. Louis, MO: Concordia, 1981.

Church Book: St. Andrews' Street Baptist Church, Cambridge, 1720–1832. Edited by K. A. Parons. London: Baptist Historical Society, 1991, 41–42.

Church of England. *Christian Initiation – A Policy for the Church of England. A Discussion Paper by Canon Martin Reardon.* London: Church House Publishing, London, 1991.

————. *Communion Before Confirmation?: The Report of the General Synod Board of Education Working Party on Christian Initiation and Participation in the Eucharist.* London: Church Information Office Publishing, 1985.

————, Liturgical Commission. *On the Way: Towards an Integrated Approach to Christian Initiation.* London: Church House Publishing, 1995.

Church of Scotland, Special Commission on Baptism. *The Biblical Doctrine of Baptism.* Edinburgh: Saint Andrew Press, 1958.

Colish, Marica L. *Peter Lombard,* Volume 2. Leiden: E.J. Brill, 1994.

Collins, A. Jefferies. *Manuale ad usum Percelebris Ecclesie Sarisburiensis.* Chichester: Henry Bradshaw Society, 1960.

Collins, Adela Yarbro. 'The Origin of Christian Baptism.' In *Living Water, Sealing Spirit.* Edited by Maxwell E. Johnson. Collegeville, MN: Pueblo, 1995, 35–57.

Connell, Martin F. *Church Worship in Fifth-Century Rome: The Letter of Innocent I to Decentius of Gubio.* Cambridge: Grove Books, 2002.

Connolly, R.H. *Anonymi Auctoris Expositio Officiorum Ecclesiae Georgio Arbelensi vulgo adscripta. Accedit Abrahae Bar Lipheh Interpretatio Officiorum,* 4 volumes 2nd edn. Louvain: Corpus Scriptorum Christianorum Orientalium, 1953–61.

————. *The Liturgical Homilies of Narsai, with an Appendix by Edmund Bishop.* Cambridge: Cambridge University Press, 1909.

———— and H.W. Codrington. *Two Commentaries on the Jacobite Liturgy.* London: Williams and Norgate, 1913.

Conybeare, F.C. 'The Character of the Heresy of the Early British Church.' *Transactions of the Society of Cymmrodorion,* 1897–98, 84–117.

Coptic Church. *Coptic Offices.* Translated by R.M.Woolley. London: SPCK, 1930.

Coster, Will. *Baptism and Spiritual Kinship in Early Modern England.* Aldershot: Ashgate, 2002.

Cottrell, Jack Warren. 'Covenant and Baptism in the Theology of Huldreich Zwingli.' Th.D. Dissertation, Princeton Theological Seminary, 1971.

Couratin, A.H. 'Justin Martyr and Confirmation – A Note.' *Theology* 55 (1953), 458–60.

Cranfield, Charles. *The Epistle to the Romans* 1. Edinburgh: ICC T&T Clark, 1975, 300.

Cranmer, Thomas. *A Catechism set forth by Thomas Cranmer.* Edited by D.G. Selwyn. Appleford: Sutton Courtenay Press, 1978.

Cressy, David. *Birth, Marriage and Death. Ritual, Religion, and the Life-Cycle in Tudor and Stuart England.* Oxford: Oxford University Press, 1997.

Crichton, J.D. *Christian Celebration.* London: Geoffrey Chapman, 1981.

Cross, Anthony R. *Baptism and the Baptists. Theology and Practice in Twentieth-century Britain.* Carlisle: Paternoster Press, 2000.

Cross, Richard. *Duns Scotus.* New York: Oxford University Press, 1999.

Cullman, Oscar. *Baptism in the New Testament.* Translated by J.K.S. Reid. London: SCM Press, 1950.

Cuming, G.J. *A History of Anglican Liturgy.* London: Macmillan and Co., 1969.

———. 'John Knox and the Book of Common Prayer: a short note.' *Liturgical Review* 10 (1980), 80–81.

———. 'The Post-baptismal Prayer in the *Apostolic Tradition*: Further Considerations.' *Journal of Theological Studies* 39 (1988), 117–19.

———. 'Thmuis Revisited: Another Look at the Prayers of Bishop Serapion.' *Theological Studies* 41 (1980), 568–75.

Cummings, Owen F. 'Is Mormon Baptism Valid?' *Worship* 71 (1997), 146–53.

Curtis, Mark H. 'Hampton Court Conference and its Aftermath.' *History* 46 (1961), 1–16.

Cyprian, Saint. *To Donatus.* In *Born to New Life.* Edited by Oliver Davies and translated by Tim Withrow. Brooklyn, NY: New City Press, 1992, 21–2.

Cyril, Saint. *St Cyril of Jerusalem's Lectures on the Christian Sacraments.* Edited by F.L. Cross. London: SPCK, 1966.

Cyrus of Edessa. *Six Explanations of the Liturgical Feasts.* Translated and edited by William F. Macomber. Louvain: Corpus SCP, 1974.

Dalby, Mark. *Open Baptism.* London: SPCK, 1989.

Danielou, Jean. 'Chrismation Prebaptismale et Divinité de l'Esprit chez Gregoire de Nysse.' *Recherches de Science Religieuse* 56 (1968), 177–98.

Daniels, Harold M. *To God Alone Be Glory. The Story and Sources of the Book of Common Worship.* Louisville, KY: Geneva Press, 2003.

Dankbaar, W.F. and Marten Micron. *De Christlicke Ordinancien der Nederlantscher Ghemeinten Te Londen (1554),* s-Gravenhage: Martinus Nijhoff, 1956.

Davies, Douglas J. *An Introduction to Mormonism.* Cambridge: Cambridge University Press, 2003.

Davril, Anselme. *The Winchcombe Sacramentary.* London: Henry Bradshaw Society, 1995.

Day, Juliette. 'The Mystagogic Catecheses of Jerusalem and their Relationship to the Eastern Baptismal Liturgies of the Fourth and Early Fifth Centuries.' Ph.D dissertation, University of London, 2003.

De Simone, Russell J. 'Modern Research on the Sources of Saint Augustine's Doctrine of Original Sin.' *Augustinian Studies* 11 (1980), 205–27.

De Vinck, Jose. *The Works of Bonaventure,* Volume 2. Paterson, NJ: St Anthony Guild Press, 1963.

Deferrari, Roy J. *Hugh of Saint Victor on the Sacraments of the Christian Faith.* Cambridge, MA: Mediaeval Academy of America, 1951.

Devotional Services for Public Worship. Glasgow: Maclehouse, 1892.

De Vries, W. 'Die Erklärung aller Göttlichen Geheimnisse des Nestorianers Johannan Bar Zo'bi (13 Jahrh.).' *Orientalia Christiana Periodica* 96 (1943), 191–203.

————. 'Zur Liturgie der Erwachsenentaufe bei den Nestorianern.' *Orientalia Christiana Periodica* 96 (1943), 460–73.

Dionysius, the Areopagite, Saint. *Dionysius the Pseudo-Areopagite.* Translated by Thomas L. Campbell. Lanham, MD: University of America Press, 1981.

Dixon, Philip. *Nice and Hot Disputes. The Doctrine of the Trinity in the Seventeenth Century.* New York: Continuum, 2003.

Dodd, C.H. *Interpretation of the Fourth Gospel.* Cambridge: Cambridge University Press, 1951.

Dolan, John Patrick. *The Influence of Erasmus, Witzel, and Cassander in the Church Ordinances and Reform Proposals of the United Duchy of Cleve During the Middle Decades of the Sixteenth Century.* Münster: Aschendorff, 1957.

Dold, P. Alban. *Die Konstanzer Ritualientexte in ihrer Entwicklung von 1482–1721.* Münster in Westfalia: Ascendorff, 1923.

Doval, Alexis. *Cyril of Jerusalem, Mystagogue: The Authorship of the Mystagogic Catecheses.* Washington, DC: Catholic University of America Press, 2001.

Draper, Jonathan A. (ed.). *The Didache in Modern Research.* Leiden: E.J. Brill, 1996.

————. 'Ritual Process and Ritual Symbol in Didache 7–10.' *Vigiliae Christianae* 54 (2000), 121–58.

Duck, Ruth (ed.). *Bread for the Journey. Resources for Worship.* New York: The Pilgrim Press, 1981.

————. *Gender and the Name of God. The Trinitarian Baptismal Formula.* Cleveland, OH: Pilgrim Press, 1991.

———— and Patricia Wilson-Kastner. *Praising God. The Trinity in Christian Worship.* Louisville, KY: Westminster John Knox Press, 1999.

Duckworth, Dennis. *A Branching Tree. A Narrative History of the General Conference of the New Church.* London: The General Conference of the New Church, 1998.

Duffy, Eamon. *The Stripping of the Altars.* New Haven, CT and London: Yale University Press, 1992.

Duncan, Edward J. 'The Administration of Baptism in the Demonstrations of Aphraates.' In *Studies in Syrian Baptismal Rites,* Volume 6 (Syrian Church Series). Edited by Jacob Vellian. Kottayam, Kerala, India: CMS, 1973.

Dunn, James D.G. '"Baptized" as Metaphor.' In *Baptism in the New Testament and the Church. Historical and Contemporary Studies in Honour of R.E.O. White.* Edited by Stanley E. Porter and Anthony R. Cross. Sheffield: Sheffield Academic Press, 1999, 294–310.

Edgeworth, Roger. *Sermons very fruitfully, godly and learned, preched and sette forth by Maister Roger Edgeworth, doctoure of diuinitie.* London, 1557.

Edwall, P., E. Hayman and W.D. Maxwell (eds). *Ways of Worship.* London: SCM Press, 1951.

Ellis, Christopher. 'Baptism and Sacramental Freedom.' In *Reflections on the Water. Understanding God and the World through the Baptism of Believers.* Edited by Paul S. Fiddes. Oxford: Regent's Park College, 1996, 23–45.

———. *Gathering. A Theology and Spirituality of Worship in Free Church Tradition.* London: SCM Press, 2004.

Elwood, Christopher. *The Body Broken. The Calvinist Doctrine of the Eucharist and the Symbolism of Power in Sixteenth-Century France.* Oxford: Oxford University Press, 1999.

Emerton, J. 'Some Problems of Text and Language in the Odes of Solomon.' *Journal of Theological Studies* 18 (1967), 372–406.

Engberding, H. *Das eucharistische Hochgebet der Basileiosliturgie. Textgeschichtliche Untersuchengen und kritische Ausgabe* (Inaugural Dissertation), Münster: no publisher, 1931.

Euchologion, 2nd edition. Edinburgh: Blackwood and Sons, 1869.

Evans, Earnest. 'Introduction.' *Tertullian's Homily on Baptism.* London: SPCK, 1964 <http://www.tertullian.org/articles/evans_bapt/evans_bapt_text_trans.htm>.

Fagan, Garrett G. *Bathing in Public in the Roman World.* Ann Arbor: University of Michigan Press, 1999.

Fawcett, Timothy. *The Liturgy of Comprehension 1689.* Southend on Sea: Mayhew-McCrimmon, 1973.

Felton, Gayle Carlton. *This Gift of Water. The Practice and Theology of Baptism Among Methodists in America.* Nashville, TN: Abingdon Press, 1992.

Fenwick, John. *The Free Church of England. Introduction to an Anglican Tradition.* London: T & T Clark, 2004.

——— and Bryan Spinks. *Worship in Transition. The Liturgical Movement in the Twentieth Century.* New York: Continuum, 1995.

Fiddes, Paul. 'Baptism and Creation.' In *Reflections on the Water. Understanding God and the World through the Baptism of Believers.* Edited by Paul S. Fiddes. Oxford: Regent's Park College, 1996,

Finn, Thomas M. 'The Ritual Process and Survival in Second-Century Rome.' *Journal of Ritual Studies* 3 (1989), 69–89.

———. *Early Christian Baptism and the Catechumenate – Volume 2: Italy, North Africa, and Egypt.* Collegeville, MN: Liturgical Press, 1992.

———. *Early Christian Baptism and the Catechumenate – Volume 1: West and East Syria.* Collegeville, MN: Liturgical Press, 1992.

Fischer, Balthasar. 'Baptismal Exorcism in the Catholic Baptismal Rites after Vatican II.' *Studia Liturgica* 10 (1974), 48–55.

Fisher, J.D.C. *Christian Initiation. Baptism in the Medieval West.* London: SPCK, 1965.

———. *Christian Initiation. The Reformation Period.* London: SPCK, 1970.

———. *Confirmation Then and Now.* London: SPCK/Alcuin Club, 1978, 128–9.

Fitzer, Joseph. 'The Augustinian Roots of Calvin's Eucharistic Thought.' *Augustinian Studies* 7 (1976), 69–98.

Flegg, Columba. *Gathered Under Apostles. A Study of the Catholic Apostolic Church.* Oxford: Clarendon Press, 1992.

Fowler, Stanley K. *More Than a Symbol. The British Baptist Recovery of Baptismal Sacramentalism.* Carlisle: Paternoster Press, 2002.

Fox, George. *The Journal of George Fox.* Edited by John L. Nickalls. London: Religious Society of Friends, 1975.

Freeman, Arthur J. *An Ecumenical Theology of the Heart: The Theology of Count Nicholas Ludwig von Zinzendorf.* Bethlehem, PA: The Moravian Church in America, 1998.

Fugel, Adolf. *Tauflehre und Taufliturgie bei Huldrych Zwingli.* Berne: Peter Lang, 1989.

Fulton, Gayle, and Karen Westerfield-Tucker. *American Methodist Worship.* Oxford and New York: University Press, 2001.

Garite, Gerard. *Documents pour l'étude du livre d'Agathange.* Vatican City, 1946, 98–100.

Garrigan, Siobhán. *Beyond Ritual.* Aldershot: Ashgate Publishing, 2004.

Gelston, Anthony. 'A Note on the Text of the *Apostolic Tradition* of Hippolytus.' *Journal of Theological Studies* 39 (1988), 112–17.

General Synod of the Church of England. *Christian Initiation and its Relation to Some Pastoral Offices*, GS Misc. 366, London, 1991.

George, Timothy. 'The Presuppositions of Zwingli's Baptismal Theology.' In *Prophet, Pastor, Protestant.* Edited by E.J. Furcha and H. Wayne Pipkin. Allison Park, PA: Pickwick Publications, 1984, 71–87.

Germanus, Saint. *Expositio Antiquae Liturgiae Gallicanae.* Edited by E.C. Ratcliff. London: Henry Bradshaw Society, 1971.

Gerrish, Brian. 'The Lord's Supper in the Reformed Confessions.' In *Major Themes in the Reformed Tradition.* Edited by Donald K. McKim. Grand Rapids, MI: Eerdmans, 1992, 245–58.

Gilbert, H.S. 'The Liturgical History of Baptism.' In *Memoirs of the Lutheran Liturgical Association*. Philadelphia, PA: 1906–07, 67–78.

Goode, William. *The Doctrine of the Church of England as to the Effects of Baptism in the Case of Infants*. New York: Stanford and Swords, 1849.

Grebaut, Selvain. 'Ordre du Baptême et de la confirmation dans l'Église Éthiopienne.' *Revue de l'Orient Chrétien* 6 (1927–28), 105–189.

Green, Robin. *Only Connect. Worship and Liturgy from the Perspective of Pastoral Care*. London: Darton, Longman and Todd, 1987.

Gregory of Nazianus. *Oration on Holy Baptism*. Nicene and Post-Nicene Fathers series <http://www.ccel.org/fathers2/NPNF2-07/Npnf2-07-52.htm TopOfPage>.

Gregory of Nyssa. *On the Holy Spirit*. Nicene and Post-Nicene Fathers series <http://www.ccel.org/fathers2/NPNF2-05/Npnf2-05-26.htm P2435 1676104>.

Gregory of Tours, Saint. *The History of the Franks*, Volume 2. Translated by O.M. Dalton. Oxford: Clarendon Press, 1927, 69–70.

Grell, Ole Peter. *The Scandinavian Reformation*. Cambridge: Cambridge University Press, 1995.

Grenz, Stanley J. and John R. Francke. *Beyond Foundationalism. Shaping Theology in a Postmodern Context*. Louisville, KY: Westminster John Knox Press, 2001.

Grimes, Ronald L. *Deeply into the Bone: Re-inventing Rites of Passage*. Berkeley, CA: University of California Press, 2000.

Grönvik, Lorenz. *Die Taufe in der Theologie Martin Luthers*. Åbo: Åbo Akademi, 1967.

Grundtvig, Nicolaj F.S. 'Elementary Christian Teachings.' *A Grundtvig Anthology*. Edited by N.L. Jensen. Cambridge: James Clarke & Co., 1984.

Hanssens, J.M. *La Liturgie d'Hippolyte*. Rome: Pontifical Oriental Institute, 1959.

Hapgood, Isabel. *Service Book of the Holy Orthodox-Catholic Apostolic Church*. New York: Association Press, 1922, 271–83.

Harding, Vincent G. 'Menno and the Role of Baptism.' *Mennonite Quarterly Review* 33 (1959), 323–34.

Harmless, William. *Augustine and the Catechumenate*. Collegeville, MN: Pueblo Liturgical Press, 1995.

Harrison, Robert and Robert Browne. *The Writings of Robert Harrison and Robert Browne*. Edited by Albert Peel and Leland H. Carlson. London: Allen and Unwin, 1953.

Hartman, Lars. *Into the Name of the Lord Jesus. Baptism in the Early Church*. Edinburgh: T & T Clark, 1997.

Hatchett, Marion. *The Making of the First American Book of Common Prayer*. New York: Seabury Press, 1982.

———. 'Prayer Books.' In *The Study of Anglicanism*. Edited by S. Sykes and J. Booty. London: SPCK, 1988.

Hauerwas, Stanley. *The Peaceable Kingdom*. Notre Dame, IN: University of Notre Dame Press, 1983, 107–108.

Hayek, Michel. *Ammar Al-Basri, Apologie et Controverses*. Beirut, 1977.

Haykin, Michael A.G. *Kiffin, Knollys and Keach – Rediscovering our English Baptist Heritage*. Leeds: Reformation Today Trust, 1996.

Henderson, W.G. *Manuale et Processionale ad usum Insignis Ecclesiae Eboracensis*. London: Surtess Society, 1875.

Hill, C.L. *The Loci Communes of Philip Melanchthon*. Boston, MA: Meador Publishing House, 1944.

Hindmarsh, Robert. *The Rise and Progress of the New Jerusalem Church*. London: Hodson & Son, 1861.

Hoffman, L.A. *Beyond the Text: A Holistic Approach to Liturgy*. Indianapolis: Indiana University Press, 1987.

Hohler, Christopher. 'The Red Book of Darley.' In *Nordiskt Kollokvium II. 1. Latinsk Liturgiforskning*. Stockholm: Stockholm University, 1972, 39–47.

Holeton, David R. *Growing in Newness of Life. Christian Initiation in Anglicanism Today*. Toronto: The Anglican Book Centre, 1993.

Holifield, E. Brooks. *The Covenant Sealed. The Development of Puritan Sacramental Theology in Old and New England, 1570–1720*. New Haven, CT and London: Yale University Press, 1979.

Holland, Bernard G. *Baptism in Early Methodism*. London: Epworth Press, 1970.

———. 'The Doctine of Infant Baptism in Non-Wesleyan Methodism.' Wesley Historical Society Occasional Paper 1 (Cyclostyled), n.p., 1970.

Holmes, Urban T. 'Education for Liturgy: An Unfinished Symphony in Four Movements.' In *Worship Points the Way. Celebration of the Life and Work of Massey H. Shepherd, Jr*. Edited by Malcolm C. Burson. New York: Seabury Press, 1981, 116–41.

The Homilies of the Anglo-Saxon Church, 2 volumes. Edited by B. Thorpe. London: The Aelfric Society, London, 1844–46.

Honders, A.C. *Valerandus Pollanus. Liturgica Sacra (1551–1555)*. Leiden: E.J. Brill, 1970.

Hope, Nicholas. *German and Scandinavian Protestantism 1700–1918*. Oxford: Clarendon Press, 1995.

Horsch, John. 'Did Menno Simons Practice Baptism by Immersion?' *Mennonite Quarterly Review* 1 (1927), 54–6.

Hough, James. *The History of Christianity in India*, Volume 2. London: Nisbet, 1845, 645–50 <http://www.nd.edu/~afreddos/translat/biel.htm>.

Huber, Raphael M. 'The Doctrine of Ven. John Duns Scotus. Concerning the Causality of the Sacraments.' *Franciscan Studies* 4 (1926), 9–38.

Hubert, F. *Die Strassburger Liturgischen Ordnungen in Zeitalter der Reformation*. Göttingen: Vandenhoek und Ruprecht, 1900.

Hunsinger, George. 'The Dimension of Depth: Thomas F. Torrance on the Sacraments of Baptism and the Lord's Supper.' *Scottish Journal of Theology* 54 (2001), 155–76.

———. *How to Read Karl Barth*. New York: Oxford University Press, 1991.

Hunt, Arnold. 'Laurance Chaderton and the Hampton Court Conference.' In *Belief and Practice in Reformation England*. Edited by Susan Wabuda and Caroline Litzenberger. Aldershot: Ashgate, 1998, 207–28.

Hürlimann, Gebhard. *Das Rheinauer Rituale*. Freiburg: Universitätsverlag Freiburg Schweiz, 1959.

Hut, Hans. *True Baptism* <http://www.anabaptistchurch.org/Baptism.htm>.

Irving, Edward. *The Day of Pentecost, or the Baptism with the Holy Ghost*. Edinburgh: John Lindsay, 1831.

―――. *Homilies on the Sacraments – Volume 1: Baptism*. London: Andrew Panton, 1828.

Isaac, J. (ed.). 'Emmanuel Bar Shahhare, Memra on the Explanation of Baptism.' *Bayn al-Nahrayn* 11 (1983), 26–66.

Jackson, Ralph. 'Spas, waters, and Hydrotherapy in the Roman World.' In *Roman Baths and Bathing*. Edited by J. DeLaine and D.E. Johnston. Portsmouth, RI: *Journal of Roman Archaeology*, 1999, 107–116.

Jacob of Serugh. *Homiliae Selectae Mar-Jacobi Sarugensis*, Volume 3. Edited by Paulus Bedjan. Paris: Harrassowitz, 1905–10.

Jacobs, Elfriede. *Die Sakramentslehre Wilhelm Farels*. Zurich: Theologischer Verlag, 1978.

Jagger, Peter J. *Clouded Witness*. Allison Park, PA: Pickwick Publications, 1982.

James,E. *The Articles of Faith*. 11th edition. Salt Lake City, UT: The Deseret News, 1919.

Jameson, Fredric. *Postmodernism or, The Cultural Logic of Late Capitalism*. Durham, NC: Duke University Press, 1991.

Jasper, R.C.D. and Paul F. Bradshaw. *A Companion to the Alternative Service Book*. London: SPCK, 1986.

Jeanes, Gordon. *The Day has Come. Easter and Baptism in Zeno of Verona*. Collegeville, MN: The Liturgical Press, 1995.

―――. 'A Reformation Treatise on the Sacraments.' *Journal of Theological Studies* 46 (1995), 149–90.

―――. 'Signs of God's Promise: Thomas Cranmer's Sacramental Theology and Baptismal Liturgy.' Ph.D. dissertation, University of Wales, Lampeter, 1998.

Jeffers, James S. *Conflict at Rome: Social Order and Hierarchy in Early Christianity*. Minneapolis, MN: Fortress Press, 1991.

Jefford, Clayton N. (ed.). *The Didache in Context*. Leiden: E.J. Brill, 1995.

Jeremias, Joachim. *Infant Baptism in the First Four Centuries*. Translated by D.Cairns. Philadelphia, PA: Westminster Press, 1963.

Jetter, Werner. *Die Taufe beim jungen Luther*. Tübingen: Mohr, 1954.

Johnson, Caroline. 'Ritual Epiclesis in the Greek *Acts of Thomas*.' In *The Apocryphal Acts of the Apostles*. Edited by F. Bovan, A.G. Brock and C.R. Matthews. Harvard Divinity School Studies, Cambridge, MA: Harvard University Press, 1999, 171–204.

Johnson, Maxwell E. 'The Postchrismational Structure of Apostolic Tradition 21, the Witness of Ambrose of Milan, and a Tentative Hypothesis Regarding the Current Reform of Confirmation in the Roman Rite.' *Worship* 70 (1996), 16–34.

———. *The Prayers of Serapion of Thmuis: A Literary, Liturgical, and Theological Analysis. Orientalia Christiana Analecta* 249, Rome: Pontifical Oriental Institute, 1995.

———. 'Reconciling Cyril and Egeria on the Catechetical Process in Fourth Century Jerusalem.' In *Essays in Early Christian Initiation.* Edited by Paul Bradshaw. Bramcote: Grove Books, 1988, 18–30.

———. *The Rites of Christian Initiation.* Collegeville, MN: Liturgical Press, 1999, 66–7.

Jones, Simon. 'Womb of the Spirit. The Liturgical Implications of the Doctrine of the Spirit for the Syrian Baptismal Tradition.' Ph.D Thesis, University of Cambridge, 1999.

Kadicheeni, Paul B. (ed.). *The Mystery of Baptism: the text and translation of the chapter 'On Holy Baptism' from the causes of the seven mysteries of the Church of Timothy II, Nestorian patriarch (1318–1332).* Bangalore: Dharmaram Publications, 1980.

Kalb, Friedrich. *Theology of Worship in 17th Century Lutheranism.* Translated by Henry P.A. Hamann. St Louis, MO: Concordia Publishing House, 1965.

Kavanagh, Aidan. *Confirmation: Origins and Reform.* Collegeville, MN: Pueblo Liturgical Press, 1988.

———. *The Shape of Baptism.* New York: Pueblo Press, 1978.

Kawerau, Gustav. 'Liturgische Studien zu Luthers Taufbüchlein von 1523.' *Zeitschrift für kirchliche Wissenschaft und kirchliches Leben* 10 (1898), 407–31, 466–77, 519–47, 578–99, 625–43.

Kay, James F. 'The New Rites of Baptism: A Dogmatic Assessment.' In *To Glorify God. Essays on Modern Reformed Liturgy.* Edited by Bryan D. Spinks and Iain R. Torrance. Edinburgh: T & T Clark, 1999, 201–12.

Keefe, Susan Ann. 'The Claim of Authorship in Carolingian Baptismal Expositions: The Case of Odilbert of Milan.' In *Fälschungen im Mittelalter: Internationaler Kongress der Monuementa Germaniae Historica, München, 16–19 September 1986.* Hannover: Hahnsche Buchhandlung, 1988, 385–401.

———. *Water and the Word. Baptism and Education of the Clergy in the Carolingian Empire,* 2 volumes. Notre Dame, IN: University of Notre Dame Press, 2002.

Keefer, Sarah Larratt. 'Manuals.' In *The Liturgical Books of Anglo-Saxon England.* Edited by Richard W. Pfaff. Kalamazoo, MI: Medical Institute Publications, Western Michigan University, 1995, 99–109.

Kelly, Henry Ansgar. *The Devil at Baptism. Ritual, Theology, and Drama.* Ithaca, NY and London: Cornell University Press, 1985.

Khs-Burmester, O.H.E. 'The Baptismal Rite of the Coptic Church. A Critical Study.' *Bulletin de la Société d'Archéologie Copte* 11 (1945), 27–86.

————. *The Egyptian or Coptic Church. A Detailed Description of Her Liturgical Services and the Rites and Ceremonies Observed in the Administration of her Sacraments.* Cairo: Publications de la Société d'Archéologie Copte, 1965.

Klijn, A.F.J. *The Acts of Thomas.* Leiden: E.J. Brill, 1962.

Knox, John. 'Answers to some Questions concerning Baptism.' In *Works.* Edited by David Laing, Volume IV. Edinburgh, 1855.

Kohlberg, A. *Die älteste Agende in der Diozese Ermland und den Deutschordensstaate Preussen nach dem ersten Druckausgaben von 1512 und 1529.* Braunsberg: Rudlowski, 1903.

Kreitzer, Larry J. 'On Board the Eschatological Ark of God: Noah-Deucalion and the 'Phrygian Connection' in 1 Peter 3.19–22.' In *Baptism in the New Testament and the Church. Historical and Contemporary Studies in Honour of R.E.O. White.* Edited by Stanley E. Porter and Anthony R. Cross. Sheffield: Sheffield Academic Press, 1999, 228–72.

Kretschmar, G. 'Die Geschichte des Taufgottesdienstes in der alten Kirche.' In *Leiturgia, Handbuch des evangelischen Gottesdienstes.* Edited by Karl Ferdinand Muller and Walter Blakenburg. Kassel-Wilhennshohe: J. Stauda-Verlag, 1970.

Kuhrt, Gordon. *Believing in Baptism.* London: Mowbray, 1987.

Kuyper, A. *Joannis a Lasca Opera*, 2 volumes. Amsterdam: F. Muller, 1866.

La Piana, George. 'The Roman Church at the End of the Second Century.' *Harvard Theological Review* 18 (1925), 214–77.

Lages, Mario. 'The Hierosolymitian Origin of the Catechetical Rites in the Armenian Liturgy.' *Didaskalia* 1 (1971), 233–50.

Lakoff, George and Mark Johnson. *Philosophy in the Flesh: The Embodied Mind and Its Challenge to Western Thought.* New York: Basic Books, 1999.

Lara, Jaime. '"Precious Green Jade Water": A Sixteenth-Century Adult Catechumenate in the New World.' *Worship* 71 (1997), 415–28.

Lausten, Martin Schwarz. *A Church History of Denmark.* Aldershot: Ashgate, 2002.

Leachman, James. 'The New Family of Common Worship Liturgical Books of the Church of England (2): An Introduction to the Initiation Services and their Theology.' *Ecclesia Orans* 21 (2004), 67–97.

Ledwich, William. 'Baptism, Sacrament of the Cross: Looking behind St. Ambrose.' In *The Sacrifice of Praise. Studies on the themes of thanksgiving and redemption in the central prayers of the Eucharistic and baptismal liturgies. In honour of Arthur Hubert Couratin.* Edited by Bryan D. Spinks. Rome: CLV, 1981.

Lee, Daniel B. *Old Order Mennonites. Rituals, Beliefs, and Community.* Chicago, IL: Burnham Inc., 2000.

Leenhardt, F.-J. *Le Baptême chrétien, son origine, sa signification.* Neuchâtel: Delachaux & Niestlé, 1946.

Leeper, Elizabeth A. 'From Alexandria to Rome: The Valentinian Connection to the Incorporation of Exorcism as a Prebaptismal Rite.' *Vigiliae Christianae* 44 (1990), 6–24.

Lentz, Harold H. *Reformation Crossroads*. Minneapolis, MN: Augsburg Publishing House, 1958.

Lester, Hiram J. 'Alexander Campbell's Millennial Program.' *Discipliana* 48 (1988), 35–9.

Lewis, A.J. *Zinzendorf the Ecumenical Pioneer.* London: SCM Press, 1962.

Linyard, Fred and Phillip Tovey. *Moravian Worship*. Bramcote: Grove Books, 1994.

Liturgic Hymns of the United Brethren, Revised and Enlarged: Translated from the German. London, 1793.

Liturgie à l'usage des Réformées. Paris, 1874.

The Liturgy of the Frankfurt Exiles 1555. Edited by Robin A. Leaver. Bramcote: Grove Books, 1984.

The Liturgy of the Holy Apostles Addai and Mari, and the Order of Baptism. London: SPCK, 1893. Reprinted Piscataway, NJ: Georgias Press, 2002.

A Liturgy: or, Order of Christian Worship. Philadelphia, PA, 1865.

Loades, Anne. 'Finding New Sense in the "Sacramental."' In *The Gestures of God. Explorations in Sacramentality*. Edited by Geoffrey Rowell and Christine Hall. New York: Continuum, 2004, 161–72.

Logan, Alastair H. *Gnostic Truth and Christian Heresy*. Edinburgh: T & T Clark, 1996.

———. 'The Mystery of the Five Seals: Gnostic Initiation Reconsidered.' *Vigiliae Christianae* 51 (1997), 188–206.

Lombard, Peter. 'Sacrum signans et sacrum signatum.' In *Sententiae in IV Libris Distinctae*, 2 volumes. Grottaferrata: Collegii S. Bonaventurae ad Claras Aquas, 1981 <http://franciscan-archive.org/lombardus/index.html#writings>.

Lukken, G.M. *Original Sin in the Roman Liturgy*. Leiden: E.J. Brill, 1973.

Lumbala, F. Kabasele. 'Black Africa and Baptismal Rites.' In *Becoming a Christian. The Ecumenical Implications of our Common Baptism*. Edited by Thomas F. Best and Dagmar Heller. Geneva: WCC Publications, 1999, 36–40.

Lumpkin, William L. *Baptist Confessions of Faith*. Valley Forge, PA: Judson Press, 1969.

Luther, Martin. *Luther's Works, American Edition*, 55 volumes. Edited by Jaroslav Pelikan and Helmut T. Lehman. St Louis, MO: Concordia Publishing House and Philadelphia: Fortress Press, 1955–86.

———. *Luthers Werke, Kritische Gesamtausgabe*, 57 volumes. Edited by J.F.K. Knaake et al. Weimer: Bühlau, 1883–2003.

Lutheran Liturgical Association. 'The Liturgical Deterioration of the Seventeenth and Eighteenth Centuries.' *Memoirs of the Lutheran Liturgical Association IV*. Philadelphia, PA: 1906–07, 67–78.

———. 'The Liturgy in Denmark.' *Memoirs of the Lutheran Liturgical Association II*. Philadelphia, PA: 1906–07, 63–73.

Lynch, Joseph H. *Christianizing Kinship. Ritual Sponsorship in Anglo-Saxon England*. Ithaca, NY and London: Cornell University Press, 1998.

————. *Godparents and Kinship in Early Medieval Europe.* Princeton, NJ: Princeton University Press, 1986.

Lyon, David. *Jesus in Disneyland. Religion in Postmodern Times.* Cambridge: Polity Press, 2000.

MacCulloch, Diarmaid. *Thomas Cranmer.* New Haven, CT and London: Yale University Press, 1996.

Mackenzie, Ross. *The Epistles of Paul the Apostle to the Romans and to the Thessalonians.* Edinburgh: Oliver and Boyd, 1961.

Macomber, W.F. (ed.). *Six Explanations of the Liturgical Feasts* (CSCO 356). Louvain: Corpus Scriptorum Christianorum Orientalium, 1974.

————. 'The Theological Synthesis of Cyrus of Edessa, an East Syrian Theologian of the Mid Sixth Century.' *Orientalia Christiana Periodica,* 1964, 1–38, 363–84, 150.

Macquarrie, John. *A Guide to the Sacraments.* New York: Continuum, 1997.

Maring, Norman H. and Winthrop S. Hudson. *A Baptist Manual of Polity and Practice.* Valley Forge, PA: Judson Press, 1963.

Martimort, A.G. (ed.). *The Church at Prayer. Volume III: The Sacraments.* London: Geoffrey Chapman, 1988.

————. *The Signs of the New Covenant.* Collegeville, MN: ET Liturgical Press, 1963.

Mateos, Juan. 'Théologie du Baptême dans le formulaire de Severe D'Antioche.' *Symposium Syriacum 1972.* Rome: Pontifical Oriental Institute, 1974, 135–61.

Matheson, Peter. *The Collected Works of Thomas Müntzer.* Edinburgh: T & T Clark, 1988.

Maurice, F.D. *The Faith of the Liturgy and the Doctrines of the Thirty-Nine Articles, Two Sermons.* Cambridge, 1869.

Mbonigaba, Elisha. 'Indigenization of the Liturgy.' In *A Kingdom of Priests: Liturgical Formation of the People of God.* Edited by Thomas J. Talley. Nottingham: Alcuin/ GROW Liturgical Study 5, 1988, 39–47.

McAllister, Lester G. and William E. Tucker. *Journey in Faith.* St Louis, MO: Bethany Press, 1975.

McClendon, James William Jr. *Systematic Theology: Doctrine.* Nashville, TN: Abingdon Press, 1994.

McGrath, Alister E. *Iustitia Dei. A History of the Christian Doctrine of Justification. Volume 2: From 1500 to the Present Day.* Cambridge: Cambridge University Press, 1986.

McHugh, John A. and Charles J. Callan (trans). *Catechism of the Council of Trent for Parish Priests. Issued by Order of Pope Pius V.* New York: Joseph F. Wagner, 1923.

McKillop, Sybil. 'A Romano-British Baptismal Liturgy?' In *The Early Church in Western Britain and Ireland.* Edited by Susan M. Pearce, BAR British Series 102 (1982), 35–48.

Mcleod, Frederick G. 'The Christological Ramifications of Theodore of Mopsuestia's Understanding of Baptism and the Eucharist.' *Journal of Early Christian Studies* 10 (2002), 37–75.

Meeter, Daniel James. *'Bless the Lord, O my Soul'. The New-York Liturgy of the Dutch Reformed Church, 1767*. Lanham, MD: Scarecrow Press, 1998.

Melanchthon, Philip. *Commentary on Romans*. Translated by Fred Kramer. St. Louis, MO: Concordia Publishing House, 1992.

Methuen, Charlotte. 'Widows, Bishops and the Struggle for Authority in the *Didascalia Apostolorum*.' *Journal of Ecclesiastical History* 46 (1995), 197–213.

Meyers, Ruth A. *Continuing the Reformation. Re-Visioning Baptism in the Episcopal Church*. New York: Church Publishing Incorporated, 1997.

Mingana, Alphonse. *Woodbrooke Studies*, Volume 6. Cambridge: Heffers, 1933.

Mirk, John. *Instructions for Parish Priests*. Edited by Edward Peacock. London: Kegan Paul, Trench, Trübner, 1902.

———. *Mirk's Festial: A Collection of Homilies*. London: Kegan Paul, Trench and Trübner (for the Early English Text Society), 1905.

———. *Quatuor Sermones*. Edited by R. Pynson. London, 1502.

Mitchell, Leonel L. 'Mitchell on Hatchett on Cranmer.' In *With Ever Joyful Hearts. Essays on Liturgy and Music Honoring Marion J. Hatchett*. Edited by J. Neil Alexander. New York: Church Publishing Incorporated, 1999, 103–38.

Mitchell, Nathan. 'Baptism in the Didache.' In *The Didache in Context*. Edited by Clayton N. Jefford. Leiden: E.J. Brill, 1995, 226–55.

Moltmann, Jürgen. *The Church in the Power of the Spirit. A Contribution to Messianic Ecclesiology*. London: ET SCM Press, 1977.

Moravian Church. *The Liturgy and Canticles authorized for use in the Moravian Church in Great Britain and Ireland*. London: Moravian Publication Office, 1914.

Morris, Richard. *Old English Homilies and Homiletic Treatises*. New York: Greenwood Press, 1968.

Mouhanna, Augustin. *Les Rites de l'initiation dans l'Église Maronite*. Rome: Orientalia Periodica Analecta, 1980.

Muller, Richard. *Post-Reformation Dogmatics. Volume 1: Prolegomena to Theology*. Grand Rapids, MI: Baker Book House, 1987.

Myers, Gilly. *Using Common Worship: Initiation*. London: Church House Publishing, 2000.

Mysteries of Initiation. Baptism, Confirmation, Communion According to the Maronite Antiochene Church. Washington, DC: Diocesan Office of Liturgy, 1987.

Myers, Susan. 'Initiation by Anointing in Early Syriac-Speaking Christianity.' *Studia Liturgica* 31 (2001), 150–70.

Nagel, Norman E. 'Holy Baptism.' In *Lutheran Worship. History and Practice*. Edited by Fred L. Precht. St Louis, MO: Concordia Publishing House, 1993.

Nevin, John W. 'The Mystical Presence: A Vindication of the Reformed or Calvinistic Doctrine of the Holy Eucharist.' In *The Mystical Presence and Other Writings on the Eucharist*. Edited by Bard Thompson and George H. Bicker. Philadelphia, PA: United Church Press, 1966.

Niederwimmer, Kurt. *Didache*. Minneapolis, MN: ET Augsburg Fortress Press, 1998.

Nischan, Bodo. 'The Exorcism Controversy and Baptism in the Late Reformation.' *The Sixteenth Century Journal* 18 (1987), 31–50.

————. *Prince, People and Confession. The Second Reformation in Brandenburg*. Philadelphia: University of Pennsylvania Press, 1994.

Noll, Mark A. *The Rise of Evangelicalism. The Age of Edwards, Whitefield and the Wesleys*. Downers Grove, IL: Intervarsity Press, 2003.

Null, Ashley. *Thomas Cranmer's Doctrine of Repentance*. Oxford: Oxford University Press, 2000.

Nümann, F.K. 'Zur Entstehung des lutherischen Taufbüchleins von Jahre 1523.' *Monatschrift für Gottesdienst und kirchliche Kunst* 33 (1928), 214–19.

Oberman, Heiko. *The Harvest of Medieval Theology*. Cambridge, MA: Harvard University Press, 1963.

Old, H.O. *The Shaping of the Reformed Baptismal Rite in the Sixteenth Century*. Grand Rapids, MI: Eerdmans, 1992.

The Old Testament Pseudepigrapha, Volume 1. Edited by J.H. Charlesworth. Garden City, NJ: Doubleday, 1983.

The Order of Baptism according to the Rite of the Armenian Apostolic Orthodox Church. Evanston, IL: n.p., 1964.

Ostervald, J.F. *A Compendium of Christian Theology*. Translated by John McMains. Hartford, CT: Nathaniel Patten, 1788.

Page, R.I. 'Old English Liturgical Rubrics in Corpus Christi College, Cambridge, MS 422.' In *Anglia. Zeitschrift für Englische Philologie* 96 (1978), 149–58.

Pahl, P.D. 'Baptism in Luther's Lectures on Genesis.' *Lutheran Theological Journal* 1 (1967), 26–35.

Pannenberg, Wolfhart. *Systematic Theology*, Volume 3. Translated by Geoffrey W. Bromiley. Grand Rapids, MI: Eerdmans, 1998.

Parenti, Stefano and Elena Velkovska. *L'Eucologio Barberini gr. 336*. Rome: Centro Liturgico Vincenziano, 1995.

Parker, Kenneth L. and Eric J. Carlson. *'Practical Divinity'. The Works and Life of Revd. Richard Greenham*. Aldershot: Ashgate, 1998.

Parons, K.A. (ed.). *Church Book: St Andrews' Street Baptist Church, Cambridge, 1720–1832*. London: Baptist Historical Society, 1991.

Pater, C.A. *Karlstadt as the Father of the Baptist Movement: The Emergence of Lay Protestantism*. Toronto: University of Toronto Press, 1984.

Payne, John B. 'Nevin on Baptism.' In *Reformed Confessionalism in Nineteenth-century America. Essays on the Thought of John Williamson Nevin*. Edited by Sam Hamstra and Arie J. Griffion. Lanham, MD: Scarecrow Press, 1995, 125–51.

Pearson, Brook W.R. 'Baptism and Initiation in the Cult of Isis and Sarapis.' In *Baptism in the New Testament and the Church. Historical and Contemporary Studies in Honour of R.E.O. White*. Edited by Stanley E. Porter and Anthony R. Cross. Sheffield: Sheffield Academic Press, 1999, 42–62.

Peaston, A.E. *The Prayer Book Tradition in the Free Churches*. London: James Clarke, 1964.

Peifer, Jane Hoober and John Stahl-Wert. *Welcoming New Christians. A Guide for the Christian Initiation of Adults*. Scottdale, PA: Faith and Life Press, Kansas and Mennonite Publishing House, 1995.

Pepperdene, Margaret. 'Baptism in the early British and Irish Churches.' *Irish Theological Quarterly* 22 (1955), 110–23.

Perkins, William. *Works*, 3 volumes. Cambridge: J. Legatt and C. Legge, 1616–18.

Peter Lombard <http://franciscan-archive.org/lombardus/index.html#writings>.

Pettigree, Andrew. *Foreign Protestant Communities in Sixteenth-Century London*. Oxford: Clarendon Press, 1986.

Pierce, Mark. 'Themes in the "Odes of Solomon" and other early Christian Writings and their Baptismal Character.' *Ephemerides Liturgicae* 98 (1984), 35–59.

Podmore, Colin. *The Moravian Church in England, 1728–1760*. Oxford: Clarendon Press, 1998.

Porter, H. Boone. 'Hispanic Influences on Worship in the English Tongue.' In *Time and Community. In Honor of Thomas Julian Talley*. Edited by J. Neil Alexander. Washington, DC: Pastoral Press, 1990, 171–84.

————. *Jeremy Taylor, Liturgist*. London: Alcuin Club/SPCK, 1979.

————. 'Maxentius of Aquileia and the North Italian Baptismal Rites.' *Ephemerides Liturgicae* 69 (1955), 3–8.

Porter, Stanley E. and Anthony R. Cross. *Baptism in the New Testament and the Church. Historical and Contemporary Studies in Honour of R.E.O. White*. Sheffield: Sheffield Academic Press, 1999.

Primus, John H. *Richard Greenham. The Portrait of an Elizabethan Pastor*. Macon, GA: Mercer University Press, 1998.

Probert, J.C.C. *The Worship and Devotion of Cornish Methodism* (cyclostyled), n.p., 1978 (copy in the Bodleian Library, Oxford).

Psalmodia Christiana. Translated by Arthur Anderson. Salt Lake City: University of Utah Press, 1993.

Pusey, Edward. *Tracts of theTimes*, 3 volumes. New York: Charles Henry, 1839–40.

Quenstedt, J. *Theologica Didactio-Polemica sive Systema Theologicum*, 1685.

Quere, Ralph W. *In the Context of Unity. A History of the Development of Lutheran Book of Worship*. Minneapolis, MN: Lutheran University Press, 2003.

Quill, Timothy C.J. *The Impact of the Liturgical Movement on American Lutheranism*. Lanham, MD: Scarecrow Press, 1997.

Randall, Max Ward. *The Great Awakenings and the Restoration Movement*. Joplin, MO: College Press Publishing Company, 1983.

Rappaport, Roy A. *Ritual and Religion in the Making of Humanity.* Cambridge: Cambridge University Press, 1999.

Ratcliff, E.C. (ed.). *Expositio Antiquae Liturgiae Gallicanae.* London: Henry Bradshaw Society, 1971.

————. 'Justin Martyr and Confirmation.' *Theology* 51 (1948), 133–9.

————. 'The Old Syrian Baptismal Tradition and its Resettlement under the Influence of Jerusalem in the Fourth Century.' In *Liturgical Studies.* Edited by A.H. Couratin and D.H. Tripp. London: SPCK, 1976, 135–54, 142–3.

Reed, Jonathan. 'The Hebrew Epic and the *Didache.*' In *The Didache in Context.* Edited by Clayton N. Jefford. Leiden: E.J. Brill, 1995, 213–25.

Reid, Alcuin. *The Organic Development of the Liturgy.* Farnborough: Saint Michael's Abbey Press, 2004.

Renoux, Charles. *Initiation chrétienne. 1. Rituels arméniens du baptême.* Paris: Les Éditions du Cerf, 1997, 5ff.

Reports to the General Assembly. Edinburgh, 1955.

Rex, Richard. *The Lollards.* New York: Palgrave, 2002.

Rican, Rudolf. *The History of the Unity of Brethren.* Bethlehem, PA: The Moravian Church in America, 1992.

Richardson, Robert. *Memoirs of Alexander Campbell,* Volume 1. Cincinnati, OH: Standard Publishing Company, 1913.

Richter, A.L. *Die evangelischen Kirchenordnungen des sechzehnten Jahrhunderts*, Volume 1. Nieuwkoop: B. Degraaf, 1967.

Ridgley, Thomas. *A Body of Divinity*, Volume 2. Edited by John M. Wilson. New York: Robert Carter and Brothers, 1855.

Riggs, John W. *Baptism in the Reformed Tradition.* Louisville, KY: Westminster John Knox Press, 2002.

————. 'Traditions, Tradition, and Liturgical Norms: The United Church of Christ Book of Worship.' *Worship* 62 (1988), 58–72.

Riley, Hugh M. *Christian Initiation.* Washington, DC: Catholic University of America, 1974.

Rittgers, Ronald. *The Reformation of the Keys. Confession, Conscience, and Authority in Sixteenth-Century Germany.* Cambridge, MA: Harvard University Press, 2004.

Roberts. Paul J. 'The Pattern of Initiation: Sacrament and Experience in the Catholic Apostolic Church and its implications for modern liturgical and theological debate.' Ph.D. thesis, University of Manchester, 1990.

Robinson, H. Wheeler. *Baptist Principles.* London: Kingsgate Press, 1938.

Robinson, J.A.T. 'The Baptism of John and the Qumran Community.' In *Twelve New Testament Studies.* London: SCM, 1962, 11–17.

Rodgers, Dirk W. *John à Lasco in England.* New York: Peter Lang, 1994.

Roman Catholic Church. *Study Text 10 CIA: Commentary.* Washington, DC, 1985.

Rordorf, Willi. 'Baptism according to the Didache.' In *The Didache in Modern Research.* Edited by Jonathan A. Draper. Leiden: E.J. Brill, 1996, 212–22.

Rorem, Paul. *Calvin and Bullinger on the Lord's Supper.* Bramcote: Alcuin/GROW Liturgical Study 12, Grove Books, 1989.

Ross, Susan. *Extravagant Affections. A Feminist Sacramental Theology.* New York: Continuum, 1998.

Ross, Woodburn O. *Middle English Sermons.* London: Oxford University Press, 1940.

Rouget, A.M. *Christ Acts Through Sacraments.* Collegeville, MN: The Liturgical Press, 1954.

Ruether, Rosemary Radford. W*omen-Church. Theology and Practice of Feminist Liturgical Communities.* San Francisco, CA: Harper and Row, 1985.

St. Thomas Aquinas, Summa Theologiae, ST 3a.60.1, 56. Edited by David Bourke. London: Blackfriars and Eyre and Spottiswoode, 1974, 5.

Samuel, Metropolitan Mar Athanasius Yeshue. *The Sacrament of Holy Baptsim according to the Ancient Rite of the Syrian Orthodox Church of Antioch.* Hackensack, NJ, 1974.

Sanders, E.P. *Paul.* Oxford: Oxford University Press, 1991.

————. *Paul and Palestinian Judaism: A Comparison of Patterns of Religion.* London: SCM Press, 1977.

Scaer, David P. *Baptism. Confessional Lutheran Dogmatics*, Volume XI. St Louis, MO: The Luther Academy, 1999.

Schaff, Philip. *The Creeds of Christendom.* Grand Rapids, MI: Baker Books, 1998.

Scharen, Christian. *Public Worship and Public Work. Character and Commitment in Local Congregational Life.* Collegeville, MN: Pueblo Liturgical Press, 2004.

Schleiermacher, F. *The Christian Faith*, Edinburgh: ET T & T Clark, 1989.

Schmid, Heinrich. *The Doctrinal Theology of the Evangelical Lutheran Church.* Translated by Charles A. Hay and Henry E. Jacobs. Philadelphia, PA: Lutheran Bookstore, 1876.

Scirughi, Thomas J. *An Examination of the Problems of Inclusive Language in the Trinitarian Formula of Baptism.* Lewiston, NY: Edwin Mellon Press, 2000.

The Scriptures, Internet Edition. The Church of Jesus Christ of Latter-Day Saints <http://scriptures.lds.org>.

The Second Helvetic Confession <http://www.ccel.org/creeds/helvetic.htm>.

Segelberg, E. 'The Baptismal Rite according to some of the Coptic-Gnostic Texts of Nag Hammadi.' *Studia Patristica* 5, Part Three (1962), 117–28.

Serra, Dominic E. *The Blessing of Baptismal Water at the Paschal Vigil (Gr. 444–448): Its Origins, Evolution, and Reform.* Diss. Pontifical Institute of Liturgy, St Anselmo, Rome, 1989.

Severus of Antioch. *The sixth book of the select letters of Severus, patriarch of Antioch, in the Syriac version of Athanasius of Nisbis.* Edited and translated by E.W. Brooks. London: Williams and Norgate, 1903.

Shaw, P.E. *The Catholic Apostolic Church.* New York: Kings Crown Press, 1946.

Shriver, Fred. 'Hampton Court Re-Visited: James I and the Puritans.' *Journal of Ecclesiastical History* 33 (1982), 48–71.

Small, Joseph D. 'A Church of the Word and Sacrament.' In *Christian Worship in Reformed Churches Past and Present*. Edited by Lukas Vischer. Grand Rapids, MI: Eerdmans, 2003, 311–23.

Smith, Joseph Jr. *History of the Church of Jesus Christ of Latter-day Saints*, Volume 4. Salt Lake City, UT: Deseret Book Co., 1976.

Soskice, Janet Martin. *Metaphor and Religious Language*. Oxford: Clarendon Press, 1985.

Spencer, Mark. 'Dating the Baptism of Clovis, 1886–1993.' *Early Medieval Europe* 3 (1994), 97–116.

Spener, Philip. *Pia Desideria*. Edited and translated by Theodore G. Tappert. Philadelphia, PA: Fortress Press, 1964.

Spinks, Bryan D. 'The Anaphora attributed to Severus of Antioch: a note on its character and theology.' In Θυσία αινέσες. *Mélanges liturgiques offerts à la mémoire de l'archevêque George Wagner*. Edited by J. Getcha and A. Lossky. Paris: Presses Saint-Serge, 2005, 345–51.

———. 'Calvin's Baptismal Theology and the Making of the Strasbourg and Genevan Baptismal Liturgies 1540 and 1542.' *Scottish Journal of Theology* 48 (1995), 55–78.

———. 'Cranmer, Baptism, and Christian Nurture; or, Toronto Revisited.' *Studia Liturgica* 32 (2002), 98–110.

———. '"Freely by His Grace": Baptismal doctrine and the reform of the baptismal liturgy in the Church of Scotland, 1953–1994.' In *Rule of Prayer, Rule of Faith: Essays in Honor of Aidan Kavanagh, OSB*. Edited by Nathan Mitchell and John F. Baldovin. Collegeville, MN: Liturgical Press, 1996, 218–42.

———. *From the Lord and 'The Best Reformed Churches.'* Rome: CLV, 1984.

———, 'Johannes Grabe's Response to William Whiston.' In *Lord Jesus Christ, Will You Not Stay. Essays in Honor of Ronald Feuerhahn on the Occasion of His Sixty-Fifth Birthday*. Edited by Bart Day et al. St Louis, MO: Concordia Publishing House, 2002, 91–104.

———. 'Karl Barth's Teaching on Baptism: Its Development, Antecedents and the "Liturgical Factor."' *Ecclesia Orans* 14 (1997), 261–88.

———. 'Luther's Timely Theology of Unilateral Baptism.' *Lutheran Quarterly* 9 (1995), 23–45.

———. 'Reflections based on a study of Church of Scotland Reports.' In *Christian Initiation – A Policy for the Church of England*. A discussion paper by Canon Martin Reardon. London: Church House Publishing, London, 1991.

———. *Two Faces of Elizabethan Anglican Theology. Sacraments and Salvation in the Theology of William Perkins and Richard Hooker*. Lanham, MD: Scarecrow Press, 1999.

———. 'Two Seventeenth Century Examples of *Lex Credendi, Lex Orandi*: The Baptismal and Eucharistic Liturgies of Jeremy Taylor and Richard Baxter.' *Studia Liturgica* 21 (1991), 165–89.

————. *Sacraments, Ceremonies, and the Stuart Divines. Sacramental Theology and Liturgy in England and Scotland 1603–1662.* Aldershot: Ashgate, 2001.

————. 'Treasures Old and New: A Look at Some of Thomas Cranmer's Methods of Liturgical Compilation.' In *Thomas Cranmer: Churchman and Scholar.* Edited by Paul Ayris and David Selwyn. Woodbridge: The Boydell Press, 1993, 175–88.

Sprengler-Ruppenthal, A. *Mysterium und Riten nach der Londoner Kirchordnung der Niederländer.* Köln: Böhlau Verlag, 1967.

Sprott, G.W. *Scottish Liturgies of the Reign of James VI.* Edinburgh: William Blackwood, 1901.

Starck (Stark), Johann F. *Tägliches Hand-Buch in guten und bösen Tagen.* Milwaukee, WI: Verlag von Georg Brumder, n.d.

Stauffer, S. Anita (ed.). *Baptism, Rites of Passage, and Culture.* Geneva: Lutheran World Federation Studies, 1998.

Stephens, Peter. *The Holy Spirit in the Theology of Martin Bucer.* Cambridge: Cambridge University Press, 1970.

————. *The Theology of Huldrych Zwingli.* Oxford: Clarendon Press, 1986.

————. 'Zwingli's Sacramental Views.' In *Prophet, Pastor, Protestant.* Edited by E.J. Furcha and H. Wayne Pipkin. Allison Park, PA: Pickwick Publications, 1984, 155–69.

Steuart, Walter. *Collections and Observations Methodiz'd Concerning the Worship, Discipline, and Government of the Church of Scotland in Four Books.* Edinburgh, 1709.

Steven, James H.S. *Worship in the Spirit. Charismatic Worship in the Church of England.* Carlisle: Paternoster Press, 2002.

Stevenson, K.W. 'The Byzantine Liturgy of Baptism.' *Studia Liturgica* 17 (1987), 176–90.

Stevick, Daniel B. *Baptismal Moments; Baptismal Meanings.* New York: The Church Hymnal Corporation, 1987.

Stewart-Sykes, Alistair. 'Manumission and Baptism in Tertullian's Africa: A Search for the Origin of Confirmation.' *Studia Liturgica* 31 (2001), 129–49.

Strabo, Walafrid. *'Libellus de exordiis et incrementis quarundam in observationibis ecclesiae.'* In *Christianizing Kinship. Ritual Sponsorship in Anglo-Saxon England.* By Joseph H. Lynch. Ithaca, NY and London: Cornell University Press, 1998.

Sutcliffe, E.F. 'Baptism and Baptismal Rites at Qumran.' *Heythrop Journal* 1 (1960), 69–101.

Swedenborg, Emanuel. *The True Christian Religion*, Volume 2. London: Swedenborg Society, 1988.

Sykes, Stephen. 'Baptisme doth represente unto us oure profession.' In *Thomas Cranmer, Essays in Commemoration of the 500th Anniversary of his Birth.* Edited by Margot Johnson. Durham: Turnstone Ventures, 1990.

Syrian Orthodox Church. 'The Baptism of the Lord Jesus.' *The Patriarchal Journal* 32 (1994), No. 131–2, 2–7 <http://syrianorthodoxchurch.org/library/sermons. baptism.htm>.

Talmage, James E. *The Articles of Faith* [1890], *The Deseret News* edition, Salt Lake City, UT: 1919.

Tanner, Sandra. 'Baptism for the Dead and the Twelve Oxen Under the Baptismal Font.' <http://www.utlm.org/onlineresources/twelveoxenbaptismalfont.htm>.

Taylor, Jeremy. *Works*, Heber-Eden edition, Volume 7. London, 1847–52.

Thodberg, Christian. 'The Importance of Baptism in Grundtvig's View of Christianity.' In *Heritage and Prophecy. Grundtvig and the English-Speaking World*. Edited by A.M. Allchin et al. Aarhus: Aarhus University Press, 1993, 133–52.

Thomas, John Christopher. *Footwashing in John 13 and the Johannine Community.* Sheffield: Sheffield Academic Press, 1991.

Thomson, Robert. *Agathangelos History of the Armenians.* Albany, NY: SUNY, 1976.

Thomson, Robert W. *The Teaching of Saint Gregory*, 2nd edition. New Rochelle, NY: St. Nersess Armenian Seminary, 2001, 120ff.

Toews, Abraham P. *American Mennonite Worship.* New York: Exposition Press, 1960.

Toon, Peter. *Evangelical Theology 1833–1856. A Response to Tractarianism.* Atlanta, GA: John Knox Press, 1979.

Torrance, Iain R. 'Fear of Being Left Out.' In *To Glorify God. Essays on Modern Reformed Liturgy*. Edited by Bryan D. Spinks and Iain R. Torrance. Edinburgh: T & T Clark, 1999, 159–72.

Torrance, T.F. 'The One Baptism Common to Christ and His Church.' In *Theology in Reconciliation.* Edited by Thomas Torrance. London: Geoffrey Chapman, 1975.

Torrance, T.F. 'Report of the Special Commission on Baptism 1955.' In *Reports to the General Assembly*, Church of Scotland, Edinburgh, 1955, 623.

Tovey, Philip. *Essays in West Syrian Liturgy.* Kottayam, Kerala, India: Oriental Institute of Religious Studies, 1998.

Tranvik, Mark David. 'The Other Sacrament: the doctrine of baptism in the late Lutheran Reformation.' Th.D. Thesis, Luther North Western Seminary, 1992.

Trigg, Jonathan. *Baptism in the Theology of Martin Luther.* Leiden: E.J. Brill, 1994.

Trobridge, G. *Swedenborg. Life and Teaching.* London: Swedenborg Society, 1935.

Truscott, Jeffrey A. *The Reform of Baptism and Confirmation in American Lutheranism.* Lanham, MD: Scarecrow Press, Inc., 2003.

Tucker, Karen B. Westerfield. *American Methodist Worship.* New York: Oxford University Press, 2001.

Turner, Paul. 'The Origins of Confirmation: An Analysis of Aidan Kavanagh's Hypothesis.' In *Living Water, Sealing Spirit*. Edited by Maxwell E. Johnson. Collegeville, MN: Pueblo, 1995, 238–58.

Turrettin, Francis. *Institutes of Elenctic Theology*, Volume 3. Translated by George Giger; edited by James T. Dennison. Phillipsburg, NJ: Presbyterian and Reformed Publishing Company, 1997.

Umble, John. 'An Amish Minister's Manual.' In *The Mennonite Quarterly* 15 (1941), 95–117.

Underwood, Grant. *The Millenarian World of Early Mormonism.* Urbana and Chicago: University of Illinois, 1993.

Underwood, T.L. *Primitivism, Radicalism, and the Lamb's War. The Baptist–Quaker Conflict in Seventeenth-Century England.* Oxford: Oxford University Press, 1997.

Van de Sandt, Huub and David Flusser. *The Didache.* Minneapolis, MN: Fortress Press, 2002.

Van Gennep, Arnold. *The Rites of Passage.* Chicago, IL: University of Chicago Press, 1960.

Van Slyke, Daniel. 'Augustine and Catechumenal "Exsufflatio": An Integral Element of Christian Initiation.' *Ephemerides Liturgicae* 118 (2004), 175–208.

The Vercelli Book Homilies. Edited by Lewis E. Nicholson. Lanham, MD and London: University Press of America, 1991.

Vial, Theodore M. *Liturgy Wars. Ritual Theory and Protestant Reform in Nineteenth-Century Zurich.* New York: Routledge, 2004.

Vogel, Cyrille. *Le Pontifical Romano-Germanique Du Dixième Siècle*, 3 volumes. Vatican City: Biblioteca Apostolica Vaticana, 1963–72.

————. *Medieval Liturgy. An Introduction to the Sources*, Washington, DC: Pastoral Press, 1986.

Vokes, F.E. *The Riddle of the Didache: Fact or Fiction, Heresy or Catholicism?* London: SPCK, 1938.

Von Rad, Gerhard. *Old Testament Theology*, Volume 2. Edinburgh: Oliver and Boyd, 1965.

Wade, Carol. *Stories of Resurrection: Traces of God in New Community*, STM Thesis. Yale Institute of Sacred Music and Yale Divinity School, 2004.

Walker, Joan Hazelden. 'A pre-Marcan Dating for the Didache: Further Thoughts of a Liturgist.' *Studia Biblica* 1978, 403–411.

Ward, Glenn. *Postmodernism.* London: Hodder Headline Ltd, 1997.

Watson, Richard. *The Works of the Rev. Richard Watson*, 12 volumes, Volume XII. London, 1834–38.

Ways of Worship: the report of a theological commission of faith and order. Edited by P. Edwall, E. Hayman and W.D. Maxwell. London: SCM Press, 1951.

Webb, D. 'The Mimra on the Interpretation of the Mysteries by Rabban Johannam Bar Zo'bi and its symbolism.' *Le Muséon* 88 (1975), 297–326.

Webster, John. *Barth's Ethics of Reconciliation.* Cambridge: Cambridge University Press, 1995.

Wedderburn, A.J.M. *Baptism and Resurrection. Studies in Pauline Theology Against its Graeco-Roman Background.* Tübingen: J.C.B. Mohr, 1987.

Weir, D.A. *The Origins of the Federal Theology in Sixteenth-Century Reformation Thought.* Oxford: Clarendon Press, 1990.

'Welcoming in the Community of Disciples.' Unpublished Draft 1, Baptist Church of Great Britain, 2004.

Wenger, John C. *The Complete Writings of Menno Simons.* Scottdale, PA: Herald Press, 1956.

Wesley, Charles. *The Journal of the Rev. Charles Wesley,* Volume 1. London: John Mason and Grand Rapids, MI: Baker Book Reprint, [1849], 1980.

Wesley, John. *The Journal of the Rev. John Wesley,* Volume 2. Edited by Nehemiah Curnock. London: Epworth Press, 1938.

————. *The Works of the Rev. John Wesley,* Volume 6. London: John Mason, 1856.

West, Charles C. 'Baptism in the Reformed Tradition.' In *Baptism, Peace and the State in the Reformed and Mennonite Traditions.* Edited by Ross T. Bender and Alan P.F. Sell. Waterloo, IA: Wilfrid Laurier Press, 1991, 13–36.

Westminster Assembly. *The Westminster Directory.* Edited by Ian Breward. Bramcote: Grove Books, 1980.

Wettach, Theodor. *Kirche bei Zinzendorf.* Wuppertal: Theologischer Verlag Rolf Brockhaus, 1971.

Wheeler, Geraldine. 'Traditions and Principles of Reformed Worship in the Uniting Church in Australia.' In *Christian Worship in Reformed Churches Past and Present.* Edited by Lukas Vischer. Grand Rapids, MI: Eerdmans, 2003, 261–79.

Whitaker, E.C. *Documents of the Baptismal Liturgy.* Revised and expanded by Maxwell E. Johnson, 3rd edition. Collegeville, MN: Liturgical Press, 2003, 18–19.

White, B.R. *The English Baptists of the Seventeenth Century.* Didcot: Baptist Historical Society, 1996.

Wickremesinghe, Francis. 'An Asian Inculturation of the Baptismal Liturgy.' In *Growing in Newness of Life.* Edited by David R. Holeton. Toronto: Anglican Book Centre, 1993, 213–17.

Wiles, Maurice. 'Triple and Single Immersion: Baptism in the Arian Controversy.' *Studia Patristica* 30, Peeters, Leuven, 1997, 337–49.

Williams, Rowan. 'Baptism and the Arian Controversy.' In *Arianism After Arius.* Edited by Michael R. Barnes and Daniel H. Williams. Edinburgh: T & T Clark, 1993, 149–80.

Williard, G.W. *The Commentary of Dr. Zacherias Ursinus on the Heidelberg Catechism.* Grand Rapids, MI: Eerdmans, 1954.

Winkler, Gabriele. 'Confirmation or Chrismation? A Study in Comparative Liturgy.' In *Living Water, Sealing Spirit.* Edited by Maxwell E. Johnson. Collegeville, MD: Pueblo, 1995.

————. *Das Armenische Initiationsrituale. Orientalia Christiana Analecta* 217. Rome: Pontifical Oriental Institute, 1982.

————. 'Nochmals zu den Anfängen der Epiklese und des Sanctus im Eucharistischen Hochgebet.' *Theologische Quartalschrift* 174 (1994), 214–31.

————. 'The Original Meaning of the Pre-baptismal Anointing and Its Implications.' *Worship* 52 (1978), 24–45.

Wolf, William J. 'Frederick Denison Maurice.' In *The Spirit of Anglicanism*. Edited by William J. Wolf, John E. Booty and Owen C. Thomas. Edinburgh: T & T Clarke, 1979.

Wolfgramm, Luke. 'An Examination of the Pietistic Content of Johann Friedrich Stark's *Tägliches Hand-Buch, in guten und bösen Tagen Gebet-Buch*, 10 February 1995 <hhttp://www.wls.wels.net/library/Essays/Authors/w/WolfgrammPietistic/WolfgrammPietistic.pdf>.

Woolley, R.M. *Coptic Offices*. London: SPCK, 1930.

Wright, David. 'Infant Baptism and the Christian Community in Bucer.' In *Martin Bucer. Reforming Church and Community*. Edited by David Wright. Cambridge: Cambridge University Press, 1994.

Wulfstan, Archbishop of York. 'Sermo de Baptismate.' In *The Homilies of Wulfstan*. Edited by Dorothy Bethurum. Oxford: Clarendon Press, 1957, 175–84.

Yarnold, Edward. *The Awe Inspiring Rites of Initiation*. Slough: St Paul Publications, 1971.

Yarnold, E.J. 'The Authorship of the Mystagogic Catecheses Attributed to Cyril of Jerusalem.' *Heythrop Journal* 19 (1978), 143–61.

Yegül, Fikret. *Baths and Bathing in Classical Antiquity*. Cambridge, MA: MIT Press, 1992, 354–5.

Yelverton, Eric E. *The Swedish Rite, a translation of 'Handbok for svenska kyrkan.'* London: SPCK, 1921.

Zakka, Patriarch Ignatius. 'The Baptism of the Lord Jesus.' *The Patriarchal Journal* 32 (131–2) (1994), 2–7, translated 1996 <http://www.syrianorthodoxchurch.org/library/sermons/baptism.htm>.

Zinzendorf, Nikolaus Ludwig Graf von. *Maxims, Theological Ideas And Sentences out of the Present Ordinary of the Brethren's Churches: His Dissertations and Discourses From the Year 1738 till 1747*. Extracted by J. Gambold, London, 1751.

Index